Long Green

The Rise and Fall of
Tobacco in South Carolina

The University of Georgia Press
Athens and London

© 2000 by the University of Georgia Press
Athens, Georgia 30602

Set in Galliard by G & S Typesetters, Inc.
Printed and bound by Maple-Vail
The paper in this book meets the guidelines for
permanence and durability of the Committee on
Production Guidelines for Book Longevity of the
Council on Library Resources.

Printed in the United States of America

04   03   02   01   00   C   5   4   3   2   1

Library of Congress Cataloging-in-Publication Data
Prince, Eldred E., 1950 –
Long green : the rise and fall of tobacco in South Carolina /
Eldred E. Prince Jr. with Robert R. Simpson.
    p.   cm.
Includes bibliographical references and index.
ISBN 0-8203-2176-1 (alk. paper)
1. Tobacco—South Carolina—History.   2. Tobacco industry—
South Carolina—History.   I. Simpson, Robert R.   II. Title.
SB273.P94   2000
633.7′1′09757—dc21   99-043773

British Library Cataloging-in-Publication Data available

for Sallye

Contents

Tables and Figures

Acknowledgments

MANY INDIVIDUALS AND ORGANIZATIONS supported this study. The Pee Dee Heritage Center has been a faithful friend and deserves first mention. Its director, Dew James, always responded to pleas for help promptly and energetically. The Pee Dee Heritage Center is co-sponsored by Coker College, Francis Marion University, the Governor's School for Mathematics and Science, and Coastal Carolina University. The South Carolina Humanities Council provided financial support in the early stages of the project. The Waccamaw Center for Historical and Cultural Studies at Coastal Carolina University funded release time for research. The center's director, Charles W. Joyner, deserves special mention not only for reading and critiquing the manuscript but for furnishing moral support as well.

We are indebted to many archivists and librarians for their assistance. Heading the list is Horace Rudisill of the Darlington County Historical Commission. We benefited from his knowledge and enthusiasm for the past as well as Darlington's incredibly rich archive. Alan Stokes of the South Caroliniana Library directed us to valuable sources, and Beth Bilderback went the second mile in locating and processing photographs. Mary Parramore of the South Carolina Division of Archives and History informed our examination of the colonial period and graciously shared her own excellent research with us. No one can do serious work on tobacco history without going to Raleigh. Thanks to Steve Massengill at the North Carolina Division of Archives and History for his hospitality to an out-of-state visitor.

Local librarians played an important role in the project as well. I am indebted to Horry County and Marion County public libraries for their assistance. The reference staff of Kimbel Library at Coastal Carolina University was especially diligent in acquiring materials from other collections. I extend special thanks to Margaret Fain, Marchita Phifer, and Jeri Traw.

Stewart Pabst of the Horry County Museum helped select and prepare images from the extraordinary William Van Auken Green collection. Bill Edmonds at Coastal Carolina University cheerfully prepared several photographs for publication. Abdallah Haddad helped create the map. The descendants of persons discussed in the book still live in the Pee Dee. John Monroe J. Holliday furnished the photograph of his grandfather Joseph William Holliday. Jimmy Daniel and Nancy Daniel Mottern provided the photograph of their ancestor William Henry Daniel. Frank M. "Buzz" Rogers furnished the photograph of his namesake, Frank Mandeville Rogers. Jack Olde at the *Progressive Farmer* and Elizabeth Dunn at Duke University provided other photographs.

Numerous scholars offered helpful critiques and suggestions. At the University of South Carolina at Columbia, Thomas Terrill, Lacy Ford, Robert Weir, and Charles Kovacik read early drafts. At Coastal Carolina University, Denvey Bowman, Beatriz Hardy, Stephen Hardy, Brian Nance, Roy Talbert, and Ken Townsend provided tough love. Anthony Badger of Cambridge University read early drafts and offered valuable insight. I extend special thanks to the anonymous referee who invested considerable effort in two readings of the manuscript. His suggestions made this a much better book than it otherwise would have been. Catherine Heniford Lewis—archivist, scholar, author, and dean of Horry County historians—shared her incomparable knowledge on a score of topics.

A great contributor to this effort did not live to see it completed. Co-author Robert R. Simpson died 6 July 1995. Bob and I met at the University of South Carolina at Columbia in the early 1990s. A common interest brought us together—the story of tobacco in the Pee Dee. I was writing my dissertation on the history of Bright Leaf, and Bob was working on a multimedia venture exploring the folklife of the Pee Dee tobacco culture. After completing our individual projects, we agreed to collaborate on a comprehensive treatment blending elements of both. Our partnership was both cordial and profitable. Bob's death did not end his contribution. As late as 1997, I was still extracting valuable information from his research legacy. May this volume serve as a memorial to that fine scholar and true southern gentleman.

My parents, Mr. and Mrs. Eldred E. Prince, merit special gratitude. Their faith in me and support for my work never wavered. I hope the result justifies their confidence. My son Michael willingly relinquished computer time for my work on the manuscript.

My wife, Sallye Brown Prince, the daughter and granddaughter of tobacco growers, was a constant source of support and encouragement. She read drafts and listened attentively to my musings. On weekends, she cheerfully accompanied me through dusty fields, dilapidated barns, and abandoned railroad beds, asking nothing more than to be at my side. It is to her, the love of my life, that this volume is dedicated.

Introduction

THE PURPOSE OF THIS BOOK is to observe and understand the history of tobacco culture in South Carolina. Given the negative image smoking has acquired, one might ask, Why study tobacco at all? and why especially in South Carolina? For better or worse, tobacco is thoroughly American. Indians grew and smoked tobacco for centuries before teaching its culture to European and African newcomers. Not only did the weed become an important export, but as the nation grew, a substantial domestic market evolved as well. Cigars, pipes, snuff, and "chew" became fixtures of everyday life.

In the 1880s, technology introduced another tobacco product to American consumers. Inexpensive and highly addictive cigarettes made of mild, aromatic Bright Leaf tobacco began to be mass-produced and aggressively marketed. Within a generation, cigarette smoking in the United States multiplied nearly one hundred–fold. To meet the demand for cigarettes, manufacturing centers arose in the historic leaf-growing regions of North Carolina and Virginia. Factories in Durham, Winston, and Richmond were soon making billions of cigarettes. In turn, rising demand for raw material expanded Bright Leaf culture beyond its traditional boundaries into new areas of cultivation. One of these was the eastern corner of South Carolina—the Pee Dee region.

The Pee Dee is an excellent site to survey the history of Bright Leaf. Unlike the "Old Belt" of North Carolina and Virginia, the Pee Dee was not a historic tobacco region that simply adapted new methods to an established crop. When Pee Dee farmers began experimenting with Bright Leaf in the 1880s, no one then living could remember when tobacco had been raised as a cash crop in South Carolina. The story of tobacco in the Pee Dee was written on a clean slate. And Bright Leaf came at a good time for Pee Dee farmers. The region's staples—cotton, rice, and naval stores— were declining in the 1880s. The Pee Dee needed a new cash crop, especially a high-value crop, to sustain the region's many small farmers. Bright Leaf tobacco seemed made to order.

The Pee Dee Bright Leaf boom of the 1890s offers a classic example of New South boosterism. Indeed, cherished tenets of the New South Creed

—industrial development and agricultural diversity—lay at the heart of the tobacco culture. Initially, the Bright Leaf boom was sparked by a New South industry—cigarette manufacture. And unlike textiles, which only deepened the region's commitment to cotton, cigarettes encouraged agricultural diversity. Many of the faces are familiar as well. The Bright Leaf drama was cast from a stock set of New South characters. Rural merchants and town boosters, elites and sharecroppers, bankers and editors, politicians and railroad men all played a part in dethroning King Cotton in favor of the seductive new pretender.

The Bright Leaf boom of the 1890s had an enormous economic impact on the Pee Dee, and the region enjoyed prosperity unknown since the 1850s. Well into the twentieth century, change was recorded on the landscape as fields were cleared, barns raised, swamps drained, rails laid, and highways paved in tobacco's name. Not only did farmers embrace a profitable new staple, but market towns flourished as well. Populations doubled and redoubled. Warehouses, banks, and stores rose, and turreted Victorian homes appeared on tree-lined streets.

Before long, however, farmers realized that in forsaking cotton for tobacco they had traded one set of problems for another. The growers' tragic tendency to overproduce compounded by their lack of solidarity made them vulnerable to a highly prejudiced marketing system. Attempts to bring reform from below ended in failure. In the crisis of the Great Depression, government intervention solved many long-term problems and stabilized the tobacco culture by introducing a very successful system of production control.

Prosperity returned to the Pee Dee in the 1940s and 1950s, but increasing concern over smoking-related illness reduced demand for cigarette tobaccos. Profits also fell. Tobacco prices, which had kept pace with inflation for thirty years, lagged far behind by the 1980s. At the same time, new technology accelerated the consolidation of traditional tobacco farms into large, capital-intensive enterprises. Technology altered traditional work routines, and sharply reduced labor requirements were met by migrant workers. By the 1980s, the traditional tobacco culture of the Pee Dee region had passed from the scene.

As often happens when pursuing history, the trail of evidence led us beyond the scope of our original topic. We set out to write a history of the tobacco industry in South Carolina and, in passing, to examine some classic issues of southern history using the Pee Dee as a test case. For example, given the enormous importance of race in southern history, we wanted to examine issues of race in Pee Dee agriculture, especially during Reconstruction, when relations between blacks and whites were being redefined.

Another objective was to learn to what extent the old planter class continued to dominate the region's economy. Further, we saw the cigarette industry as an especially appropriate setting in which to examine New South issues. While some believe the New South was little more than a northern colony—and much evidence can be marshaled to support this view—the tobacco industry offers an exception.[1] From seedbed to cellophane, cigarettes were a southern enterprise. The capital, labor, technology, manufacturing, and entrepreneurship of the new industry were all southern.

We started with several questions: How did new forms of labor, land tenure, finance, and marketing evolve in the Pee Dee after the Civil War? How did the cotton depressions of the 1870s and 1890s affect the region? When and how did Bright Leaf tobacco culture enter the region? How did elites—both old and new—view the change of staple crops? How did tobacco change the Pee Dee? What were the effects of the New Deal and World War II? How has technology altered traditional tobacco culture more recently? What has been the impact of health issues?

We made some interesting discoveries. For one, the portrait of emancipated slaves unveiled in these pages is more flattering than the traditional image of them as the passive victims of southern racism and northern paternalism. Pee Dee freedpeople emerged from slavery stronger, bolder, and more competent than they have sometimes been portrayed.[2] In the confusing, even frightening post–Civil War environment, Pee Dee freedpeople typically showed good judgment in the choices they made for themselves and their families. For example, freedpeople asserted themselves to win important concessions from employers as a new labor system emerged after the Civil War. We learned that sharecropping was not forced on freedpeople in the Pee Dee; they preferred it to less equitable labor alternatives. Moreover, in the 1880s and 1890s, a substantial percentage of Pee Dee blacks were upwardly mobile, evolving from sharecroppers to renters and proprietors.

Other questions were harder to answer. For example, there is no clear pattern of the persistence of antebellum planters. In the Pee Dee, descendants of planter families shared the limelight with a rising mercantile class in the towns and rural crossroads. Both groups welcomed diversification, and both played crucial roles in bringing Bright Leaf to the region. Some elites planted experimental tobacco crops and recruited experienced tobacco growers to cultivate them. Others built warehouses and extended credit to novice tobacco growers. Both worked hard to make the new crop a success, and both shared in the prosperity that accompanied it.

Discovering the cooperative movement was another surprise. In the 1920s, Bright Leaf growers in the Carolinas and Virginia mounted a vigorous campaign to reform the tobacco marketing system. Pee Dee farmers were deeply involved, and several rose to positions of leadership in the movement. Far from the popular image of farmers as staunch conservatives, the co-op movement produced a wave of agrarian activism in the Pee Dee that crossed boundaries of race and class. Landlords and tenants alike joined, and black farmers were welcomed as full participants. Indeed, in the reform movement of the 1920s, Pee Dee tobacco farmers of both races cooperated to a degree remarkable for the times. Ironically, other Pee Dee farmers opposed reform.

Perhaps our greatest discovery was that the tobacco boom of the 1890s was the crop's third appearance in the Palmetto State. Twice before tobacco had become a major money crop only to vanish virtually without a trace. Parallels to the present were obvious and compelling. As tobacco culture is retreating yet again in the 1990s, we believed studying earlier instances of change could inform our understanding of the present. Moreover, considering the current state of the tobacco industry, a more complete history would underscore the ephemeral nature of the human condition. Certainly, such motives would tempt any historian. Therefore, the first chapter examines tobacco's earlier advances and retreats in South Carolina and seeks to understand the forces that compelled them.

From the earliest days of European colonization, South Carolina has been a player on world commodity markets. Tobacco's fortunes in the Palmetto State have risen and fallen not only as farmers responded to market forces but also as government—especially the national government—has involved itself. This volume considers the rise and fall of tobacco in South

Carolina against the backdrop of market forces on one hand and government policy on the other.

This book is written from the growers' perspective, but more is examined here than the age-old quest to maximize return and minimize risk. Although Pee Dee tobacco growers endured differences of race and class and often argued among themselves, they were united by common experiences and interests. For a very long time, a common experience was exploitation by tobacco companies. Only direct intervention by the federal government ended the abuse. If our characterization of tobacco companies seems harsh or occasionally verges on the polemical, we ask readers to consider the evidence and decide for themselves if our judgment is just.

But while we sympathize with farmers, we have not hesitated to point out their mistakes, follies, and failures. Indeed, we maintain that many of the farmers' troubles were of their own making. Even so, we believe the thousands of men and women who toiled in the fields, barns, and packhouses of the Pee Dee—often for very little recompense—deserve a compassionate hearing. It is to that task that we now turn.

The Pee Dee region takes its name from two rivers, the Great Pee Dee and the Little Pee Dee, that drain the eastern quarter of South Carolina. The name memorializes a Native American people who once inhabited the area. Setting boundaries to the Pee Dee is ultimately an act of consensus. The region is bounded on the north by North Carolina and on the east by the Atlantic Ocean. Although the region's southern and western boundaries are less definite, regional scholars usually include counties touched by either of the Pee Dee Rivers. This model includes Chesterfield, Darlington, Dillon, Florence, Georgetown, Horry, Marion, Marlboro, and Williamsburg Counties. Contiguous areas of Clarendon, Lee, and Sumter Counties are typically included in the Pee Dee for cultural reasons. (See A. S. Salley, "Pee Dee or Not Pee Dee," in Claude H. Neuffer, ed., *Names in South Carolina,* vol. 4 [Columbia: Department of English, University of South Carolina, 1957], 41; James A. Rogers, *Theodosia and Other Pee Dee Sketches* [Columbia: R. L. Bryan, 1978], xvii–xxiii; James McBride Dabbs and Carl Julien, *Pee Dee Panorama* [Columbia: University of South Carolina Press, 1951], 3.)

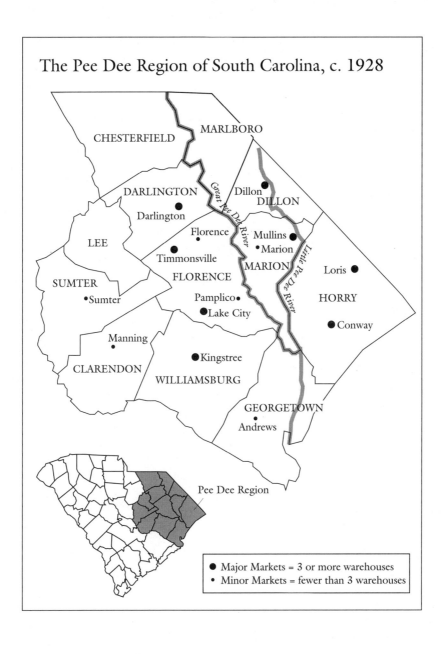

The Pee Dee Region of South Carolina, c. 1928

CHESTERFIELD

MARLBORO

DARLINGTON

Dillon

DILLON

Darlington

LEE

Florence

Mullins

Marion

Timmonsville

MARION

Loris

SUMTER

FLORENCE

HORRY

Sumter

Pamplico

Lake City

Conway

Manning

Kingstree

CLARENDON

WILLIAMSBURG

GEORGETOWN

Andrews

Pee Dee Region

Great Pee Dee River

Little Pee Dee River

● Major Markets = 3 or more warehouses
• Minor Markets = fewer than 3 warehouses

Long Green

Tobacco . . . they have of an excellent sort,
mistaken by some of our English Smoakers
for Spanish.
THOMAS ASHE, 1682

I Tobacco Doth Here Grow Very Well, 1670–1810

AGRICULTURE is the world's oldest commercial activity, and farmers have long felt the fickle arrogance of the marketplace. The laws of supply and demand and comparative advantage have dominated agriculture since Babylonian peasants traded omers of wheat for baskets of olives. The ancient logic of market forces is well known and requires only a brief summary here. For a crop culture to be economically viable, supply must be great enough to support an active market but not so great as to bury consumers under an avalanche of surplus, smothering prices and profits. On the other side of the equation, demand must be sufficiently vigorous to ensure a reliable and satisfactory rate of return.

The theory of comparative advantage suggests that producers in a given place tend to specialize in activities that the environment and resources will support and that provide the greatest rates of return. In agriculture, therefore, the profitability of a given crop must be as great as any that could be produced with the means at hand. When a commodity no longer answers this requirement, effort, acreage, and capital shift to one that will.[1]

Three times in the history of South Carolina, tobacco has risen to the status of a major crop, and three times it has declined. The three periods of tobacco culture are separated by time and place. Tobacco was first planted near Charles Town during the city's infancy. The crop flourished there for nearly twenty years, giving way to rice about 1690. Tobacco reappeared in the backcountry in the 1760s. The crop became a major economic force on the frontier in the 1780s and 1790s, supporting a network of warehouses and aftermarket services. Backcountry tobacco culture continued until about 1800, when it gave way to cotton. The crop made its third appearance in the Pee Dee region when farmers began experimenting with Bright Leaf in the 1880s.

Although the main focus of this book is the third period of tobacco culture, some understanding of the first and second is desirable. Since the earlier periods were relatively brief, some questions naturally arise. Why did South Carolina farmers twice turn to tobacco and twice abandon it? How did the market encourage and discourage tobacco production? Finally, does the decline of tobacco culture in the late twentieth century bear any resemblance to earlier periods of decline?

When the colony of South Carolina was established at the mouth of the Ashley River in 1670, settlers began their quest for a crop suited to its soil and climate for which a dependable market existed in Europe. The English investors who underwrote the Carolina venture, known to history as the Lords Proprietors, encouraged many agricultural experiments in the early days of the colony. The Proprietors originally intended Carolina to fill a niche in the English mercantile system by supplying commodities not produced elsewhere in the empire. Because Charles Town fell along the same latitude as North Africa and the Middle East, the Proprietors hoped the colony could produce silk, citrus, olives, and wine. Attempts to establish these crops in South Carolina persisted for many years with little success. Ironically, experiments with cotton and rice, crops destined to have massive impact on South Carolina, were initially disappointing as well.[2]

As costs of maintaining the colony mounted, the Proprietors were understandably eager for the venture to become self-supporting. Aware of tobacco's success as a money crop in Virginia and Europe's growing appetite for smoking leaf, the Proprietors urged their dependents in Carolina to plant tobacco as a temporary staple. Besieged with requests for aid, the Proprietors responded that "Supplyes of all sorts and at moderate rates ye would not want if ye would make a rational proposall how they should be paid for; or would bee but soe industrious as to plant Tobacco or any other thinge to draw a trade to you, untill we can furnish ye with more proffitable plants."[3]

These instructions indicate that the Proprietors believed tobacco was not a permanent solution but could help to support the colony until something better was found. Indeed, the Proprietors knew tobacco had served Barbados as a temporary staple until sugar replaced it as that colony's leading export. Moreover, many Carolinians had once lived on Barbados and were acquainted with tobacco culture. The colony's need for a crop that would generate at least some hard cash made tobacco South Carolina's first link with world markets.[4]

The timing was unfortunate. Although tobacco had brought prosperity to Virginia and Maryland in earlier decades, by the 1670s overproduction had glutted the market. As South Carolinians were nurturing their first tobacco crop, Virginians were selling leaf for a penny a pound, and their governor was lamenting "the contemptible price we are allowed for our tobaccoes."[5] Clearly, the empire did not need another tobacco colony. Nevertheless, tobacco flourished in South Carolina. Indeed, colonists reported their greatest successes with watermelons, potatoes, pumpkins, and tobacco "as good as ever was smoakt."[6] Encouraged by the high quality of Carolina leaf, the Proprietors advised their clients to visit Virginia and refine their tobacco-growing skills. What Virginia farmers thought of this advice is not recorded.[7] Furthermore, the Carolina lobby in London persuaded Parliament to extend valuable incentives and protection to Carolina tobacco growers by granting a seven-year waiver of export duties on the crop and outlawing leaf production in England.[8]

Tobacco prices advanced a little in the mid-1670s, and for a while the crop seemed promising. Letters from South Carolina planters described tobacco as a "maine commodity" and reported that "tobacco doth here grow very well."[9] It did well enough for colonists to repay loans from the Proprietors in leaf. Soon, tobacco became currency for a variety of purposes, including passage to the New World. Immigrants to South Carolina could reimburse the Proprietors for their passage "with the sume of five hundred pounds merchantable tobacco" raised in the colony.[10]

And the new colony raised very merchantable tobacco, indeed. Some observers rated South Carolina's crop above Virginia's and equal to the highly regarded Spanish leaf. Such claims should be taken with a pinch of salt, however. Colonial promoters often composed their reports more with an eye on encouraging immigration than achieving absolute veracity. In any event, by 1675 South Carolinians judged tobacco exports important enough to warrant hiring "viewers" to inspect tobacco shipments.[11] Although no production data exist for the 1670s and 1680s, surviving colonial documents suggest that tobacco was widely planted around Charles Town.[12]

Just as tobacco culture was becoming firmly rooted in the South Carolina lowcountry, dramatic price swings whipsawed growers from boom to bust. At its peak, tobacco had retailed in England for its weight in silver. London merchants spooned shredded tobacco on one side of the scales while customers stacked silver coins on the other, measure for measure. As one wit noted at the time, "As the nostrils are filled, purses are emptied."[13] Once again, however, high prices stimulated a huge increase in production. In the 1680s, leaf prices fell drastically. Tobacco that formerly brought forty-two pence per pound fell to three pence. In Virginia, common grades sold for a penny a pound, and Maryland leaf sank to five pounds for three pence. The tobacco depression was so severe that the Virginia House of Burgesses petitioned King Charles II to outlaw tobacco planting for a year.[14]

In the mid-1680s, Carolina tobacco growers were hit with political troubles that compounded their economic ones. Virginia planters were abusing the duty-free status of South Carolina tobacco by shipping their leaf to Charles Town and then reexporting it to evade the king's tax. Not only did the Virginia planters gain by cheating the Royal Exchequer, but Charles Town merchants doubtless profited from this illicit trade as well. Fearful of losing their tax-exempt status, the Proprietors assured the king that they were taking steps to prevent this abuse so "Your Majesty may be no waies defrauded of Your Customs . . . that may happen by carrying tobaccos to Carolina from the bordering plantations of Virginia." [15]

The Proprietors' assurances apparently left the king unconvinced. Writing from London, the Proprietors informed Governor Joseph West that the commissioners of the customs had appointed George Muschamp as "King's Collector of the Duty upon Tobacco" for Charles Town. Apparently, the challenge of enforcing unpopular tax laws overwhelmed him. Muschamp complained to London that it was "difficult to maintaine the Acts of Navigation in due force here" and requested transfer to Maryland.[16]

The issue was further complicated when King Charles's younger brother James II ascended the throne. The new monarch immediately raised taxes on tobacco and sugar to finance naval construction.[17] That the tax was not collected from growers and shippers but paid by retail consumers hardly mattered. Imposing a tax on retail sales of tobacco weakened demand in a market already softened by abundant supply. The South Carolina planter Thomas Ashe expressed a sentiment shared by many when he wrote that while the colony produced high-quality tobacco, "Finding a great deal of trouble in the Planting and Cure of it, and the great Quantities which Virginia and other of His Majesty's Plantations make, rendering it a Drug [on the market] all over Europe; they do not much regard or encourage its Planting, having already before them better and more profitable Designs of Action." [18] This unrewarding situation led South Carolinians to begin dedicating their energies and acreage to more promising crops.

One of these crops was rice. In the late 1680s, colonists obtained from Africa seed rice that flourished in the lowcountry's semitropical climate. Soon, hundreds of fields were cleared and thousands of enslaved Africans imported to toil in them. The lowcountry enjoyed a further environmental advantage. While it is possible to cultivate rice on higher ground, it grows best in the swampy, marshy areas that rendered the lowcountry virtually useless for anything else. Thus the marshy, miasmal landscape helped to confine the profitable tidewater rice culture to a fairly small area. The threat of overproduction of rice was far less—and its profitability far greater—than tobacco. Indeed, demand for the famed "Carolina Gold" rice remained strong enough to drive expansion of the rice culture for decades.[19]

Besides being protected by geography, tidewater rice culture enjoyed other important advantages over tobacco. Foremost among these was its greater consumer base. Obviously, rice was a food, and as such its potential consumer base was virtually unlimited. By the 1730s rice was becoming an integral part of the European diet, and ships laden with Carolina rice made regular calls on Hamburg, Rotterdam, Amsterdam, and Danzig.[20] Tobacco, in contrast, was a luxury article that provided neither nourishment nor sustenance. Furthermore, by the mid-seventeenth century some of the plant's harmful aspects were already being discovered, and tobacco was being damned in tracts and sermons throughout Europe.[21] Thus, while economic and societal constraints confined tobacco consumption chiefly to adult males, rice growers could aspire to fill every stomach in Europe.

Another "more profitable Design of Action," as Thomas Ashe put it, was naval stores: the tar, pitch, and turpentine used to waterproof and maintain hulls and cordage. All are products of the long-leaf "pitch" pine that grew by the millions throughout South Carolina.[22] As the world's foremost maritime power, England had a vital strategic interest in naval stores. The Royal Navy and commercial shipping interests had formerly obtained these products from Scandinavia. In 1689, however, a war broke out in Europe that threatened access to Scandinavian naval stores at a critical time. Prices responded predictably, soaring to record levels. Realizing that reserves of these materials were easily accessible in America, the Admiralty encouraged naval stores production there. Parliament agreed and voted impressive subsidies to stimulate production of these commodities. Moreover, the English government appropriated £10,000 for surveyors, engineers, and equipment to launch the new colonial industry. By the early 1700s, South Carolinians were reaping handsome profits from the humble yellow pine.[23]

Thus the greater possibilities of rice and naval stores soon drove low-country planters out of the tobacco business. By the 1690s, tobacco culture had virtually disappeared in South Carolina, and former tobacco growers were busy planting rice and tapping pine trees. Edward Randolph, chief customs inspector for North America, paid an official call on Charles Town in 1699. His report to the Lords of Trade made no mention of tobacco but showed great enthusiasm for rice and naval stores.[24] Furthermore, shipping lists for 1699–1720, while noting shipments as small as four barrels, fail to list tobacco but reveal shipments of rice and naval stores numbering in the tens of thousands of barrels.[25] Thus as the tobacco market weakened because of overproduction and rising taxes and rice and naval stores seemed promising, tobacco succumbed to the relentless efficiency of the market-place. South Carolina's first tobacco period was over.

South Carolina's second tobacco period was separated from the first by time and place. In 1730, Governor Robert Johnson began an immigration policy that ushered in three decades of rapid population growth and geographical expansion in South Carolina. Johnson's "township scheme" sought to enlarge the colony's tax base and balance the large numbers of black slaves arriving in the lowcountry with white immigration in the backcountry. The plan offered incentives designed to attract "poor Protestant settlers" from Europe and other English colonies.[26] The lodestone was land. Families received fifty acres per person virtually free. Moreover, the government subsidized transportation, tools, and provision costs to lure immigrants. Ironically, much of the funding for these subsidies came from taxes collected from the slave trade. Thus forced immigration of Africans funded voluntary immigration of Europeans.[27]

Drawn by this impressive package of incentives, settlers began moving into the South Carolina backcountry. Europeans arrived through the Atlantic ports and made their way up the Ashley, Cooper, Edisto, Pee Dee, Santee, Savannah, and Waccamaw Rivers. Later, others came overland from North Carolina, Virginia, Maryland, and Pennsylvania to take up homesteads. The Pennsylvanians who eventually settled in the north-central area of the colony named their new homes—Chester, Lancaster, and York—after their former ones.[28]

The backcountry differed from the lowcountry in important ways. While the coastal region was characterized by large plantations worked by a growing black majority, the interior was dominated by German, Welsh, and Scots-Irish yeomen who tilled their own land, earning their daily bread by the sweat of their brows.[29] Another important difference was crop selection. While rice remained the staple of the tidewater lowcountry, geography hindered its cultivation in the piedmont. The bonanza in naval stores had about run its course as well. Indeed, thirty years of government subsidies had worked rather too well. By 1719, imports of naval stores from the Carolinas had overwhelmed the English market. Predictably, questions were raised about fostering excessive production at taxpayers' expense. Two years later, Parliament reduced the subsidy and thus the profitability of naval stores. Within a few years, exports of naval stores from South Carolina had declined 75 percent.[30] Unable to grow rice and unwilling to tap pine trees for no profit, settlers in the backcountry were slower to form a cash economy. Thus barter remained the piedmont's primary means of exchange for several years.

Just as lowcountry settlers brought knowledge about tobacco with them from Barbados, so many backcountry pioneers brought tobacco seed and experience from Virginia and the middle colonies. At first, tobacco played a minor role in the piedmont economy, being grown in small amounts for barter and home consumption. Clearly, none was exported in those years. Shipping lists from the 1740s make no mention of tobacco.[31] Even as late as 1761, Governor James Glen stated, "The only commodity of Consequence produced in South Carolina is rice."[32] Once again, however, market forces were about to compel a change in the South Carolina landscape.

Backcountry folk were a sturdy, self-sufficient lot, little acquainted with the refinements of civilization even by eighteenth-century standards. At first, these hardy pioneers practiced subsistence farming, producing or bartering for what they needed. But as subsistence yielded to rising expectations, backcountry folk sought a cash crop to supplement their corn cribs and smokehouses.[33] Their search coincided with rising tobacco prices, which almost doubled in the 1760s, climbing more than 83 percent by 1771.[34] Since backcountry farmers were already producing small amounts of tobacco and understood its culture, they had only to grow greater quantities, not just to smoke or barter but to sell. As these resourceful pioneers established commercial tobacco culture in the South Carolina backcountry, they took the first critical steps from subsistence toward a market economy.[35]

Backcountry tobacco of the 1770s was a rustic ancestor of what later became the Burley variety. It was not a difficult crop to grow. Plants were set in small patches of an acre or less. The crop might be hoed once or twice but otherwise got little attention. The tobacco ripened through the summer, and by September all the leaves were yellow. Farmers cut the plants and hung them to dry or "cure" in well-ventilated sheds. Air-curing could take several weeks. In late autumn, farmers stripped the dry, brown leaves from the stalks, packed them in wooden hogsheads, and hauled them to market.

Between 1769 and 1773, leaf exports from South Carolina more than trebled, rising from 160,000 pounds to more than half a million pounds per year.[36] Charles Town merchants welcomed the new trade. In December 1771, the *South Carolina Gazette* boasted that "no less than 113 waggons [are] on the Road to Town, most of them loaded with two Hogsheads of tobacco."[37] The backcountry tobacco trade continued to thrive well into the 1770s, bringing much-needed cash into the backcountry and welcome commerce to Charles Town merchants.

The War for Independence (1775–83) seriously interrupted foreign trade, and during the war South Carolina produced small amounts of tobacco for the domestic market. But when the war ended and commerce with Europe resumed, prices rose and production soared. The tobacco crop of 1783 topped 2.6 million pounds, four times the 1773 figure. Good prices continued for several years, and in 1790 backcountry farmers shipped more than 6.8 million pounds of leaf through Charleston, about twelve times the pre-war level.[38]

Large-scale production brought large-scale problems. As early as 1770, South Carolina governor William Bull had identified a major obstacle facing up-country tobacco farmers. "Tobacco," Bull reported, "tho' a bulky commodity, is planted from one hundred & fifty to two hundred miles from Charleston, . . . [but] they cultivate it with great advantage notwithstanding the distance of carriage to market."[39] Moreover, most of the state's tobacco was produced above the fall line. Thus shippers attempting river transport encountered rapids, rocks, and shoals.[40] These hazards to navigation stimulated overland wagon trade, and some determined farmers put axles through the hogsheads and rolled them to Charleston behind mules or oxen.[41] The difficulties of pulling thousand-pound barrels over one hundred miles of muddy, gullied roads behind cantankerous draft animals transcend the imagination.

Government acted to solve the transportation problem. In 1784, Governor William Moultrie called a special legislative session to cope with a host of problems facing South Carolina. High on the list were roads, bridges, and ferries to move "that Valuable but Bulky Article of Tobacco," which, Moultrie predicted, would "in a few years be one of our great staples."[42] Over the next two decades, government cleared rivers, built bridges, improved roads, and dug canals that stimulated agriculture in the backcountry and funneled trade to Charleston.

But transportation was only part of the problem. Since tobacco was shipped in wooden hogsheads, buyers were not always sure what they were getting. Removing the lid revealed the uppermost contents, but some planters "nested" hogsheads with lower-quality tobacco topped off with high-grade leaf. Moreover, since tobacco was sold by weight, dishonest planters sometimes hid rocks, bricks, even fragments of gravestones deep in the hogsheads. Casual inspection did not usually reveal the ruse, and only when buyers uncased the tobacco in Europe did they discover the deception. Buyers sometimes reacted by withdrawing from the offending market or lowering their bids to protect themselves. In either case, the consequences of dishonesty undermined the market and penalized the innocent along with the guilty.[43]

Even before the War for Independence, the colonial legislature took steps to regulate the tobacco trade and protect the reputation of South Carolina leaf. South Carolina's first tobacco law went on the books in 1771. The act provided for inspection warehouses to be located in the port cities of Charleston, Georgetown, and Beaufort and on the Pee Dee River at Cheraw, the Wateree at Camden, and the Savannah at Silver Bluff.[44] The law also provided for official tobacco inspectors to examine each hogshead. Following the example of Maryland and Virginia inspectors, officials removed not only the lids but also random staves from the sides of hogsheads to view the contents in cross section. Hogsheads could also be probed for foreign matter. Inspectors weighed the hogshead and branded the lid with the letters "SC." Officials usually assigned a quality grade as well. Over time, the state's inspection system enhanced the reputation of South Carolina leaf and the confidence of buyers.

The warehouses also served as marketplaces, bringing buyers and sellers together. After changing hands, the tobacco was stored in the warehouse until shipment. Warehouses on the Pee Dee, Wateree, and Savannah Rivers enabled farmers to sell their crop closer to home, freeing them from the necessity of further travel and expense. If the leaf did not sell on the premises, officials issued bonded receipts, called manifests, to growers. Manifests recorded the quantity and grade of leaf. Farmers could redeem the manifests for cash after the goods were paid for and safely aboard ship. The General Assembly was deadly serious about safeguarding South Carolina's reputation. Hogsheads found to contain offending "dirt or trash" were burned by inspectors, and the law prescribed a draconian penalty for forging or altering a tobacco manifest—death by hanging.[45]

The warehouse inspection system was very popular. Several times in succeeding years, the state government authorized creation of additional tobacco inspection and storage facilities. Floor space and services were enlarged in the port cities and new facilities established in the upcountry to serve more remote areas. In 1784, warehouses opened on the Congaree River and "near the head of navigation" on the Savannah River. By 1786, warehouses were receiving tobacco at Winnsboro and the north fork of the Edisto River.[46] In 1789, planters in the westernmost districts of the state—Chester, Greenville, Spartanburg, Union, and York—reminded the General Assembly of "their extreem remoteness from a Tobacco inspection" and petitioned for the same to be "established more convenient to the Planters, where they could send Tobacco with equal advantage."[47] Government responded by establishing ten more inspection warehouses. By 1799, South Carolina's annual leaf exports approached ten million pounds, and the General Assembly had chartered fifty-two tobacco inspection warehouses.[48]

The central figure of the up-country tobacco period was Thomas Singleton. A native of Virginia, Singleton moved to South Carolina and became customs inspector for the port of Charles Town in the 1760s. Informed by a lifetime of tobacco production and inspection, Thomas Singleton was uniquely qualified to advise all interested parties.[49] He traveled the backcountry, instructing farmers on cultivation and curing techniques and suggesting ways to improve quality and profits. Singleton published a pamphlet on tobacco culture that circulated widely in the backcountry. The esteem Singleton enjoyed among tobacco growers is evident in correspondence received by the legislature. Farmers in Ninety-Six praised Singleton's "Thorough knowledge" and concluded that "where there is bad Tobacco . . . he can inform us the cause and point out The Remedy."[50] Spartanburg planters urged the General Assembly to appoint Singleton chief inspector for South Carolina, charging that the incumbent "Never Raised a plant in his Life" and acclaiming Singleton "the fitemest inspector that ever Belonged to a warehouse."[51] Thomas Singleton set high standards for South Carolina's tobacco inspection system, and his Charleston warehouse was a model for facilities throughout the state. A man of eclectic interests, Singleton was experimenting with ways of protecting ships from water worms when he died in Charleston in October 1798, aged seventy-seven years.[52]

Thomas Singleton's death coincided with the zenith of backcountry tobacco culture. The second tobacco period peaked in 1799 at about ten million pounds production, then declined sharply. Indeed, by 1840 tobacco production was only fifty-one thousand pounds, a decrease of 99.5 percent.[53] Only an event of sweeping economic significance could account for the disappearance of a crop culture that previously showed steady gains. The cause, of course, was the advent of the Industrial Revolution and its raw material—cotton.

The origins of the cotton textile industry are so well known that a brief summary will suffice. In the closing decades of the eighteenth century, British and American engineers developed a cluster of technologies that revolutionized both manufacturing and agriculture.[54] By the early 1800s, two thousand steam-powered spinning and weaving machines were operating in Great Britain, and worldwide sales of inexpensive cotton cloth increased apace.[55]

The American South responded to the need for raw material. Small amounts of cotton had been raised in America since the early colonial period. The Sea Islands of Georgia and South Carolina produced a luxurious, long-fiber cotton highly regarded in Britain. As late as 1791, these two states were responsible for the entire American cotton crop of two million pounds. So strong was the demand for this long-fiber cotton that a pound of it brought sixty pence on the Liverpool docks.[56] Another advantage enjoyed by Sea Island cotton was that its shiny black seed was easily separated from the fibers, making it inexpensive to clean and process. Climatic peculiarities necessary for this variety confined its culture to coastal regions of South Carolina and Georgia, thus limiting production to a few million pounds per year.

A far more common variety, upland or short-staple cotton, was more adaptable and could grow almost anywhere in the American South. Though its shorter fiber was less desirable than the Sea Island type, it was perfect for mass-produced, inexpensive cloth. The problem lay with its fuzzy green seed. Unlike Sea Island cotton, upland fibers clung so tenaciously to the seed that cleaning a single pound of lint required a day's work.[57] Obviously, this labor-intensive cleaning process was the bottleneck restraining a potentially vast supply to meet British demand.

No college student's summer vacation was more momentous than Eli Whitney's journey south in the summer of 1793. When Whitney left New

Haven he had never seen a cotton plant. While visiting near Savannah, Whitney learned of the pressing need to mechanize the seed cleaning process. His hostess introduced him to a neighbor who agreed to underwrite his attempt to develop a "cotton engine." Whitney's efforts were so successful, he later informed his father, that with his invention "one man and a horse will do more than fifty men."[58]

Although experiments with other ginning devices were also under way, Eli Whitney's "cotton engine" was the last link in the chain of technology that raised the floodgates of cotton production in the American South. In 1793, the year Whitney built his first gin, about 5 million pounds of cotton were grown in the United States. Within a decade, annual production reached 60 million pounds, a rate of increase exceeding 100 percent per year. In 1825, machines based on Whitney's design ginned 250 million pounds of cotton. In 1850, cotton production in the United States passed 1 billion pounds, two hundred times the 1793 figure.[59]

South Carolina farmers kept pace with the region's enthusiasm for cotton. The climate and soils of the South Carolina backcountry were ideally suited to short-staple cotton, and the fleecy staple spread through the region with remarkable speed. Backcountry farmers began acquiring land and slaves and turned to cotton farming with a will. Within a single generation, the rolling hills and fertile valleys of the South Carolina piedmont were literally made white (see Table 1).[60]

The demand for inexpensive cotton goods seemed insatiable, and the looms of Leeds and Manchester, Lowell and Fall River had a ravenous appetite for the white fiber. This demand translated into high prices and high profits for South Carolina cotton growers. Adding to cotton's appeal was its low start-up costs. Unlike rice culture, which required an expensive infrastructure and substantial labor, cotton farmers could get by with smaller capital outlays. Indeed, the new staple could be cultivated in small plots by family labor. Thus small farmers could profit from cotton as they never could from rice. In 1805, observers calculated that a small family could "make provisions" and show a $212 profit from only four acres of cotton. Some large planters made fortunes from cotton. For example, Wade Hampton I cleared $75,000 on his first cotton crop.[61]

Cotton enjoyed a price advantage over tobacco as well. This price differential was even more telling because tobacco was more labor intensive and costlier to produce than cotton. As Table 2 confirms, although prices of

TABLE I

Cotton Production in South Carolina
for Selected Years, 1791–1849

Year	Millions of Pounds
1791	1.5
1796	10.0
1801	20.0
1806	30.0
1811	40.0
1816	44.0
1821	50.0
1826	70.0
1833	73.0
1839	61.7
1849	120.0

Sources: Stuart Bruchey, comp. and ed., *Cotton and the Growth of the American Economy, 1790–1860* (New York: Brace and World, 1967), 18; Alfred G. Smith, *Economic Readjustment of an Old Cotton State: South Carolina, 1820–1860* (Columbia: University of South Carolina Press, 1958), 47.

both crops varied in response to market influences such as the War of 1812 and the Panic of 1819, cotton consistently outperformed tobacco.

Cotton's economic impact was immediate and dramatic. David Ramsay, South Carolina physician and historian, noted in 1809 that "cotton trebled the price of land suitable to its growth . . . and the annual income of those who plant it is double to what it was before."[62] If anything, Ramsay's estimates were conservative. During the previous two crop years, 1808 and 1809, cotton prices were unusually low at about thirteen cents.

The transition from tobacco to cotton in the South Carolina backcountry was consistent with market forces. World markets in the early 1800s clearly favored cotton over tobacco, and this preference was reckoned in cold, hard cash. Backcountry farmers, accustomed to little more than subsistence, plunged into cotton culture. Cotton flourished in the piedmont environment, and profits from the new staple funded increasing land and labor requirements as cotton culture expanded throughout the region.

TABLE 2

Wholesale Prices of Cotton and Tobacco at Charleston, 1806–1824

Year	Cotton	Tobacco	Year	Cotton	Tobacco
1806	20.0[a]	5.2	1816	27.5	15.0
1807	19.6	6.5	1817	29.0	9.5
1808	13.3	5.5	1818	32.0	8.5
1809	13.8	6.5	1819	15.4	8.0
1810	14.4	6.0	1820	18.8	5.3
1811	12.6	4.8	1821	14.5	4.5
1812	10.6	4.5	1822	13.3	4.7
1813	9.7	4.2	1823	12.4	3.7
1814	15.0	11.0	1824	14.4	4.4
1815	24.2	11.5			

Source: Arthur H. Cole, *Wholesale Commodity Prices in the United States, 1700–1861*
(1938; rpt. New York: Johnson Reprint Co., 1969), appendix C, passim.
[a] Prices are in cents per pound.

While the South Carolina backcountry was becoming a cotton kingdom, tobacco retreated to its former status as a minor subsistence crop. Ironically, tobacco had served backcountry farmers in the 1780s and 1790s as it served the lowcountry a century earlier, that is, as a temporary cash crop until something better came along. As lowcountry tobacco culture gave way to rice and naval stores about 1690, so backcountry tobacco culture fell to cotton about 1800.[63]

The change in staple crops involved more than land use alone, and much of the commercial infrastructure that served the tobacco trade was soon adapted to cotton. About 1804, cotton growers and traders petitioned the legislature to rent them space in state-owned tobacco warehouses because cotton had "in a great measure superseded tobacco as an article of extensive cultivation." Moreover, cotton interests soon adapted idle tobacco equipment to serve the new staple. Screw presses used to prize leaf into hogsheads were modified to compress cotton into bales.[64]

Within a decade, tobacco farming again disappeared from South Carolina. By the 1820s, Charleston factors who still handled tobacco recorded it as originating in "Kentucky, Georgia, and Fayetteville."[65] Indeed, tobacco's decline was so complete that the census of 1850 failed to find a single farm in South Carolina producing as much as three thousand pounds. By comparison, the number of farms producing that amount of cotton exceeded eleven thousand.[66] By the early 1800s, South Carolina's second tobacco period was over. Cotton's greater value—often three or four times greater—pushed tobacco from the red hills of the piedmont.

The triumph of rice over tobacco in the 1690s was entirely consistent with market forces. In the first place, rice enjoyed a broader consumer base than tobacco. Furthermore, tidewater rice planters were protected by the environmental peculiarities necessary for large-scale production, and the lowcountry had a comparative advantage for producing rice. Indeed, Peter Coclanis's award-winning study of the lowcountry argues that rice culture was the best hope the region's swampy terrain and semi-tropical climate ever had for sustained economic growth.[67]

The backcountry tobacco period was superseded by the first great cotton boom about 1800. A cluster of technologies in the late eighteenth century focused the Industrial Revolution on cotton. Mass production and marketing made high-quality cotton goods affordable, and demand drove expansion of cotton culture and manufacture for decades. Like lowcountry rice growers before them, backcountry cotton growers responded to the siren song of the marketplace, acquiring land and slaves.

Tobacco was South Carolina's original staple crop. In both lowcountry and backcountry, tobacco served as a temporary staple until displaced by crops offering greater possibilities. In the 1670s, tobacco helped establish South Carolina's first fragile links to world markets, links soon commandeered by rice. In the 1770s, tobacco put the backcountry on a cash basis and established the essential market orientation, commercial networks, and physical plant that assured a smooth transition to cotton after 1800.

More than seventy-five years passed before technology revolutionized the tobacco industry and demand for tobacco products again justified its cultivation in South Carolina. While the state's tobacco culture languished during the middle decades of the nineteenth century, the momentous events of those years altered the economic landscape so profoundly that some understanding of what emerged from the crucible of the Civil War is essential.

*Here is a country capable of supporting
ten times the present population with
lands in order . . . [yet] there is not now
enough in this parish to give the people one
dinner.*

DANIEL JORDAN, 1868

2 Years of the Locust, 1865–1885

MORE THAN SEVENTY-FIVE YEARS passed before to-
bacco was again cultivated as a cash crop in South Carolina. Over these
eight decades, South Carolina deepened its commitment to rice, cotton,
and slavery and marched in lockstep with world markets to the cadence of
the overseer's lash. In the 1820s, South Carolina's preeminence in cotton
production was supplanted by vast new areas of cultivation in Mississippi,
Alabama, and Texas. The state's competitive edge was further dulled by
tariffs that South Carolinians believed discriminated against them. In 1832,
the tariff issue brought South Carolina and the national government face-
to-face in the first great crisis of union. It would not be the last.

Alarmed by the mounting strength of the antislavery movement in the 1840s, South Carolinians countered abolitionist rhetoric with strident defenses of the peculiar institution. Again in 1850, the shrill cry of secession was heard in the Palmetto State. South Carolinians rushed to the brink in 1850 and drew back only because no other state would accompany them, and they were loath to make the leap alone. The famous compromise of that year was but a lull in the storm. During the last antebellum decade, voices of reason on both sides of the sectional conflict faded as the howl of extremism swelled. Finally, in 1860, South Carolina led ten sister states out of the Union and into catastrophe.[1]

On the Fourth of July 1881, a traveler passing through the Pee Dee region of South Carolina gazed upon scenes of grinding poverty. As he entered the region from North Carolina, the landscape presented "the dreariest picture of desolation and desertion imaginable." Along the twenty-five-mile post road from the state line to Conway the traveler noticed only four residences that "bore any semblance of culture and refinement. The habitations of the populace were crude log cabins with mud chimneys as if gruesome sentinels placed there to challenge the entrance of improvement or progress."[2] In other parts of the Pee Dee, railway passengers could cross miles of worn-out cotton fields where men and women toiled for fifty cents a day.[3]

In the decades following the Civil War, the Pee Dee region was afflicted with a host of deficiencies, which, like a virtual plague of locusts, ravaged the quality of life and stripped the land of everything but hope. Poverty in all its crippling manifestations beset the region: economic stagnation, lack of opportunity and capital, illiteracy, inadequate transportation and communication, all compounded by poor diet and health care.[4]

Lack of economic diversity underlay much of the region's troubles. The remarkable industrial development that transformed South Carolina's piedmont in the 1880s and 1890s largely bypassed the Pee Dee, and agriculture remained the bedrock of the region's economy.[5] The Pee Dee's few industries were mostly lumber or grist mills engaged in low value-added processing of raw materials. In 1886, the *Marion Star* echoed a lament typical for the region: "Manufacturing in this county is, we are sorry to say, at a very low ebb. Along the Pee Dee River are some flouring mills, and here and there a saw mill, but aside from these trifling concerns . . . there is nothing in the line of manufacturers."[6] Thus the scarcity of employment opportunities off the farm deepened the region's dependence on agriculture and forced thousands to scratch a living from the land.

To make matters worse, agriculture, on which the prosperity of the Pee Dee depended almost entirely, was in a miserable state. Indeed, the 1870s and 1880s were difficult years for most American farmers. Government policies favored industry over agriculture, capital over labor, creditors over debtors, and the Northeast over the rest of the nation. But in addition to these national issues, southern farmers faced a special set of problems stemming from the Civil War and its aftermath. The events of the 1860s wrought profound change in Pee Dee agriculture, affecting labor, land tenure, finance, and marketing. Traditional economic institutions and commercial linkages had to be modified or reinvented altogether, and transitions were not always smooth. Moreover, by the 1880s, cotton, the crop that virtually defined the southern economy, had fallen on hard times. Despite their best efforts, Pee Dee farmers were slow in regaining antebellum levels of prosperity. For example, the census of 1880 found the value of farm property in South Carolina to be only half the 1860 assessment.[7]

Certainly the most important consequence of the Civil War for the Pee Dee was emancipation. Indeed, since most South Carolinians had been slaves before the war, it could be argued that in demographic terms at least, South Carolina was actually on the winning side. But even as emancipation solved old problems, it created new ones. Liberation of the enslaved labor force in the spring of 1865 essentially halted agriculture in many communities. Pee Dee landowners were eager to plant, anxious that precious time was being lost. But beyond the immediate needs of the current crop lay the larger issue of devising an entirely new production system based on free labor. Emancipation ended the two-hundred-year slave regime without creating a free labor system to replace it. Indeed, there was no consensus on how the need for labor would be met. Just then, however, the historic labor force was occupied with other matters.[8]

The first weeks of freedom were an epiphany for many former slaves. Motivated by years of longing and the anxieties of war, they began to probe the perimeters of their new status with a hope and excitement only free people can feel, free people beginning a long journey whose outcome is uncertain. Many sought to affirm their new condition and enjoy the novelty of freedom. Understandably, this meant doing things they were forbidden to do as slaves. An obvious means for freedpeople to assert their freedom was simply to leave the places of their former bondage. Abandoning their customary places—even if many later returned—was an important gesture of confirmation. One South Carolina freedperson spoke for many in declining a job offer from her former mistress: "No, Miss, I must go. If I stays here I'll never know I'm free."[9]

Emancipation provoked a wide range of responses, of course, and some former slaves chose to stay with their former masters.[10] Some who remained included older people and those whose health or family obligations compelled their continued presence. For some, practical considerations were paramount. They looked upon the plantations as home; they felt secure there; friends and family were nearby and material necessities available. For them, the idea of abandoning the only home they knew seemed more like exile than emancipation, more folly than freedom. Still others, bewildered by unfamiliar, even frightening postwar conditions, stayed put to see what would happen.

The reaction of whites to emancipation ranged from compassion to condemnation. In March 1865, a white South Carolinian wrote, "There is quite a difference of manner among the negroes, but I think it proceeds from uncertainty as to what their condition will be . . . and their manner is a sort of feeler by which they will find out how far they can go."[11] Observed another South Carolinian, "They are wandering about the countryside enjoying their new freedom, and, to my mind, wonderfully civil under the circumstances."[12]

Other observers were less generous. Many whites doubted that freedpeople would work without coercion and pronounced large-scale agriculture as dead as slavery. Some arrogantly dismissed the notion of free black labor. In July 1865, a correspondent signing himself "Pee Dee" told the *Darlington New Era,* "We can have no further use for them [freedpeople] in their present status. We will work our lands ourselves or hire white men to work for us." As for the freedpeople, the writer concluded, "We would be pleased for you to take them from among us."[13]

Old attitudes died hard. Governor Benjamin F. Perry voiced an opinion shared by many South Carolinians when he asked the *New York Times,* "If all the children in New York City were turned loose to provide for themselves, how many would live, prosper, and do well?" The governor continued, "Negroes are as improvident as children and require the guardian protection of someone almost as much as they do."[14] Others, confident that free blacks could not care for themselves, gloomily predicted the extinction of the race. Horry planter Daniel Jordan asked his diary: "How many years will pass before he is like the Indian—gone?"[15]

To understand the striking pessimism of such sentiments, one must look beyond the obvious racism to observe the overwhelming difficulties planters faced in the postwar period. Much of their wealth had been written off at Appomattox. In common with their class throughout the South, most Pee Dee planters had invested the bulk of their capital in slaves, land, and banknotes. With emancipation, the cash value of their human property had vanished in an instant.[16] Confederate notes and bonds were worthless, and much of the other currency circulating in the Pee Dee was nearly so. After four years outside the national monetary system, genuine United States notes and coins were scarce, and the currency issues of private banks traded at deep discounts. For example, the Bank of Georgetown's notes traded at 12 percent of face value, the Merchants' Bank of Cheraw's at 8 percent, and the Bank of South Carolina's at just six cents on the dollar.[17]

Real estate values were depressed as well. Postwar conditions were so uncertain that farmlands depreciated sharply. Contemporary sources abound with examples. In April 1867, the *Charleston Daily Courier* reported that a farm in Williamsburg District worth $5,000 before the war had just sold for $700. In some communities, the price of farmland plummeted to about a dollar an acre. Near Marion, farms of 158 acres and 381 acres brought $160 and $400 respectively.[18] Thus the utility of farmland as a basis of credit was severely limited. Predictably, credit was scarce and very expensive. Desperate for operating capital, some Pee Dee planters paid as much as 3 percent interest per month for production credit.[19]

Despairing of ever rebuilding their shattered fortunes, a few Pee Dee planters cashed in their holdings as best they could and left the region. Some immigrated to Florida and Texas, while others sought opportunity in the Far West. After watching his children depart for California in 1868, Anthony W. Dozier, a former mayor of Georgetown, sold his plantation on Snow's Island for $2.25 per acre and followed them. He later wrote that San Jose was the handsomest city he ever saw, except Kingstree.[20]

For planters who stayed, however, rumors of land confiscations added to their woes. Indeed, uncertainty over the land question was a source of confusion for both blacks and whites. Rumors persisted that large landholdings would be seized, subdivided, and sold to blacks and poor whites and the proceeds applied to the federal war debt. Appearances in print gave such rumors an especially long life, and some Pee Dee papers rushed to print gossip as if it were gospel. For example, in August 1865, the *Darlington Southerner* reported that federal authorities would soon establish a "Confiscation Department" to carry out seizures of "agrarian property."[21]

Rumors of land confiscation further impeded the revival of commerce in the Pee Dee. Fears that plantations of former Confederates would be seized prompted some merchants to deny credit to landowners even with the security of a first mortgage.[22] Although the feared confiscations did not occur, many estates were worth less than the sums already owed on them, and a strict accounting would have reckoned many planters' net worth in negative values. Indeed, some Pee Dee planters retained their holdings only because their creditors were themselves insolvent.[23] For what it was worth, all most planters had left was land.

Most freedpeople lacked even that. Although there was much talk of lands being made available to freedpeople, and rumors of "forty acres and a mule" flew thick and fast, few actually acquired any land. Fewer still kept lands where they had "squatted" awaiting permanent titles. Adding to the confusion, swindlers posing as government agents passed through the Pee Dee selling bogus "land certificates" to hopeful freedmen for a few dollars.[24] Legitimate government policies were nearly as flawed. In many cases, lands reserved for free black families in South Carolina were sold to Republican politicos and northern businessmen eager for quick profits. The failure to provide needed economic underpinnings for the freed-peoples' newly won liberty was ultimately the greatest disappointment of Reconstruction.[25]

By the autumn of 1865, many freedpeople were beginning to feel the sting of hardship. As the novelty and exhilaration of their new status began to wear off, they took stock of their circumstances. The sobering conclusion was that freedom, with all its intangible benefits, could not sustain them. A South Carolina freedman, Ezra Adams, recalled the sentiment with a familiar analogy: "Slaves . . . soon found out that freedom ain't nothing 'less you got something to live on. Livin' on liberty is like young folks livin' on love after they gits married. It just don't work."[26]

As autumn gave way to winter, many began to suffer real want. Although federal authorities and private relief agencies distributed emergency rations to the destitute of both races, it was never intended to be more than a supplement to indigenous food supplies. Years later, former slave Tinney Shaw recalled the bitter winter of 1865: "The first winter after the war was the worst I ever knowed. I'm telling you it was bad. Maybe you don't think so, but nigh 'bout every nigger in the world cussed ole Abe Lincoln that winter."[27] Thus the specter of want impelled former masters and former slaves toward each other in a groping search for survival.

For most people in the Pee Dee, survival meant cotton. By the spring of 1866, everyone—blacks and whites alike—wanted to grow cotton. In June, the *Marion Star* declared, "No subject interests our people more at present than the next cotton crop."[28] They had good reason to be concerned. Low production levels during the war and uncertainties afterward sent cotton prices soaring. In the autumn of 1866, middling grade cotton was bringing forty-three cents a pound. Even corrected for wartime inflation, this was more than double its 1860 value.[29] Landowners wanted to cash in on the cotton boom and needed labor; freedpeople wanted work on favorable terms and needed land. Thus both sides of the agrarian equation, each with its own doubts, fears, and prejudices, began to experiment with free labor economics.

Of the many obstacles impeding the revival of Pee Dee agriculture, the greatest was the method of paying for labor. Most freedpeople were willing, even eager, to work, but they expected to be paid. And who could blame them? After a lifetime of unrequited toil, freedpeople wanted regular wages. The problem was that almost no one had any money. Here and there, a planter had managed to save a few bales of wartime cotton to sell on the postwar market, but he was very much the exception. "The South is thoroughly depleted of means and material," declared the *Charleston Daily Courier,* "and time must be given to recover. . . . Should freedmen refuse to labor unless paid in full before the crops can be brought to market, it is not clear how the soil is to be tilled to advantage."[30] The idea of accepting promises in lieu of payment did not appeal to most freedpeople. Few were inclined to trust those who had until very recently waged war to keep them enslaved.

Into the breach between land and labor stepped the Bureau of Freedmen, Refugees, and Abandoned Lands, called the Freedmen's Bureau. The agency, acting with the authority of the War Department, brought land and labor together through use of employment contracts. Government policymakers believed labor contracts were the best means of educating former masters and former slaves to the realities of free labor. Further, it was hoped the binding character of the contract would provide needed stability and encourage freedpeople to settle down and return to work.

Contracts obligated freedpeople to work for an individual landowner for a given period, usually a crop season. They specified tasks, compensation, and other particulars. To provide for immediate needs, weekly distributions of rations—typically bacon, cornmeal, rice, and molasses—were specified, and housing for working families was furnished as well. Wages were payable when the crop was sold. To planters, the contract guaranteed adequate labor to make a crop. To freedmen and women, the contract offered food, housing, and a surety that their wages would be paid. With federal troops on hand to compel payment, freedpeople could labor with the assurance that promises would be kept.[31]

In the Pee Dee, federal officers met with planters at county seats to explain the new labor system and distribute model contracts. For example, Colonel George H. Nye of the Twenty-ninth Maine Infantry met with Darlington and Marion planters at their respective courthouses, and Lieutenant Colonel B. H. Smith met with Georgetown planters. Junior officers and Freedmen's Bureau agents canvassed the countryside, meeting with freedpeople and reassuring them that their interests would be protected. The agents negotiated with landowners, resolved differences, and approved contracts.[32]

Several labor contracts circulated in the Pee Dee. Details varied from place to place and reflected local conditions. Contracts specified a variety of compensation packages including cash, crop shares, food and housing, use of implements and draft animals, garden space, firewood, and other benefits. For example, Georgetown contracts specified that landowners would furnish mules, wagons, and plows, and workers were to keep fences and ditches in good repair.[33] Wages payable in produce were common in Pee Dee labor contracts. Planters in Marion District promised workers one-third of the cotton crop, and Georgetown contracts pledged workers two-fifths of the rice harvest. Field hands on Peter Bacot's plantation near Mars Bluff got one-third of the cotton plus one-third of the corn, peas, and potatoes. Bacot paid house servants cash wages of $10 to $16 per month. A contract widely used in Darlington District assigned laborers half the crop after deductions for fodder and cotton baling materials.[34]

Aware that emancipation implied more than solely economic considerations, Freedmen's Bureau agents sometimes inserted clauses memorializing the laborers' new status. For example, Woodward Manning of upper Marion District (later Dillon County) agreed to treat his workers "in a manner consistent with their freedom."[35] Model contracts distributed to Marion and Darlington planters pledged landowners to treat freedpeople "with justice and kindness." Darlington's Unionist newspaper *New Era* reminded readers that "the slaves are now free, and the old usages of slavery in the government of the plantation must be abolished. The whip, the paddle, and the stocks must be put away . . . [and] the rule of the planters over the laborers should be worthy of men not actuated by malice."[36]

Like the road to hell, the contract system was covered with good intentions. Initially, federal authorities imposed the system because they felt it embodied principles of free labor economics as they were then understood in the North. Simply stated, the free labor ideology maintained that independent farmers, shopkeepers, and artisans were (or should be) the backbone of the republic. Furthermore, in a free labor environment, every worker, though he might begin as a wage earner in the field or forge of another, could aspire to proprietorship and self-sufficiency. In the case of the South, federal authorities believed that once the constraints of slavery were removed, labor would flow to areas of comparative advantage, and supply and demand would find equilibrium. Moreover, the theory went, diligent laborers could aspire to yeoman status as slaves could not.[37]

As logical and reasonable as this thinking seemed, however, the difficulty lay in transplanting these principles into an environment where neither labor nor management had much experience with them. Slavery had deprived blacks of valuable decision-making experience, and most planters had little background with free labor, especially free black labor.[38] But lack of experience was not just a southern problem. Few federal policymakers knew much about large-scale staple agriculture. Northern farms tended to be smaller and more diversified than southern plantations, and northerners often lacked understanding of southern conditions and attitudes.[39]

Racial differences complicated the situation more than northern theorists had predicted. In the North, employers and employees were typically the same color. In the Pee Dee, however, bosses and workers were usually

TABLE 3

Black/White Population Ratios,
Pee Dee Counties, 1880

County	Population black/white	Percentage black/white
Chesterfield	6,847/9,498	41.9/58.1
Clarendon	12,908/6,282	67.3/32.7
Darlington	21,556/12,929	62.5/37.5
Georgetown	16,146/3,466	78.5/21.5
Horry	4,942/10,632	31.7/68.3
Marion	18,226/15,881	53.4/46.6
Marlboro	12,571/8,026	61.1/38.9
Williamsburg	16,352/7,758	71.4/28.6
Total	109,548/74,472	59.5/40.5

Source: Computed from Julian J. Petty, *The Growth and Distribution of Population in South Carolina* (1943; rpt. Spartanburg:
Reprint Company, 1975), 228.

of different races. As Table 3 shows, as late as 1880, blacks still outnumbered
whites three to two in the Pee Dee. In fact, every county in the region but
Horry and Chesterfield had a black majority throughout most of the nineteenth century. Race relations were further strained by the recent, bitter
memory of slavery. No northern employer ever had to face workers he had
formerly owned and possibly abused. Truly, for all its lip service to freedom, federal sponsorship of labor contracts in the postwar South was neither enlightened nor imaginative.

There were problems with the contract system from the beginning. First,
contracts perpetuated slave-style work routines such as gang labor, which
focused on groups rather than individuals and tended to make labor a collective responsibility. Contracts were typically collective, covering many
workers on the same plantation.[40] Although workers were often paid a
share of the crop, the communal nature of the division did little to encourage individual effort. "Full hands" received a certain amount, "half hands"
less, and so on (see example of a labor contract in Appendix).[41] Thus workers were paid according to their capacity rather than their output. Moreover, rewards for greater effort on the part of one did not accrue entirely

to him or her but were disbursed among the group. Conversely, penalties for an individual's lack of effort were largely borne by the group.[42] Such a wage scheme tended to penalize rather than reward diligent workers. As one Cheraw farmer put it, "The hardworking, industrious laborer fares no better than the veriest slouch."[43] Lack of positive incentives, therefore, must be added to the indictment against the contract system.

Typically, contracts were designed to give landowners control over labor. Believing that only strict discipline would assure the constancy of labor needed to grow cotton or rice, Pee Dee planters clearly intended the new regime to impose order on the labor force. On the Allston rice plantations in Georgetown District, for instance, a bushel of rice was deducted from a worker's share for each day of unexcused absence. The contract further provided that repeat offenders could be dismissed with forfeiture of all interest in the crop. Penalties were also imposed for nonspecific offenses vaguely defined as "insubordination."[44]

In some cases, planters sought to retain a vestige of the authority and deference they had enjoyed as slave masters. For example, Adele Petigru Allston required laborers on Chicora Wood plantation in Georgetown District "to conduct themselves honestly & civilly and to exact the same from their families."[45] Workers on Peter Bacot's plantation near Mars Bluff were forbidden to "introduce or invite visitors, or leave the premises without permission." Employees further agreed "to keep nothing whatsoever upon the premises except what he [Bacot] may see fit to allow." And all were "subject to the orders of the employer at all hours."[46]

Many northerners shared these paternalist sentiments. Model contracts circulated by federal officials in the Pee Dee admonished laborers to be "orderly and quiet in their conduct" and forbade them to "leave the plantation without permission from their employer." That these conditions were often spelled out in printed, standardized forms attests to their widespread application. Predictably, freedpeople found such conditions galling. Indeed, many believed labor contracts perpetuated aspects of slavery and suspected their hard-won liberty was somehow being beguiled from them.[47]

Such suspicions appear justified in some cases. Nuances of language reveal much about planters' attitudes toward the newly freed blacks. Peter Bacot's contracts furnish an excellent example. The Freedmen's Bureau furnished Bacot—like all planters—with model contracts. Planters were expected to make copies as needed, faithfully following the model. In making copies, however, Bacot departed from the model in subtle but critical ways. For example, the model referred to workers as "Freedmen and Women." In place of this respectful form of address, Bacot substituted "servants," a term traditionally used as a euphemism for slaves. Moreover, the model stipulated that fines could be levied for absenteeism but that such fines would be divided between employer and employees "in proportion to their relative shares" of the crop. Bacot rendered this provision "All such fines & forfeitures shall inure to the benefit of the employer." Ironically, the model included a promise by the landowner to treat employees "with justice and kindness." Bacot omitted this phrase entirely.[48]

Persistent rumors of government-sponsored land grants also undermined the contract system in the Pee Dee. Understandably, those who stood to gain from such a policy were reluctant to abandon it. A reporter for the *Nation* touring the region in the autumn of 1865 reported that many freedpeople were reluctant to enter contracts, preferring instead to draw emergency rations from the Freedmen's Bureau and northern charities and await land distributions they believed would take place at Christmas. The *Nation* further related that freedpeople in Marion District were refusing to contract even for half the crop, waiting instead for bureau authorities in Columbia to "tell what they'll do" about the land question.[49]

Federal authorities recognized that rumors of land grants were interfering with economic recovery and could result in even greater hardship. In November 1865, the Freedmen's Bureau ordered its agents to "correct the false impression prevailing amongst the Freedmen with regard to land . . . [and] urge the negroes to enter into contracts by every reasonable inducement."[50] Hope died hard. Although Freedmen's Bureau and military personnel dutifully denied the rumors and urged freedpeople to sign contracts, many continued to refuse, believing that doing so would compromise their chances of ever receiving land.[51]

Among the thousands who did contract, however, disappointment undermined morale even further. Clearly, freedpeoples' expectations of a better life were not being met. Besides the demeaning nature of gang labor, they also found fault with the housing arrangements. Under the contract system, housing patterns were often carried over from slavery. Contract workers were usually housed in the plantation slave quarters, sometimes within sight of the landlord or overseer. Specialists in the history of slavery agree that most slaves resented living and working under the watchful eyes of their masters and overseers. Even domestic servants—who were generally better fed, clothed, and housed than field hands—often chafed under the scrutiny of whites.[52] Under the contract system, then, freedpeople saw little improvement in two critical areas—work routines and living conditions. Simply put, had Rip Van Winkle fallen asleep on a Pee Dee plantation in 1846 and awakened in 1866, he would have noticed little change.

Desperate to free themselves from the hopeless drudgery they had known as slaves, many freedpeople acted out their frustrations. Throughout the Pee Dee region, reports mounted of freedpeople breaking contracts, refusing to work, and deserting their employers. Some were willing to fight for what they believed was due them. In December 1866, three hundred freedpeople met near Kingstree to voice their discontent with contract labor and demand land of their own. The freedpeople organized themselves into militia companies, practiced military maneuvers, and declared that "the damned rebels have had their way long enough."[53]

The general dissatisfaction with the new labor scheme alarmed federal authorities. Freedmen's Bureau and army personnel felt considerable ownership in the contract system and were clearly dismayed by its failure. Bureau agents traveled the rivers and dirt roads of the Pee Dee, pleading with freedpeople to respect their contracts. Others, seeing their efforts come to naught, vented their frustrations. In a pessimistic report of the labor situation in Georgetown, the agent there complained that "every contract made in 1865 has been broken by the freedmen."[54]

Facing loss of their property to creditors, Pee Dee planters appealed to federal authorities to enforce the labor contracts. In what could be the crowning irony of Reconstruction, Union troops were dispatched to Pee Dee plantations to compel former slaves to work for their former masters. At Brookgreen, Woodstock, Mount Arena, and Oak Lawn plantations in Georgetown District, Union soldiers were welcomed by former rebels. In fact, some planters wanted troops permanently stationed on their lands. Dr. Allard Flagg asked the military commander at Georgetown if he could keep the two privates sent to Oak Lawn.[55]

Sometimes, however, not even troops could intimidate unhappy freedpeople. At Keithfield Plantation on the Black River in Georgetown District, workers chased superintendent Dennis Hazel, a black man, off the property. Hazel returned with two Union soldiers and manager F. S. Parker Jr. The four faced angry workers armed with hoes and axes, who pelted them with bricks and stones and took away the gun of one soldier. Parker escaped by swimming across the Black River.[56]

Union troops were also sent to discipline troublesome whites. Once the harvest was safely in, some planters tried to provoke freedpeople into leaving before receiving their wages. In the autumn of 1866, the Freedmen's Bureau investigated a "labor disturbance" near Florence in which a planter refused to distribute rations, hoping to starve workers into leaving. Moreover, the report continued, the landlord had forced freedpeople to work at night and on Sundays and had hung one man by his thumbs for refusing. Understandably, the workers became "uneasy" and fled the plantation without their wages.[57]

Predictably, given the unstable labor situation, crop yields were down sharply. For example, Pee Dee rice lands that produced 1,200 pounds per acre before the war yielded only 540 pounds in 1868, a decline of 55 percent. In many places, cotton production also lagged behind prewar levels.[58] Discouraged by their experience with contract labor, Pee Dee planters routinely blamed the workers and the Yankees, ignoring their own contribution to the debacle. Others, persuaded by their own racist assumptions, believed blacks had been "ruined" by freedom and considered importing an entirely new labor force to replace them.[59]

The search for "reliable" labor took some strange turns. The idea of importing European immigrants to work on Pee Dee farms gained popularity for a while. In August 1865, the Darlington Agricultural Society was investigating the "introduction of white foreign laborers" to the region.[60] The following month, the Unionist *New Era* reported that "the new and interesting proposition" of immigrant labor was gaining "active favor" around Darlington. The paper's editor, Benjamin F. Whittemore, championed the idea, citing prosperous Irish and German settlements in the North and concluding that "the settlement among us of industrious and frugal foreigners will be of great value."[61]

A few European laborers actually moved to Darlington and tried cotton farming, albeit briefly. In one instance, Benjamin F. Williamson, a prominent Darlington planter, recruited about thirty Germans to work on his plantation. The Germans were unhappy with their circumstances, however, and drifted away in a few months. This experience taught at least one planter that reliability, or lack of it, was not a matter of color.[62]

Some planters considered importing Chinese workers to meet their labor requirements. Marion planters were sold on the idea, resolving that "in coolie labor only can be found the rehabilitation of the shattered prosperity of the country."[63] In Georgetown, the Agricultural and Mechanical Society debated importing Chinese labor to grow rice. Chinese workers would be well acquainted with rice culture, the planters reasoned, and were believed to be "a race of People of a higher type of civilization and ingenuity." Both groups eventually discarded the idea, however. Pee Dee planters were beginning to realize that the solution to the labor problem lay not in importing foreign workers but in striking a better bargain with free black labor.[64]

Of course, what free blacks wanted was land of their own. But out of the whirlwind of rumor and counterrumor that characterized the land issue in Reconstruction, the plain truth was that relatively few freedpeople ever stood on an acre of their own. Failing that, they wanted freedom to mean something—that their living standard would improve, that they could make some decisions for themselves, that they could exercise more control over their lives and fortunes. They wanted something to change. Clearly, the contract system was not the answer. Disappointed in their ambitions for land of their own, freedpeople began to demand what they hoped would offer the next best thing.

Sharecropping did not originate in the postwar period. The custom of landowner and laborer dividing a crop was well established in the Pee Dee decades before the Civil War. Most sharecropping arrangements were oral understandings (or misunderstandings) between neighbors or family members and left no paper trail. Nevertheless, enough documentation survives to attest to the practice of sharecropping in the Pee Dee as early as the 1820s.[65] The landowner was typically older and better established and was recognized as the senior partner in the sharecropping arrangement. But notwithstanding the difference in status, both parties were usually white, often neighbors, and sometimes related by blood or marriage. Thus issues of race and the former enslavement of one by the other did not complicate the matter.

After emancipation, however, the demographics of sharecropping began to change. Although some whites continued to sharecrop, the arrangement increasingly involved white landowners and black laborers. Besides racial differences, the landowner was typically a former slave owner whose

disposition toward free blacks was paternal at best. And though the occasional exception will prove the rule, most freedpeople were resentful and
mistrusting of former slave owners. Differences of race and class as well
as the legacy of slavery were soon compounded by conflicting economic
interests.

Ironically, share payments began as an accommodation to planters who
lacked cash to pay regular wages. Because there was little hard currency in
circulation after the Civil War, federal officials typically permitted Pee Dee
landowners to pay workers in produce. Freedpeople, who usually wanted
cash wages, at first objected to share payments.[66] By the spring of 1866,
however, the situation began to change. As Pee Dee landowners sold their
first postwar cotton crop and accumulated some working capital, they began to resist sharecropping, preferring instead to pay cash wages and retain
full interest in the crop. When cotton prices were high, paying cash wages
made good economic sense for landowners because they were cheaper. For
example, in 1866 the going rate for prime hands in the Pee Dee was about
$12 a month plus "quarters and rations" for the eight-month cotton sea-
son.[67] The staple averaged forty-three cents in 1866, so this wage level afforded the landowner a far greater profit than paying half the crop for labor. Even when cotton fell to thirty-one cents in 1867, planters preferred
paying cash wages to halving the crop.[68]

Pee Dee planters reckoned more than money in the free labor equation.
By paying cash wages, the landowner retained control of the production
process. That is, he or she decided when and how planting, cultivation,
and harvesting would take place. Planters also believed more was at stake
than purely agricultural issues. Most landowners were also former slave
owners and resisted the idea of entering into partnerships with former
slaves. Landowners wanted to keep labor in a subordinate position, and
even the limited prerogatives of sharecropping implied far too much equal-
ity to suit them. The *Charleston Mercury* summarized the sentiment: "The
freedman, having a direct interest in the crop, is too apt to undertake to
judge what shall and shall not be done in the management and working of
the crop—when he shall labor and when he shall not, and where he shall
labor and where he shall not."[69] Conditioned by a lifetime of ordering
blacks to work, many landowners resented having to negotiate with freedmen and women for the terms of their labor.[70]

The press echoed this sentiment and advised planters to reject share-

cropping. Editors cited examples of failure and warned of dire consequences if freedpeople were permitted to exercise their own judgment. The
Charleston Mercury deemed granting blacks any voice in farm management
"simply absurd." The *Marion Crescent* urged readers to "Pay Money
Wages!" and declared, "The joint crop plan has failed with the negro."
Blacks were blamed, of course. "The free negro partner objects to your
mode of planting, tilling, and harvesting . . . but fails not to commit waste
everywhere." Indeed, said the *Charleston Mercury,* only lack of money
could compel a prudent landowner to undertake this folly.[71]

Freedpeople preferred sharecropping for the same reasons landowners
disliked it. Freedpeople knew the price of cotton was high and working for
half the crop paid better than cash wages at prevailing rates. Through
sharecropping, freedpeople hoped to achieve greater independence and
self-reliance than contract labor would allow. South Carolina's emerging
black press took a firm stand on the issue. The Charleston *South Carolina
Leader,* a black newspaper widely circulated in the Pee Dee, condemned
the monthly wage plan and urged readers to insist on sharecrop arrangements with employers. Only thus could they hope to "retrieve the mistakes
of the past."[72]

Besides the greater tangible rewards, many freedpeople saw sharecropping as a chance to raise their status as well as their living standard. Having
input in decision making, however limited and begrudged, was an important advancement for former slaves. Furthermore, living and working more
or less independently as families appealed to people accustomed to gang
labor and the crowded indignities of the slave quarters. Receiving no land
of their own and disillusioned by the contract system, most freedpeople
wanted to salvage something from the unkept promises of Reconstruction.
They saw sharecropping as a more equitable place in the new agrarian capitalism emerging in the postwar Pee Dee and hoped it would provide a
pathway to proprietorship.

Labor was scarce in parts of the Pee Dee, and freedpeople quickly
learned to press their advantage.[73] In fact, far from meekly accepting whatever landowners offered them, Pee Dee freedpeople aggressively negotiated better compensation and working conditions for themselves. In most
cases, Pee Dee landowners had little choice but to acquiesce. Walter Gregg,
a Mars Bluff planter, told his wife in December 1867, "I have not as yet
gotten all the labor I wish for another year as I am trying to hire for wages,

and a portion of the crop is the popular idea of the freedmen."[74] Although Gregg may have engaged a few workers on his terms, other Pee Dee planters despaired. The *Charleston Daily Courier* reported that some landowners around Cheraw had failed to secure a single hand for the crop season.[75]

Unaccustomed to blacks asserting themselves, whites complained bitterly of the freedpeople's strong bargaining position and willingness to press their advantage. In August 1866, the *Darlington Southerner* complained: "By the [sharecropping] arrangement, labor is made scarce, and capital is forced to court its capricious favor by unreasonable concessions and ruinous indulgence."[76] In November 1867, the *Marion Crescent* indignantly condemned the greed of those who had toiled a lifetime without pay: "The negro partner got, in 1865, one-tenth; in 1866, one-quarter; in 1867, one-third; for 1868, he demands one-half. How long will his native modesty prevent him from claiming the other half?"[77]

The debate over competing work styles in the Pee Dee was well documented by both the local and national press. In September 1866, the *Sumter Watchman* reported that an increasing number of local landowners were determined to abandon sharecropping in favor of cash wages, believing the latter would encourage workers to "greater industry." Freedpeople, however, were coming to the opposite conclusion. A *New York Times* correspondent visiting Sumter in the autumn of 1866 attended a freedpeople's meeting where the group discussed terms for the coming season. With the harvest done and cotton bringing forty-three cents a pound, the majority opposed working for cash wages, preferring to "farm on shares" for half the crop. The reporter noted their optimism and praised their "increasing capacity to adapt themselves to novel circumstances."[78]

Pee Dee planters were also adapting to circumstances, although sometimes with considerable reluctance. The prestigious Darlington Agricultural Society offered leadership in educating planters to the new realities. Hoping to secure an adequate supply of reliable labor, the society resolved to encourage "just compensation & proper treatment" for freedpeople as a general policy. As early as August 1865, the society was exploring ways of balancing planters' interests with "contentment and justice" for the labor force. The society took the extraordinary step of calling a general meeting of area farmers to hear its case for "organization and harmony within the new [labor] system." A year later, the society charged a committee to monitor "the proper treatment of the laborers of the Country."[79] Whether willingly or grudgingly, by the late 1860s more and more Pee Dee land-owners were accepting sharecropping as a fact of life.

Sharecropping differed from contract labor in important ways. For one, the individual character of sharecropping addressed important issues of status. If the arrangement fell short of recognizing landlords and laborers as equals, at least it acknowledged former slaves as free people and free agents, an important distinction in the South of the late 1860s. Perceptions obviously counted for much. In 1869, the *Southern Cultivator*, a popular agricultural journal, reported that freedpeople near Society Hill preferred sharecropping over contracts, considering it a "higher form of laboring." Their preference had convinced area planters that sharecropping was "more likely to secure labor, especially in undesirable localities."[80]

But more was at stake than mere perceptions of status. Freedpeople be-lieved sharecropping gave them more control over their own labor, and some were willing to reject well-paying jobs that placed them under the close supervision of whites. For example, in January 1867 a Mr. Edgecombe informed the *Charleston Mercury* that freedpeople in his community were refusing offers as high as $15 per month and rations to work under a white manager, "being desirous of farming on shares where they can do so with-out a manager over them."[81]

Sharecropping also provided better incentives. Since the system was based on individual production, industrious workers benefited more di-rectly. The fruits of their labors were divided only with the landlord rather than disbursed among several co-workers who might not share the same commitment to effort and efficiency. Freedpeople liked the greater security and privacy the sharecropping lifestyle provided. Housing was furnished on a yearly basis, and fringe benefits could enhance the cropper's living standard. Garden space was routinely provided, and croppers cut firewood from the landlord's forest. Hunting and fishing rights were commonly ex-tended as well, though often limited to certain areas of the property. More-over, since cropper families were often housed some distance apart, they were generally subject to less supervision by the landlord and less scrutiny by their neighbors.[82]

After emancipation, freedpeople wanted to break with the demeaning patterns and usages of the past, and no desire was stronger than the urge for greater independence and mobility. Thus from the freedpeoples' point of view, an intangible but crucial advantage of sharecropping over contract labor was its more definite break with the past. It offered former slaves important affirmation of their freedom by affording them at least a modicum of independence. It was more than most of them had ever known.

Sadly, the economic advantages of sharecropping were short-lived. Within a few years the labor situation stabilized, cotton production increased, and prices declined. Falling cotton prices dulled any economic edge the croppers had enjoyed. In fact, as prices fell, the value of the crop share approached that of wage labor.[83] Ironically, many freedpeople had rejected wage labor because it limited their earnings and had embraced sharecropping because it afforded greater opportunity. They soon learned, however, that exploring the possibilities of free enterprise meant assuming the risks as well.

Lower cotton prices also changed the minds of many landowners about sharecropping. Many Pee Dee landowners had accepted sharecropping in the late 1860s for the simple reason that freedpeople preferred it and the need for labor compelled them to adopt it. But as cotton prices fell and share payments sank to the value of wage labor, landowners became more comfortable with the arrangement. Under the share system, labor costs were not a fixed expense but declined at the same rate as the staple price. Indeed, planters soon discovered other aspects of sharecropping that served their interests. Landowners came to prefer that laborers be vested in the success of the crop, something wage labor did not provide. After all, wage earners could strike, be absent, even desert altogether with little risk; sharecroppers could not. Rather, because croppers did not receive their due until the harvest was in, the system compelled them to stay and work.

By the early 1870s, contract labor had all but disappeared in cotton-producing areas of the Pee Dee, and sharecropping had become the pragmatic accommodation between land and labor.[84] But though sharecropping was better than the system it replaced, it had many drawbacks. Sharecroppers typically purchased necessities on credit from the landlord or an obliging merchant. In lean years—and there were many lean years in the 1870s and 1880s—their share was sometimes insufficient to settle their accounts, and many slid into debt. Even so, sharecroppers were not helpless drudges. If they felt ill-used or if a better situation offered, they could move and often did. Sometimes a new landlord would "pay-out" a cropper family's debt and move them to his farm. Hoping to improve their lot, some moved every few years. But for better or worse, landowners always held the upper hand in the unequal relationship.[85]

Scholars have focused much attention on sharecropping in the postwar South, and although it is unlikely a consensus will emerge, some synthesis of the debate is possible. Some have suggested that anything short of universal land ownership condemned freedpeople to a lifestyle little better than slavery. Others contend that sharecropping, though falling well short of proprietorship, offered a meaningful improvement in the living standard of former slaves.[86] Essentially, the issue seems to be one of perspective: of idealism versus pragmatism, of pessimism versus optimism, of scholars using the same evidence to arrive at different conclusions.[87]

Perhaps the best perspective to bring to the question, however, is that of the croppers themselves. The transition from gang labor as slaves to sharecropping as free people was an important one. At the time, most freedpeople viewed the arrangement as a temporary, transitional stage between slavery and proprietorship. Indeed, given the high price of cotton after the war, they had every reason to believe sharecropping could provide a means to acquire land. But while most freedpeople were ultimately disappointed in their hopes for land of their own, the modest advantages of sharecropping seemed far removed—in their minds, at least—from their former bondage.[88]

Despite the difficulties black farmers faced in the postwar decades, a surprising number were upwardly mobile. By the 1880s, sharecropping was evolving into renting. And by the 1890s, "tenant farming," as it was sometimes called, was commonplace in the Pee Dee. Under this system, considered a step above sharecropping, tenants rented land outright rather than work for a share of the crop. Rents might be paid in cash or produce. For example, good cotton land in the Pee Dee might rent for one hundred pounds of cotton per acre, about a quarter of what it would produce. The tenant usually furnished a mule and implements and had the capital, or at least the credit, to finance his own crop. By the 1890s, a significant number of freedpeople, now middle-aged, had acquired a mule and established credit with a local merchant.[89]

From the tenant's point of view, the advantages of renting over share-cropping were the greater opportunity and autonomy it afforded. The landlord did not supervise the tenant's farming operation or share his profits. Once the rent was covered, the tenant kept everything else. The tenant family usually occupied a house on the rented farm, so housing was a valuable benefit of tenantry. Sometimes tenants performed certain tasks for the landlord such as ditching or fence mending. In exchange, they might receive a small cash wage or other benefits such as firewood or fodder.[90]

As cotton prices fell, landowners came to prefer renting to sharecropping. Rather than gamble on recouping their investments in land, draft animals, and fertilizer from an uncertain partnership, renting minimized the landlord's risk and assured a more definite return. By the 1890s, many Pee Dee landowners were dividing their holdings into several small farms that they rented for cash or cotton. Sometimes the landlord retained a portion, known as the "home place," to cultivate on his own.

Just as sharecropping replaced contract labor in the postwar period, so renting began to replace sharecropping late in the century. The eagerness of blacks to rent land and the willingness of whites to rent to them is clearly revealed by the census of 1900. In Marion County, for example, 50 percent of black farmers were renting and 29 percent were sharecropping by 1900. In Darlington County, the disparity was even greater with 71 percent of black farmers renting and only 15 percent sharecropping. Of Pee Dee counties, only in Horry did sharecroppers outnumber tenants, at 23 percent and 15 percent, respectively. From a distance, distinctions between sharecroppers and tenants may seem subtle, especially since rentals were sometimes paid in kind. Nevertheless, renting offered meaningful advancements over sharecropping, and rural folk were very conscious of them at the time.[91]

Finance and marketing also suffered when the war severed traditional links between Pee Dee fields and northern and foreign markets. Before the war, produce flowed through commission agents called factors. Firms in Georgetown, Charleston, and Wilmington numbered Pee Dee farmers among their clients.[92] Factors received cotton, rice, and naval stores from growers, sold and delivered the commodities to buyers, and collected the proceeds. Factors could also serve as purchasing agents, filling clients' orders with the merchants of the city and shipping the goods upriver. Factors received a commission for their services, and the better capitalized of them sometimes extended credit to selected clients. Improving rail and wire service to the interior began undermining the factors' traditional place in the Pee Dee even before the Civil War. When war came, the naval blockade of southern ports and other disruptions of commerce bankrupted many factors. Those who survived the war were in no condition to meet the capital needs of their clients.[93]

Banks were also hard-pressed to meet capital needs. Indeed, commercial banking had almost ceased in the Pee Dee by 1865. Federal banking regulations enacted during the Civil War made it difficult to establish banks in rural communities, especially in the impoverished South. Capital requirements were steep. National banks were required to have $50,000 paid-in capital to charter—an immense sum in an economy in which farmland sold for $10 an acre and workingmen labored for $14 a month. By 1871, only six banks in South Carolina had met this requirement, none in the Pee Dee. By comparison, Rhode Island, with less than one-third of South Carolina's population, had sixty-two national banks. Not until 1881—sixteen years after the Civil War ended—was a national bank chartered in the Pee Dee.[94]

In addition to high capital requirements, national banking regulations imposed strict limits on real estate loans. Thus the most important store of value in rural communities was limited as a credit resource. Further restrictions limited a bank's currency issues to 90 percent of its treasury bond holdings. State banks were easier to organize, but Congress imposed a stiff tax on their note issues, essentially removing that form of currency from the money supply. Clearly, another source of farm credit was needed.[95]

The financial vacuum in Pee Dee agriculture was filled by entrepreneurs called supply merchants.[96] Businessmen established general stores at strategic places throughout the Pee Dee, often where a well-traveled road crossed a railway or river. The Holliday Company, for example, located by the Little Pee Dee River on the Conway-Marion road in 1869. These merchants carried not only farm supplies and equipment but groceries, clothing, even medicines and furniture. Most storekeepers obtained merchandise on credit from manufacturers and sold it on credit to farmers. To circumvent usury laws, merchants typically priced goods two ways: a cash price and a higher "time price" if the item went on the books. Surveys of rural credit conducted by the *Progressive Farmer* in the 1900s found that time prices were routinely 20 percent higher than cash prices. Indeed, since the 20 percent was added regardless of the term of credit, it could more accurately be called a surcharge. For example, a $100 advance in April was payable at $120 in October. Thus the debtor paid 20 percent for six months' credit, an annual percentage rate of 40 percent. Each customer had a credit line called a "run." The amount of a farmer's run was determined by the size of his farm, his farming skills, livestock or other assets, reputation, and other criteria used to evaluate credit risks. The customer drew on his credit during the growing season and made settlement at harvest time.[97]

Payment was secured by the crop lien, a specialized debt instrument that mortgaged the growing crop. In common with other southern states, South Carolina enacted a lien law soon after the Civil War. The crop lien, like any mortgage, was designed to protect the lender against default by the borrower. Sometimes the crop alone was deemed insufficient collateral and further security was demanded. Cattle and draft animals were often pledged to secure farm credit in the Pee Dee. For example, in 1880, Henry Spain, a Sumter County tenant, pledged his crop and "one small White and Brown Bull" to secure his $45 debt with James M. Carson. Another tenant, Jack Drayton, offered his crop and a "dark brown Mare" as surety for $75 owed Carson.[98]

In much of the Pee Dee, creditors specified cotton to secure advances. Cotton was excellent collateral. It was easily stored, nonperishable, and less likely to be pilfered than food crops or animals. There was a year-round market for cotton so it could be turned into cash anytime. This liquidity appealed to bankers and wholesalers who accepted assignment of crop liens as security against advances made to merchants. Although the cotton lien system may have met immediate needs, there is some evidence that the practice intensified the region's dependence on cotton and thereby retarded much-needed diversification.[99] In the eastern Pee Dee, especially Horry County, naval stores often served as the basis of credit; they had many of the same advantages for this purpose as did cotton.[100]

Besides the formal obligation represented by the lien, payment was further compelled by isolation. Rural people did not usually travel farther than a day's round-trip by wagon. In remote areas of the Pee Dee, therefore, merchants often enjoyed a captive market, having no competitor within a dozen miles or more. Thus some farmers were deterred from defaulting by the lack of an alternate source of supplies. Remoteness could work to the merchant's advantage in other ways. Although isolation may have kept some farmers honest, lack of competition could tempt merchants in remote areas to pad their profit margins.[101]

Despite the increasing market orientation of Pee Dee agriculture, cash was still scarce, and barter remained a common means of exchange. Many area merchants received payment in produce as well as cash. As late as 1886, the Holliday Company of Galivants Ferry was accepting barrels of tar and turpentine to settle accounts. One customer, Fred Williamson, squared his account and left a small credit balance in exchange for "3 Bbls dip." The next day, C. K. Gerrald traded four barrels of "dip" for bacon, flour, molasses, and some empty barrels, presumably to hold more turpentine. Indeed, contemporary advertising confirms that Pee Dee merchants encouraged farmers to spend their staple as an alternative to cash. In the *Horry Weekly News*, Burroughs and Cooper urged patrons to "bring your greenbacks or heavy bbls. of turpentine and watch merchandise fly off the shelves!" [102]

Of course, more was at stake in barter arrangements than the customer's convenience. Merchants expected to profit from handling the staple. Rural merchants also bought produce outright and shipped it by river or rail to brokers in Charleston, Wilmington, or Columbia. With his hand in farming from seedtime to harvest, channeling merchandise in and produce out, financing it all and profiting from it all, the rural merchant was the pivotal figure in his Pee Dee community.

Names long prominent in the commerce of the region began their rise behind the counters of such stores. James Lide Coker, founder of Coker Seed Company and a chain of retail stores, opened his original business in Hartsville in 1865.[103] The Holliday Company began at Galivants Ferry in 1869. The Burroughs and Collins Company in Conway and Daniel Supply Company of Mullins were organized during the first decade after the Civil War.[104] These firms and many more that did not survive had similar customers. Sharecroppers, tenants, yeomen, and planters alike looked to the merchant for the means to make another crop. Thus the merchant bound land and labor together as the Pee Dee climbed slowly to its feet after the Civil War.

Crop selection is a fundamental component of agriculture and affects not only the economics of a community but its very way of life. Well into the 1890s, crop selection divided the Pee Dee region into western and eastern areas. The western area, including the present counties of Darlington, Dillon, Florence, Marion, Marlboro, and Williamsburg, was part of the cotton culture. The eastern Pee Dee—Horry and parts of Georgetown County—were more inclined to subsistence agriculture supplemented by a little cotton, rice, and naval stores. After nearly disappearing, naval stores reemerged as an important cash crop in the early 1870s. Horry and Georgetown farmers "tapped," "dipped," and "scraped" their pine trees for a few extra dollars per year. Commercial operations such as the Burroughs and Collins Company of Conway leased immense tracts of timber and employed scores of workers to collect and process the raw material.[105]

Populated by few planters and many yeomen, Horry had a fundamentally different economic and demographic structure than other Pee Dee counties. Both were carryovers from the antebellum period. For example, in 1850 fully two-thirds of Horry farms were valued under $600. By comparison, in Georgetown District small farms made up only about one-quarter of the total.[106] Horry's demographics offer even sharper contrast. The county's white population of 77 percent was not only the Pee Dee's highest but was second only to the mountain county of Pickens in the whole of South Carolina.[107]

Horry's land distribution and demographics show the county's lesser commitment to slavery before the war and to tenantry afterward. For example, despite its larger area, Horry County was home to only 687 black farmers in 1900 compared to 1,452 in Marion and 2,064 in Darlington. Furthermore, black farmers in Horry were more likely to own land than their counterparts in other Pee Dee counties. By 1900, 62 percent of black farmers in Horry County were proprietors compared to 20 percent in Marion and only 13 percent in Darlington. And the size of the average holding was larger in Horry. In 1900, Horry farms averaged 143 acres compared to 111 in Marion and 70 in Darlington.[108]

A greater commitment to subsistence farming also distinguished Horry County. Horry farms produced enough food for the small, hardy population with some to spare. Contemporary records confirm that Horry County exported food in the postwar decades, even in tough economic times. Table 4, listing shipments from the port of Little River during the depression year of 1873, reveals the diversification of Horry agriculture. The relative values of naval stores, foodstuffs, and cotton are clearly shown as well. Since Horry had no railroads until the 1880s, maritime shipments are especially significant.

The Franco-Prussian War of 1870–71 sent the price of naval stores soaring.[109] The windfall benefited many eastern Pee Dee farmers and pumped much-needed cash into the economy of the region. But the bonanza of the

TABLE 4

Produce Shipments from the Port of
Little River, South Carolina, 1873

Quantity	Unit	Product	Value
14,000	barrels	rosin	$31,500
1,750	barrels	turpentine spirits	28,000
1,000	barrels	tar	2,500
500	barrels	crude turpentine	500
100	bales	cotton	6,000
1,500	bushels	peanuts	3,000
50	–	cowhides	100
1,000	–	other skins	425
300	pounds	bee's wax	90
1,000	bushels	sweet potatoes	600
500	barrels	mullets [fish]	3,300
1,000	gallons	oysters	800
1,000	head	chickens	250
1,000	dozen	eggs	200
100	head	beef cattle	2,000
200	head	turkeys	250
		total	$79,515

Source: "Records of the Port of Little River, S.C.," *Independent Republic Quarterly* 3 (October 1969): 15.

early 1870s was the last the Carolina naval stores industry would enjoy. Changes in naval architecture were gradually undermining demand for wood preservatives and caulking as shipbuilders moved from timber to iron and from sail to steam.[110] At the same time, petroleum products were replacing rosin, pine tar, and turpentine in industrial applications, further eroding demand. The softening market for naval stores coincided with dwindling reserves of pitch pine. More than two hundred years of exploitation and inadequate conservation had diminished the supply, and the industry left the Carolinas for the forests of Georgia, Florida, and Alabama. Confronted with vanishing resources within and waning markets without, the eastern Pee Dee clearly needed a new cash crop.[111]

The western Pee Dee had its problems too. The litany of troubles caused by overdependence on cotton has been voiced elsewhere and needs no elaboration here. The economic decline of the cotton South, and the Pee Dee with it, was hastened by overproduction.[112] By the 1870s, the focus of the Industrial Revolution was moving away from textiles, and demand for cotton was tapering off. At the same time, Egypt, India, and Brazil were producing sizable amounts of cotton, thus becoming serious competitors on the supply side.[113] The economist Gavin Wright has calculated that the world supply of cotton grew at least twice as fast as demand for the staple. Between 1866 and 1895, demand increased an average of only 1.3 percent per year while acreage devoted to the white fiber grew about 5 percent per year.[114] Cotton values responded predictably to slackening demand and increasing supplies. The 1870s saw a drastic decline of cotton prices deepened by the general depression, especially after 1873. Although relieved by occasional upswings, cotton prices continued their downward trend throughout the 1880s and 1890s.

Lower profits from cotton and naval stores reduced incomes throughout the Pee Dee and intensified the poverty of the region.[115] Nearly every component of the living standard bent beneath increasing economic pressure. In many places the diet was reduced to the cheapest foods available. Salt-cured "fatback," corn bread, and molasses raised blood pressure and cholesterol levels without supplying needed vitamins and nutrients. Malnutrition contributed to chronic anemia, goiter, pellagra, and other diseases.[116] High fat and salt consumption doubtless increased the incidence of cardiovascular disease as well.

Education was another casualty. Although a few good private schools such as St. John's Academy in Darlington and St. David's in Society Hill were available for the few who could afford them, public education in South Carolina was miserably inadequate. Most Pee Dee schools were one-room buildings staffed by one poorly paid, overworked teacher who attempted to instruct all ages and grade levels. In 1897, white teachers were paid an average of $147 and blacks about $90 for the five-month school term. Teacher-student ratios are more revealing because, unlike dollars, they need no correction for inflation. Forty-one white pupils were enrolled for every teacher; in black schools there was one teacher for every sixty-nine students. The racially segregated, dual school systems were funded separately, and outlays for black schools actually declined in the 1890s. In 1897, South Carolina spent only $4.21 per white pupil and a pathetic $1.36 each for blacks.[117]

Although racism surely motivated this discrepancy, the state's thin tax base underlay inadequate funding for both races. At the turn of the century, South Carolina could draw on $434 of taxable wealth per pupil while every school-age child in Massachusetts, for example, was supported by $1,449 of assessed valuation. The consequences of this starvation diet for education are revealed by South Carolina's illiteracy rate of 55 percent compared to the national average of 17 percent.[118] Thus fewer than half the citizens of South Carolina could have read the words a Florence-area farmer wrote to his brother in 1885: "We in this section are wondering if there is another way. If the world has lost its appetite for cotton, what does it want? We shall grow that."[119]

By 1885, fluid postwar conditions in the Pee Dee were hardening into permanent patterns. New models of land tenure, marketing, and finance were in place. In both eastern and western areas of the Pee Dee, however, the decline of traditional cash crops hobbled the economy. But soon, a cluster of interlocking developments would impel the Pee Dee toward a new staple for which the world was indeed developing an appetite. Out of the smoke would come the light.

As for me, I'm going into the cigarette business.
JAMES BUCHANAN DUKE, 1884

We need something to take the place of six cent cotton.
MULLINS FARMER, 1894

3

Pearl of the Pee Dee, 1885–1918

FEW CULTURAL PHENOMENA in American history have equaled the spectacular rise of cigarette smoking in the late nineteenth and early twentieth centuries.[1] As a way of consuming tobacco, cigarettes were latecomers. Before the 1870s, few Americans outside major cities had seen a cigarette, let alone smoked one. Americans puffed pipes and cigars, dipped snuff, and chewed flavored tobacco, but cigarettes were uncommon even in the tobacco country. As recently as 1868, a Virginian could mark someone a stranger because "he was smoking a cigarette, which is unheard of in these parts."[2] Within a generation, however, Americans were consuming billions of cigarettes, and Virginia and the Carolinas had become the center of cigarette manufacturing. Moreover, as demand for raw material soared, tobacco culture spread beyond the historic Old Belt of North Carolina and Virginia into new areas of production. One of these was the Pee Dee region of South Carolina, where the need for a new staple met the demand for a new product and sparked an economic revolution.

One reason for the increasing popularity of cigarette smoking was the development of Bright Leaf tobacco, a new mild variety especially well suited to cigarettes. Before the advent of Bright Leaf, tobacco culture had changed little in the previous two centuries. In late summer, the mature plants were harvested and hung in wooden sheds to dry or "cure." Sometimes, farmers lit small fires on the dirt floors of the drying sheds to speed the process. Even so, curing could take weeks, and the result was a strong, dark brown tobacco preferred by chewers and pipe smokers. This robust tobacco was far too strong for cigarettes and could make users dizzy, even nauseous. Though a hearty few tried rolling this pungent tobacco in paper and lighting up, the result was so harsh that one who tried it reported he "could not yet Smoke the whole . . . without revulsion."[3] Indeed, attempts to inhale the pungent smoke often induced a coughing, retching spasm.[4] Before Bright Leaf, there was no smoke mild enough to be inhaled comfortably. The lighter, more palatable tobacco that became the staple of the cigarette industry and, ultimately, the Pee Dee region, was discovered by accident.

It happened in the 1840s. On the Slade brothers' tobacco farm in Caswell County, North Carolina, a teenage farm hand assigned to maintain the low, smoldering fires in the curing barn fell asleep at his post. Waking to find the fire almost completely out, he quickly added several large, burning logs from a nearby blacksmith's forge. The sharp rise in temperature accelerated curing dramatically, and the leaf was ready in a matter of days rather than weeks. It also produced a barn full of mild-smoking, yellow leaf that cigarette manufacturers were eager to buy.[5] Soon, news of the Slades' milder, brighter tobacco and shorter curing time traveled through the North Carolina–Virginia Old Belt tobacco region. Tobacco growers began experimenting with curing methods and equipment, seeking to duplicate by design the lemon-colored accident at the Slades' farm.[6]

There were several obstacles to be overcome. Although hotter fires cured the tobacco faster, the leaves were darkened by smoke and soot. Moreover, it was difficult to keep several small fires at uniform temperatures. Tobacco in hotter areas of the barn cured too fast while leaf in cooler areas cured too slowly. Uneven curing yielded an undesirable mixture of colors and textures. To achieve a uniform cure and color, farmers settled on "flue-curing." A furnace distributed heat through a network of stove pipes (or flues) running parallel to and a few inches above the floor. The flues distributed heat evenly through the barn. The tobacco plants were hung overhead in evenly spaced rows to effect a uniform cure. Because the furnace chimney carried exhaust outside the barn, the leaves were untainted by smoke and soot. The light-colored, yellow product was named Bright Leaf to distinguish it from the darker varieties.[7]

Equally critical as the hardware involved was the schedule of temperature changes needed to dry and color the leaves. Thus variables of humidity and moisture content were accounted for as well. In the years that followed, farmers explored several flue-curing techniques with varying degrees of success. Through trial and error, word-of-mouth, and a helpful press, a reliable method was gradually worked out and entered the public domain. By the 1870s, virtually every tobacco grower in the Old Belt was flue-curing at least part of his crop, and the method became so commonplace there that the term "flue-cured" became synonymous with Bright Leaf tobacco. The mild, yellow leaves were no longer an accident but a culture.[8]

This smoother, milder tobacco found an eager market. In fact, Bright Leaf changed the way smokers consumed cigarettes. Before Bright Leaf, cigarettes were so harsh tasting that only the hardiest user could inhale the smoke. Most smokers were content to puff their cigarettes without inhaling, like cigar and pipe smokers. But the milder smoke of flue-cured tobacco was more easily drawn into the lungs, and this deep inhaling enhanced the smoker's satisfaction with the experience. Inhaling also accelerated the smoker's physiological addiction to the product. Thus Bright Leaf's very mildness was the insidious mechanism that ensured its success.

Before the advent of Bright Leaf tobacco, cigarettes were little more than an expensive novelty and commanded no great following. Americans smoked only 16 million manufactured cigarettes in 1870. But the introduction of increasing amounts of mild, flue-cured leaf in cigarette blends together with improving economic conditions in the late 1870s greatly enhanced the popularity of cigarette smoking. And not only were more

Americans smoking, but they were smoking more. By 1880, Americans were smoking 500 million cigarettes per year, more than thirty times the 1870 figure.[9]

In the 1880s, demand for cigarettes rich in Bright Leaf tobacco continued to rise, while technical innovations made meeting the demand easier, cheaper, and more profitable. One hundred years after the Industrial Revolution turned the American South into a cotton kingdom, technology came calling on the tobacco industry. The Bright Leaf boom of the 1890s, like the cotton boom a century earlier, resulted from a series of technical breakthroughs that revolutionized the tobacco industry. The result was mass production and mass marketing of cigarettes and an even greater demand for Bright Leaf.

Until the 1880s, "manufactured" cigarettes were actually handmade by laborers who rolled and packaged the product in Manhattan sweatshops. Hand rollers—mostly East European immigrants—earned eighty cents per thousand cigarettes. The high price of cigarettes reflected this labor-intensive method of manufacture, and most Americans continued to smoke cigars or roll their own cigarettes with inexpensive shredded tobacco and cigarette papers. Tobacco companies believed a cigarette-rolling machine could lower prices to within reach of the average consumer and greatly expand their potential market. Cash prizes as high as $75,000 were offered to anyone who could build a workable rolling machine.[10]

The first obstacle was preparing leaf tobacco for mechanical processing. In the 1870s, Albert Pease of Dayton, Ohio, patented a cutting machine that rendered leaf tobacco into particles suitable for cigarettes. Furthermore, the speed and output of the Pease Cutter, as it was called, was several times that of manual labor.[11] Now that proper raw material was available, the industry approached the next hurdle: an efficient means of rolling and packaging the product.

The development of rolling technology had as profound an impact on cigarette manufacture as the cotton gin had on textiles. The Eli Whitney of the tobacco industry was James Albert Bonsack of Roanoke, Virginia. Bonsack was a third-generation machinist, his father and grandfather having been successful woolen manufacturers. When the New York firm of Allen and Ginter offered $75,000 for a viable cigarette-rolling machine, Bonsack rose to the challenge. His natural mechanical skills had been honed by years spent tinkering in the family mill, and his efforts proceeded apace. He registered the Bonsack Cigarette Machine with the Patent Office in September 1880, one month before his twenty-first birthday.[12]

The revolutionary potential of the Bonsack machine lay in its speed and volume of output. A single Bonsack machine could produce as many cigarettes as forty-eight hand-rollers, resulting in dramatically lower per-unit cost. Impressed with the machine's potential, James Buchanan Duke of Washington Duke and Sons (later American Tobacco Company) installed several Bonsack machines in his Durham, North Carolina, plant in the spring of 1884. Duke engineers improved the machines, lowering the manufacturing cost of a thousand cigarettes from eighty cents to thirty cents. Negotiations with Bonsack further lowered costs to twenty-four cents per thousand, less than one-third that of the handmade product.[13]

The potential of the rotary cutter and rolling machine was limited by the lack of suitable packaging for the finished product. Cigarette packages were then of two extremes: expensive boxes for luxury goods and flimsy paper wrappers for the general trade, neither satisfactory for merchandising on the scale Duke envisioned. Again improving on the work of another, Duke patented a cardboard sliding tray package for his new Cameo brand in 1886. The new box was attractive, durable, and cheap—perfect for mass marketing. The package could also serve as an excellent advertising medium. The Cameo package was very popular and widely imitated throughout the industry.

The cigarette industry also benefited from government policy. Cigarettes were first taxed during the Civil War. The tax rate began at $1 a pound in 1864 and rose to $1.75 a pound in the 1870s. In 1883, Congress, embarrassed by large surpluses generated by high tariffs, reduced the tax on cigarettes from $1.75 to 50 cents a pound. The new rate, which remained in effect for nearly fifteen years, lowered manufacturers' laid-in costs still further.[14]

Lower costs enabled Duke and his competitors to drop the price of the standard ten-unit package of machine-made cigarettes from ten cents to five cents. Vigorous advertising accompanied the price cut.[15] Public response to nickel-a-pack cigarettes confirmed the wisdom of Duke's marketing strategy. Riding the crest of a growing national market for consumer goods, cigarette sales doubled in two years and doubled again in another two years, passing one billion units in 1884 and two billion in 1887.[16]

British smokers were also developing a taste for cigarettes rich in Bright Leaf tobacco. Transatlantic exports of the yellow variety merited mention in the 1880 census. A special report on tobacco included in the census stated that Bright Leaf was "growing in appreciation, not only in this country but in Great Britain, where rapidly increasing demand for it promises large extension in the future." Of course, the addictive character of the product doubtless contributed to increasing demand on both sides of the Atlantic.[17]

The popularity of cigarette smoking and the ensuing demand for Bright Leaf tobacco were being felt in southern agriculture. Southern farmers had not seen anything like the demand tobacco was enjoying in a generation. True, the Civil War had raised cotton prices for a few years, but since the early 1870s the fleecy staple had languished. By 1885, the price of cotton had fallen to eight cents a pound—half its former value. Of course, the costs of producing cotton did not decline at the same rate, and profit margins were shaved closer and closer. By the 1880s, low prices were beginning to nudge cotton growers out of their traditional culture.[18]

Surging demand for Bright Leaf contrasted sharply with the sluggish cotton market. Indeed, from the 1880s through the end of the century, demand for Bright Leaf steadily increased. So did production. By the 1880s, farmers in eastern North Carolina were learning to flue-cure, and markets for yellow tobacco were opening in Wilson, Rocky Mount, and other towns. Soon, Bright Leaf culture had spread far enough to require designating a "New Belt" in eastern North Carolina. And deep in South Carolina, lured by the promise of high profits, Pee Dee farmers were beginning the quest for the fancy yellow leaf.

Tobacco reemerged as a cash crop in South Carolina in the late 1880s, about seventy-five years after it succumbed to cotton. In the interim, some farmers continued to plant and air-cure a little of the ancient, rustic variety for home consumption, but the amounts were negligible. For example, the census of 1880 reported only 45,678 pounds of tobacco grown in South Carolina. Thus the state's entire tobacco crop would not have filled one boxcar. Before the census-takers came around again, however, the Pee Dee region was becoming a tobacco empire.[19]

Bright Leaf culture entered the Pee Dee from the top down as prominent farmers, merchants, and bankers took the lead in establishing the new crop in their communities. By the 1880s, the Pee Dee's agricultural and commercial elite was painfully aware that another cash crop was needed to supplement cotton. While many yeomen and tenants shared this sentiment—the cotton problem was as well known as the weather—only elites possessed the vision and resources actively to seek a successor to the old monarch. As substantial landowners and merchants, their fortunes were solidly rooted in the region's agrarian economy, and they realized it was easier to change crops than professions.

Furthermore, large farmers tended to be more market-oriented than their less affluent neighbors. For them, substantial investments in land and equipment made agriculture more a commercial enterprise than a subsistence activity. Indeed, some top-tier farmers managed a diverse entrepreneurial portfolio in which farming was but one of several ventures. In many Pee Dee communities, elites balanced agriculture with banking, mercantile, and professional interests. Moreover, elites were well connected in local politics and wielded influence to further their material goals. Such diversity could provide greater insight and sensitivity to shifts in the economy. Far from resistant to change, Pee Dee elites were resourceful and innovative in the transition to Bright Leaf tobacco.

To this end, the region's prominent farmers and businessmen brought important resources to bear. Perhaps the most significant was information. Because fewer than half of the Pee Dee's citizens were literate, awareness of broader issues and influences was more the exception than the rule. The Pee Dee's agricultural and commercial leadership was well informed. Elites read newspapers and agricultural journals and corresponded with their counterparts in other communities. Such exchanges were valuable. Linked by commerce and friendship, Pee Dee elites drew on personal networks in the Carolinas and Virginia. As Bright Leaf began to outgrow its cradle in the Old Belt, elites recognized the crop's possibilities and dedicated their energies and assets to exploring them. With land, labor, and capital to spare, they planted experimental crops, hired experts, and proved that tobacco could thrive in South Carolina. Later, elites established markets and financed the expansion of the crop throughout the region. In a very real sense, these Bright Leaf pioneers were the nuclei of tobacco culture in their communities.

Although no person was solely responsible for introducing Bright Leaf into South Carolina, Frank Mandeville Rogers merits first mention. The son of a prominent Darlington County family, Rogers benefited from the privileges of his class. He attended private schools in Charleston, returning in 1874 to the life of a country squire. He could afford it. Besides his fine education and family connections, Rogers had fifteen hundred acres of prime farmland near Black Creek. If the former inspired Rogers to experiment, the latter furnished the means.[20]

Like many in the Pee Dee, Rogers was dismayed by declining cotton prices and the general economic malaise of the region. In 1881, a visiting Episcopal clergyman from North Carolina suggested Bright Leaf tobacco as a possible alternative.[21] Acting on this semidivine inspiration, Rogers sought advice of Old Belt growers about the possibility of introducing the crop into the Pee Dee. Their response was not encouraging. Tobacco could never thrive in South Carolina, they argued, citing unsuitable soils and climate. Of course, the Old Belt growers may have sincerely doubted the Pee Dee's potential for tobacco culture, but faced with the prospect of another region competing with their staple, they may have had other motives.[22]

Despite their gloomy predictions, however, Rogers remained convinced "that we had both the soil and climate to grow tobacco successfully and profitably." Given the Pee Dee's longer growing season, Rogers reasoned, tobacco plants would produce more leaves at no greater cost. In 1884, Rogers planted a small plot of Orinoco, the standard variety of the Old Belt. He did not intend to market the tobacco, only observe its development. As the crop ripened, Rogers continued to seek advice from knowledgeable growers. Major R. L. Ragland of Virginia sent instructions by mail. "The leaves grew to fine size," Rogers wrote, "and mellowed on the hill satisfactorily."[23]

Encouraged, Rogers increased his tobacco plantings in 1885 to three acres and built a sixteen-foot-square barn to cure his crop. His three acres yielded about twenty-one hundred pounds of cured leaf. Rogers shipped his curings to a North Carolina market—probably Henderson—where veteran tobacconists mistook its rich, yellow color for Granville County leaf. The three-acre crop averaged more than twenty-eight cents a pound —returning Rogers about $600. Frank Mandeville Rogers proved that Bright Leaf culture was not only viable in the Pee Dee but offered great promise to the region's farmers.[24]

His judgment confirmed, Rogers increased his tobacco acreage again in

1886. Recognizing the need for experience in this larger undertaking, Rogers hired Richard E. Rives of Battleboro, North Carolina, to assist and advise him in growing and curing the crop. Another Tar Heel, nineteen-year-old Robert Eugene Currin of Henderson, North Carolina, joined Rogers in 1887. Rives and Currin were the first of many North Carolina tobacco growers hired to teach Pee Dee farmers Bright Leaf culture. Of course, experienced cotton growers could adapt their considerable farming skills to cultivating a new crop, but flue-curing posed special challenges. Building curing barns, installing furnaces and flues, and managing the complex schedule of temperature changes needed to flue-cure a tobacco crop were completely new to them. "Tobacco instructors," as they came to be known, were typically young North Carolinians recommended by Old Belt warehousemen. They were lured to the Pee Dee by offers of a good salary, housing, and an interest in the crop. Eugene Currin later remarked that when he arrived, all Pee Dee farmers knew about tobacco was "how to chew it and spit it out." [25]

Any lingering doubts about Bright Leaf's potential in South Carolina were dispelled in 1887. Rogers and Currin sold their twenty-acre crop for $4,611, paid expenses of $1,681, and earned a net profit of $2,930—a phenomenal $146 per acre. [26] Such returns were revolutionary to South Carolina farmers in the 1880s. Indeed, the implications can be fully appreciated only in comparison with cotton. An acre of good cotton land, well fertilized, would yield about five hundred pounds of cotton. At eight cents a pound, a Pee Dee farmer of 1887 grossed about $40 an acre. With production costs of about five cents a pound, the grower netted roughly $15 from an acre of cotton. Thus Rogers's tobacco profits were nearly ten times greater, acre for acre, than those for cotton. [27]

With the zeal of a convert, Frank Mandeville Rogers preached the Bright Leaf gospel to all who would listen. He invited neighbors to inspect his crop, visit his curing barn, and ponder his profits. The advantage of leaf over lint was not lost on the thoughtful farmers of Mars Bluff. Tobacco's high value per acre was especially attractive to farmers whose modest holdings limited their opportunities. Assured that Bright Leaf would not interfere with their regular cotton crop and with Eugene Currin to advise them, Rogers persuaded some of his neighbors to plant a few acres of tobacco. Soon, Thomas Ashby, John C. Calhoun Brunson, Smilie A. Gregg, Eli

Gregg, Captain John McSween, and Thomas W. Williamson were tending tobacco fields.[28]

Frank Mandeville Rogers also reported his Bright Leaf ventures—and profits—to the press. He corresponded with several newspapers, relating his experiences and forwarding articles from other journals. Most editors were quick to recognize the crop's potential and eagerly spread the news about Bright Leaf. Cotton was so closely linked with the past and universally blamed for the region's economic woes that the press warmly embraced anything that offered hope for a brighter future. Indeed, for some editors, the tobacco movement evolved into a crusade, and their advocacy went beyond merely promoting a new crop. The tobacco movement came to embody cherished New South ideals of progress, resource development, and economic diversity. Truly, the enthusiasm of the press for Bright Leaf is the most striking feature of the crop's early history in South Carolina.

Predictably, the first reports of Rogers's experiments appeared in the *Darlington News*. The paper showed hometown pride in Rogers's success and monitored his efforts with interest.[29] Although planting, cultivating, and harvesting were duly noted, it was the crop's value that fascinated the press and public. With eight-cent cotton as a frame of reference, a crop worth twenty-two cents a pound was news. In 1888, when Rogers declined an offer of $8,000 for his thirty-acre crop, it made the front page. As Rogers and others continued to reap handsome profits from their Bright Leaf experiments, the *Darlington News* heralded the coming of another cash crop to the Pee Dee.[30]

By far the most important advocate for tobacco culture was South Carolina's largest newspaper, the *Charleston News and Courier*. As early as 1885, its editor, Francis Warrington Dawson, was recommending tobacco as an alternative to cotton and urging farmers to give the crop a trial.[31] To encourage the experiment, Dawson obtained a supply of Cuban cigar leaf seed thought to be suitable for the lowcountry and offered it free along with a pamphlet on tobacco culture. In return, Dawson asked recipients to report their results so others might profit by their experience.[32] Dawson ultimately furnished seed to more than five hundred farmers. The occasional report that resulted kept tobacco in the pages of the *News and Courier* while providing valuable information for pioneer tobacco growers.[33] After Dawson's death in 1889, the new editor, James C. Hemphill, continued the paper's strong support of tobacco culture. Clearly, the *News and Courier*'s enthusiasm for the crop was a major factor in its success.[34]

Columbia's new daily, the *State,* took an active interest in the tobacco movement as well. Lamenting South Carolina's thralldom to the white fiber, the *State* exhorted farmers to "throw off the yoke of King Cotton."[35] The appeal assumed greater urgency as cotton prices sank ever lower. The paper's editor, Narcisco G. Gonzales, deplored farmers' stubborn loyalty to cotton in the face of tobacco's greater promise: "If the farmer will cease to ask 'Will the price of cotton be higher next year?' and will intelligently determine whether he can profit more in tobacco than in cotton, he will be nearer the solution of his difficulties."[36] The *State* promised to continue its tobacco crusade "until that great crop shall be elected to the control of this now cotton-besotted section."[37]

The universal appeal of the Bright Leaf story is confirmed by the diversity of publications that carried it. The *Baptist Courier,* a statewide denominational weekly, kept readers informed of economic as well as religious news through the reports of traveling clergymen. In 1889, the *Baptist Courier* reported the Pee Dee's emerging Bright Leaf culture, naming Frank Mandeville Rogers, John C. Calhoun Brunson, Thomas Ashby, D. H. Hamby, and Captain John McSween as leading tobacco growers.[38] In 1890, a pastor assisting with revival meetings in Darlington reported that David M. Smoot, a local tobacco pioneer, had made $125 per acre after expenses. Since cotton profits were less than $16 per acre, the *Baptist Courier*'s pious readers doubtless pondered this message in their hearts.[39]

That cotton and tobacco could be grown simultaneously on the same farm was a decisive factor in Bright Leaf gaining a foothold in the Pee Dee. Very few farmers would have abandoned a familiar crop for an unfamiliar one, no matter how promising. From the very beginning, however, Rogers, Dawson, and other Bright Leaf boosters assured farmers that the two crops were compatible, even complementary, in their labor requirements. Indeed, Dawson argued, an industrious farmer could produce two cash crops rather than one.[40] Having the old crop to fall back on gave farmers the confidence to experiment with a new one. They could enter the tobacco culture gradually, learning new skills as they continued to apply old ones. That Bright Leaf employed labor that would otherwise be idle during July and August added to the crop's appeal. The evolution of a work routine that included both crops gradually changed the Pee Dee into a bi-cultural economy.[41]

State government gave the tobacco movement needed direction in 1886. Aware of private experiments in the Pee Dee and elsewhere, the commissioner of agriculture, Andrew P. Butler, was eager to determine whether South Carolina had real potential as a tobacco producer and if so, what plant types and methods of culture were best suited to the state. For example, while Pee Dee farmers were planting Bright Leaf, others were attempting to establish Cuban cigar leaf on the Sea Islands. Curing was a source of confusion as well. Some were flue-curing, others fire-curing, and still others clung to old-fashioned air-curing.[42]

To bring order to this chaos, Commissioner Butler organized comprehensive tobacco experiments throughout the state. Advisory committees selected one farmer in every county to plant an acre of tobacco. These farmers agreed to record the types of seed and fertilizer used, as well as methods of planting, cultivating, harvesting, and curing. Moreover, farmers were asked to record every item of expense and keep a weather log. When the crop was ready, each farmer would submit ten pounds of his curings. Fifty dollars expense money was payable upon receipt of the sample. To provide an incentive, an expert would be retained to evaluate the samples and a $100 prize awarded for the sample judged best. All farmers could keep whatever they might earn from their crop.[43]

Throughout the autumn of 1886, packages of cured tobacco leaves arrived at the Department of Agriculture in Columbia. After all the samples were received, Butler retained E. M. Pace of the Banner Warehouse in Danville, Virginia, to judge them. The thirty-seven bundles were displayed in the lobby of the state agricultural building. Each sample was identified by grower, county, seed type, and curing method. Pace examined the samples and wrote a brief and very candid appraisal of each.[44]

Fully two-thirds of the samples were adjudged "poor," "inferior," or "sorry." Pace laid much of the blame on Cuban seed, which he deemed "very unsuited" to South Carolina. He advised cigar leaf growers to sell their crop for whatever they could get and abandon the culture. He praised the samples grown from the Orinoco and Hester varieties, however, remarking on their good body and color. As expected, another problem was improper curing. Lacking flue-curing skills and equipment, many growers had simply air-cured their tobacco, hanging the harvested plants to dry naturally for several weeks. Pace was especially harsh in his judgment of "shade curing," stating that, excepting Burley varieties, "no good can result" from this method.[45]

After criticizing most entries, Pace lauded the few yellow tobaccos that met Old Belt standards. Finest was the sample submitted by Frank Mandeville Rogers. Awarding Rogers first prize, Pace praised the rich lemon color and "good handling" of his sample. Pace further stated that not only was Rogers's leaf the best in South Carolina, but he "had never seen better" in the Old Belt. Of course, Rogers had raised two previous tobacco crops and had the further advantage of drawing on Richard E. Rives's skills and experience. Nevertheless, Pee Dee Bright Leaf had triumphed. Before boarding the train for Danville, Pace concluded that South Carolina had proven it could produce high-quality tobacco.[46]

The statewide tobacco competition had accomplished that and more. South Carolina farmers had learned what types of tobaccos to grow, what curing method to employ, and where the crop was likely to flourish. Cuban cigar leaf was out and Old Belt varieties were in; archaic air-curing must be abandoned for modern flue-curing; and tobacco thrived in the Pee Dee region. Moreover, the contest was well publicized, and Rogers's victory likely convinced other Pee Dee farmers to plant a few acres of their own.

By the early 1890s, well-informed people throughout the Pee Dee were aware of the movement toward Bright Leaf and alive to its potential. In every community, enterprising people began to experiment with the new crop. Clarendon County farmers first planted Bright Leaf in 1892. Pioneer growers included J. E. Beard, W. H. Coker, R. H. Green, and J. E. Tomlinson. They soon learned that the new crop thrived in the rich soils of Pudding Swamp.[47]

The first tobacco grower in Mullins was Dr. C. T. Ford, the town physician. A man of keen intellect and broad interests, Ford tended a small patch of Bright Leaf behind his home during the summer of 1892. In July, Dr. Ford built a curing barn—the first in Mullins—and hired Israel Fowler to help cure the crop. By August, Ford and Fowler were showing off their handmade crop of bright yellow "wrapper," described as "silken in texture, and worth about 60 cents a pound." Fowler suggested that their success would likely "induce others in the vicinity of Mullins to engage in tobacco culture." Fowler's prediction would prove a monumental under-statement.[48]

The fate of Mullins changed forever when William Henry Daniel, the town's leading merchant, threw his support behind Bright Leaf in 1893. Daniel was a classic "new man" of the postwar South. Born near Raleigh, North Carolina, the son of a wagon-master, Daniel joined the Confederate army in 1861. He was captured and spent much of the war as a prisoner in Elmira, New York. After the war, Daniel settled in the Pee Dee and tried the naval stores business for a while. When naval stores began declining in the mid-1870s, Daniel moved to Mullins and established the W. H. Daniel Supply Company, trading with farmers in the surrounding country. Success followed, and Daniel acquired property and standing in the community.[49]

By the mid-1890s, Daniel was seeking a way out of the cotton dilemma. Possessing the resources and entrepreneurial spirit of a successful business-man, Daniel recognized tobacco's possibilities. Aware of Dr. Ford's success with Bright Leaf, Daniel planted eight acres in 1894 to judge the crop for himself. The tobacco flourished. Observers remarked on the bright yellow color and fine texture of Daniel's curings. Daniel shipped his crop to Danville, where it brought a very satisfactory price.[50] Convinced of the crop's potential, Daniel persuaded some of his customers to plant Bright Leaf and hired a North Carolina tobacco grower, J. C. Teasley, to advise them. By the spring of 1895, "tobacco fever" was said to be sweeping the countryside around Mullins.[51]

In neighboring Horry County, Bright Leaf had been gaining ground since James C. Bryant planted an experimental crop on his Green Sea farm in 1889.[52] Although Samuel Sarvis of Socastee had represented Horry in the 1886 tobacco competition, he had air-cured his crop. The result was a disaster. E. M. Pace had judged Sarvis's leaf as "neither flesh nor fish nor fowl," that is, unfit for cigarettes, pipes, or chewing.[53] Bryant, in contrast, employed "the modern style of artificial heat" and achieved stellar results. Seeking to promote his sweet-smelling yellow tobacco, Bryant sent a sample to the *Charleston World* for evaluation. A *World* reporter showed Bryant's curings to Charleston tobacconists who praised the "delicate yellow" leaf, describing it as "splendid" and "the equal to any."[54] By the early 1890s, farmers at Green Sea, Floyds, and Wannamaker were planting Bright Leaf. At Galivants Ferry, tobacco pioneer Joseph William Holliday recruited Peter Raspberry, an experienced Bright Leaf grower from Weldon, North Carolina, to oversee his crop and teach the culture to his neighbors.[55]

The quickening pulse of Pee Dee agriculture was also being felt in Horry's tidewater rice areas. Before the Civil War, the Bucks of lower Horry District were substantial rice planters. The 1850 census estimated the Buck estate at $100,000, a fabulous sum for the time and by far the greatest in Horry District. By 1860, the Bucks' human property alone exceeded that value, and Woodbourne Plantation, valued at $45,000, had been added to their holdings as well.[56]

Although the Civil War and emancipation reduced their fortunes, the Bucks remained prominent in the postwar decades. In the 1890s, as rice and naval stores declined, Henry Lee Buck began experimenting with Bright Leaf. To build curing barns, Buck cut timber from his own forest and dressed it at his sawmill. Buck's son later recalled that his father selected poor land for his initial plantings to achieve the lightest color possible. Buck's original curing barn was still standing in the 1940s.[57]

Across the Pee Dee River in Georgetown County, farmers were also showing interest in the new crop. Like the Bucks, Georgetown farmers had once prospered from rice and naval stores, but by 1890 both crops were on the way out. The once great lowcountry rice industry had been declining since at least the 1860s, and some have argued that rice culture peaked in the 1830s.[58] Competition from new rice areas in Louisiana and old ones in Asia had supplanted South Carolina's tidewater rice culture. The decline of naval stores paralleled that of rice. As naval architecture evolved from wood to steel, demand for wood preservatives diminished. Moreover, as railroads replaced rivers as the primary means of transportation, Georgetown was yielding commercial leadership of the Pee Dee to Florence, a city built to serve the railroad. Georgetown boosters saw the tobacco trade as a means of reviving Georgetown's fading fortunes.

In the early 1890s, *Georgetown Times* editor Josiah Doar watched the tobacco story unfolding in neighboring counties. Citing successes in Florence, Darlington, and Horry, Doar encouraged Georgetown farmers to "get a move on" and begin planting Bright Leaf.[59] By 1895, industrious Georgetown farmers were planting experimental tobacco crops and reaping profits. Edward Harper was the first Georgetown farmer to flue-cure a tobacco crop and was "highly delighted" with the results. Harper was soon joined by the colorful J. B. Steele, whose tobacco farm on the Waccamaw River was often visited by others seeking to learn the culture. Within a few years, farmers in Rhems, Carver's Bay, Black Mingo, and Pennyroyal communities were producing yellow tobacco.[60]

By the early 1890s, Bright Leaf was flourishing in a score of Pee Dee communities, but lack of local markets was a serious obstacle to further expansion. Without home markets, Pee Dee tobacco growers were compelled to ship their crop to North Carolina and Virginia markets. Some growers consigned their leaf to local merchants as they did their cotton and naval stores. For example, Joseph William Holliday received customers' tobacco at Galivants Ferry and shipped it to C. D. Noell & Company and Lee's Warehouse in Danville.[61] Old Belt tobacco interests were beginning to recognize the Pee Dee as an important source of leaf, and Danville, Durham, and Richmond warehouses were sending "drummers" into the region to solicit business.[62] But notwithstanding the good offices of Old Belt warehousemen, shipping their crop north cost Pee Dee farmers time and money. Recognizing the need for home markets—and possibilities for investors—local businessmen began establishing tobacco markets in the Pee Dee.

Frank Mandeville Rogers again played a central role in fastening Bright Leaf to the region. By 1890, Florence was emerging as the center of the state's flue-cured tobacco culture, and Rogers was determined to establish a leaf market there. Indeed, the city's excellent rail connections made Florence an obvious site for a tobacco market.[63] In 1890, Rogers visited North Carolina and Virginia to study marketing methods. While in Durham, he met with James Buchanan Duke of the American Tobacco Company to arrange for buyers to be sent to Florence. Returning home, Rogers persuaded other Florence-area leaf growers and businessmen to invest in the Florence Tobacco Manufacturing and Warehouse Company, South Carolina's first Bright Leaf market. Joining Rogers in the venture were John C. Calhoun Brunson, Eugene F. Douglas, Gus McSween, Captain John McSween, and Thomas W. Williamson. P. A. Willcox served as secretary and legal counsel. The investors subscribed $15,000 in capital stock and hired R. A. Croxton of Danville to manage the new enterprise.[64]

The Pee Dee's first Bright Leaf marketing venture established a model for future warehouse partnerships. Rogers and his partners were prosperous farmers with considerable tobacco acreage of their own and would, of course, form the nucleus of the warehouse's patronage. Moreover, some of the partners had banking and mercantile interests in addition to their farming operations. For example, Eugene F. Douglas was a prominent merchant and director of a local bank; P. A. Willcox was well connected politically and acknowledged as one of the city's social and professional elite.[65]

Besides their diverse financial interests, the partners were well connected socially. They attended church and belonged to fraternal organizations. Three of the six were members of Florence's Committee of Fifty, a civic club active in local politics. In the Pee Dee's emerging capitalist environment, entrepreneurs valued personal networks and nurtured them with great care. They expected to draw on their social capital to help assure the success of their business ventures. Rogers and his partners, like hundreds of Pee Dee warehousemen who followed them, plied their influence with friends, neighbors, and acquaintances to fill their sales floors.[66]

The first auction, or "break," of flue-cured tobacco in South Carolina took place in the Florence Tobacco Warehouse on Thursday, 1 October 1891. The event was acclaimed on the front pages of South Carolina's leading newspapers. The *News and Courier* titled its four-column story "A 'Break' for Liberty." Citing its long advocacy of tobacco as a cash crop, the paper devoted considerable space to reminding readers of its own role in promoting Bright Leaf.[67] The *State* observed that tobacco growers had brought their crops to Florence "the old-time North Carolina way"— in covered wagons. Besides local growers from Florence and Darlington Counties, there were wagons from Clarendon, Horry, Lancaster, Marlboro, Marion, and Sumter Counties as well.[68]

The opening of the Pee Dee's first tobacco market was recognized as an event of great significance. Few Florentines had ever seen a tobacco auction, and it drew a large crowd. About three hundred persons packed into the narrow wooden building on Darlington Street to watch the sale.[69] Shopkeepers left their counters, and the Florence County Court adjourned so the judge, jurors, lawyers, and litigants could attend the auction. For some, the event afforded an opportunity to see and be seen; several politicians were on hand and made their presence known to all. The *News and Courier* also noted the presence of "not a few colored farmers who watched the proceedings with interest."[70]

Industry leaders from Winston, Durham, Danville, Richmond, and New

York were on hand to launch the new market. Henry Harmon, editor of the *Southern Tobacco Journal*, ceremonially bought the first pile of Bright Leaf ever auctioned in South Carolina—ten pounds of mahogany wrapper grown by Charles S. McCullough of Darlington—for $2.05 a pound. Harmon generously distributed the leaves among the excited onlookers, giving each a souvenir of the historic occasion. In the next few hours, about five hundred piles of leaf were auctioned at prices ranging from nine to twenty-six cents a pound. That evening, Florence merchants treated the buying corps to dinner at Barringer's Hotel.[71]

The success of the Florence market prompted a group of Darlington planters and businessmen to open a market in that city in 1892. Investors in the Darlington Warehouse included W. F. Dargan, Charles S. McCullough, J. J. Ward, and Paul Wipple. Besides being tobacco growers, all were involved in other enterprises. For example, Charles S. McCullough owned a cotton gin and a fertilizer company; W. F. Dargan was a prominent attorney and the solicitor of Darlington County. The Darlington Warehouse measured 60 feet by 120 feet and boasted sixteen skylights. The first auction took place on 27 September 1892. "The Great" Garland E. Webb, a celebrated tobacco auctioneer of Winston, North Carolina, presided. Farmers were generally pleased with prices as was the business community with the lively tempo of trade. Thus by 1892, the Pee Dee boasted tobacco markets at Florence and Darlington, each with a single warehouse.[72]

The progress of the Bright Leaf movement in South Carolina was not entirely even. After several years of vigorous expansion, momentum slowed in 1893 and 1894. For two years, no new tobacco markets were founded or new warehouses built in existing market towns. Two warehouses, one each in Florence and Darlington, sold nearly all the leaf grown in South Carolina. Tobacco acreage seems to have increased only slightly. Even the enthusiasm of the press for the new crop waned. Clearly, the Bright Leaf movement had reached a plateau.

The explanation rests on two concurrent disasters—one natural and one of human making. In August 1893, when the tobacco harvest was at its zenith, a powerful hurricane struck South Carolina. Crossing the coast below Charleston, the storm moved north through the Pee Dee. Along its path, more than one thousand people died. Besides the human toll, uncounted draft animals perished, hundreds of buildings were damaged, and crops were devastated. Most of the cotton was simply blown away; corn and tobacco fields were flattened. Some farmers gathered half a crop, some less. For tobacco growers, damage to curing barns and packhouses came at the worst possible time. The surviving leaf cured thin and light, an undesirable condition for produce sold by weight.[73]

As if wind and rain were not bad enough, the contraction of already tight credit added to the general misery of the Pee Dee. The depression of 1893 created a "financial stringency" in the United States, and none were pinched tighter than Pee Dee farmers. In the towns, commerce practically stopped. Bankers and merchants addressed the cash shortage in novel ways. Many banks limited withdrawals to $50 per day, and desperate merchants drew cashiers' checks for small sums made payable to the bearer that circulated in place of currency.[74]

Worse, with little cash available to commodity buyers, farmers could not sell their crops. In some communities, "cotton certificates" were used to settle accounts. Cotton growers placed their crop in bonded storage and handed over receipts to creditors.[75] Tobacco markets were also hit hard. Even the Durham market, the oldest and largest in the Carolinas, was forced to close. In the Pee Dee, the cash shortage caused tobacco markets to open three weeks late. Prices for the 1893 leaf crop were lower than expected, but most growers at least broke even.[76]

Although both cotton and Bright Leaf growers suffered in 1893, tobacco recovered the following year. Cotton did not. Lint prices went down in 1893 and stayed down for three years. The cotton depression of the mid-1890s quickened the pace of change in the Pee Dee. Although Bright Leaf was becoming commonplace in many Pee Dee communities, some cotton growers had resisted change. They had always planted cotton, they liked the easy pace of cotton culture, and they were resolved to continue.

But even the most loyal cotton growers were shaken by the events of 1894. Middling-grade cotton fell to five cents a pound—what experts reckoned as the cost of production. At best, therefore, a cotton grower might recover the costs of seed, fertilizer, and hired labor but nothing for his own hard work or capital investment. Worse, many farmers had borrowed against anticipated earnings. And by the autumn of 1894, hundreds were facing foreclosure and ruin. Some storekeepers were as broke as their customers. Powerless to collect their accounts, many merchants defaulted on their obligations. Others simply walked away from their barren shelves and sought other employment.[77]

For the cotton-based economy of the Pee Dee, prospects for 1895 seemed bleak. On the first day of the year, a Kingstree merchant declared that "the agricultural outlook is more gloomy in this county to-day than it has been since the spring of 1865."[78] Throughout the region, journalists echoed the tale of woe. In Marion, cotton had become the object of grim sarcasm. In one scathing sentence, the *Marion Star*'s editor Junius Evans summarized the plight of area farmers: "The price of cotton is rising; if it advances a little more, the farmers may recover the cost of producing it."[79]

In Clarendon County, farming prospects were described as "suicidal." Many small farmers and tenants were being "closed out" by their creditors. Merchants in Manning had repossessed so many mules that they were overwhelmed by the cost of feeding them. Credit was nearly impossible to obtain, even with the offer of a first mortgage. Indeed, some merchants were reluctant to extend credit to cotton growers on any terms. At current prices, they reasoned, even the most creditworthy would likely default. Cotton simply did not repay the expense of growing it.[80]

Contemporaries knew their economic problems were linked to cotton. Lamenting the lack of business in Manning, a correspondent wrote: "The cause and effect has never been so marked before. It shows absolutely in what our whole interest and apparent welfare lies."[81] Still, many cotton growers balked at change. Cotton had been the centerpiece of agrarian life for nearly a century, and many kept hoping it would rebound. But time was running out. "For ten years this depressed state of affairs has been going from bad to worse," declared one observer, "and every year the people, thinking they had at last reached bottom, have taken hold with renewed vigor and greater resolution, all to no avail." Said another, "It would not be unsafe to say we are in a worse fix than ever before."[82]

In parts of the Pee Dee, tobacco profits moderated the cotton catastrophe. In Williamsburg County, for example, where "not more than one farmer in twenty-five" could pay his debts in full, tobacco growers were the exceptions. S. P. Brockington, a merchant in Williamsburg County, reported that tobacco growers were among the few to "pay out." In communities where Bright Leaf was well established, conditions were somewhat better. According to sources in Darlington County, the performance of tobacco was "simply beyond any comparison" with cotton. Indeed, Darlington and Florence tobacco growers reported substantial profits and plans to increase their acreage in 1895. Said S. H. McGill, "The outlook [for tobacco] is as bright as a fine grade wrapper." At nearly every crossroads in the Pee Dee, people were agreeing, however reluctantly, that tobacco seemed their only hope.[83]

Others with a stake in the Pee Dee economy were joining the chorus in praise of Bright Leaf. As the Pee Dee's primary rail carrier, the Atlantic Coast Line (ACL) was vitally interested in the region's prosperity. As cotton prices sank ever lower in the mid-1890s, ACL president T. M. Emerson became convinced that Bright Leaf offered hope for the region's farmers. Emerson commissioned Henry Harmon, editor of the *Southern Tobacco Journal,* to write an instructional booklet for novice Bright Leaf growers. The outcome was *The Tobacco Planters' Guide,* a clear, step-by-step handbook. Railroad agents ultimately distributed twenty thousand copies free of charge along the ACL's routes through the Carolinas. Harmon was subsequently flooded with requests for the pamphlet and more information about Bright Leaf.[84]

Eighteen ninety-five was the pivotal year of the Bright Leaf movement in South Carolina. Tobacco acreage made tremendous gains, and the number of warehouses more than tripled. Shaken by the "cotton crash" of 1893–94, many farmers were eager to try the new crop. Throughout the spring and summer of 1895, merchants reported unprecedented interest in tobacco. In communities that had never raised a leaf, hundreds of acres were planted and scores of curing barns raised.[85] Indeed, locals learned to track the expansion of tobacco culture by counting barns. Darlington County furnishes good examples. Between 1894 and 1895, the number of curing barns at Antioch rose from six to twenty-two, at Lamar from seventeen to ninety-one, and at Lydia from one to sixty-two. By 1895, the sturdy wooden curing barn had become the ensign of Bright Leaf culture, attesting to its expansion and underscoring its permanence.[86]

In 1895, the advent of new markets and enlargement of existing ones confirmed the vigor of Bright Leaf in the Pee Dee. In a single year, the number of markets increased from two to five and warehouses from two to seven. Timmonsville became South Carolina's third tobacco market when the Timmonsville Tobacco Warehouse held its first sale on 27 August 1895.

The venture was underwritten by a group of local planters and business-men headed by bankers Charles A. Smith and John McSween.[87] On open-ing day, the warehouse was so crowded that many farmers could not get inside to auction their leaf, and several wagon loads changed hands outside after the sale. Within days, Timmonsville was challenging Florence as the county's leading tobacco market.[88]

The Sumter tobacco market opened two days later on 29 August 1895. Sumter hoped to draw farmers west of Lynches River, especially from the tobacco-rich Pudding Swamp section of Clarendon County. Some of the biggest merchants in town were backing the enterprise. Foremost was Abraham Ryttenberg, whose large mercantile establishment dominated downtown Sumter. On opening day, all business was suspended during the auction so the entire community—even attorneys and physicians—could attend. A converted railway depot served as a sales facility until a new ware-house could be built. The auctioneer Garland E. Webb was on hand to do the honors. Sumter merchants happily reported that many farmers were raising both cotton and tobacco and were settling their debts with tobacco money and still had their cotton to sell.[89]

In 1895, both Florence and Darlington added new warehouses, increas-ing their count to two each. Florence's new house, the Farmers', opened on Coit Street under the management of A. J. Ellington and A. E. Miles of Reidsville, North Carolina.[90] Darlington's second warehouse, Planters' Tobacco Warehouse, opened on 22 August 1895. It boasted twenty thou-sand square feet of floor space and was the largest sales floor yet built in South Carolina. The new house was owned and operated by Benjamin F. Smoot and Eli McGill of Darlington. The first sale commenced with a trumpet fanfare played by an employee called, appropriately, Gabriel. Be-sides the new warehouse, Darlington investors chartered a small factory that made smoking tobacco from local leaf. The Darlington Tobacco Works turned out two rum-flavored mixtures called "Palmetto State" and "Pride of Darlington."[91]

The most important event of the momentous 1895 season was the estab-lishment of the Mullins tobacco market. As the cotton depression deep-ened in 1894, more and more Marion County farmers turned to tobacco. From Dothan, Fork, Zion, and Gapway came reports of seedbeds sown and curing barns raised.[92] Mullins elites were leading the way. Encouraged by their own Bright Leaf experiments, William Henry Daniel, Dr. C. T.

Ford, and a few others were striving to meet the need for a local market with characteristic vigor. Construction of Planters' Warehouse began late in 1894. Daniel recruited several "tobacco instructors" from the Old Belt to help nurture and cure the crop. Indeed, by the spring of 1895, Mullins was said to be "well furnished with Tar Heels." Daniel hired D. K. Mc-Duffie of Durham to manage the warehouse and Captain John Hutchings of Danville as auctioneer.[93]

On Wednesday, 28 August 1895, crowds poured into Mullins from all points of the compass. Wagons loaded with fragrant leaf and eager farmers had been arriving throughout the night. Many wagons came from neighboring Horry County, some waiting several hours for the ferry at Sandy Bluff. Many farmers boarded with townsfolk or slept under their wagons as horses and mules grazed on front lawns. The morning train delivered many interested visitors from nearby Marion. All converged on the new Planters' Warehouse, an ornate wooden structure adorned with gables, turrets, flagpoles, and a belfry.[94]

The warehouse floor was so congested there was hardly room to walk. From the sheer numbers, it was obvious that Daniel and his partners had underestimated the extent of Bright Leaf culture in Marion and Horry Counties. Daniel admitted surprise at the turnout and vowed to enlarge the warehouse. Crowding the floor were farmers, merchants, and onlookers, most of whom had never seen a tobacco auction. Aware that many novice growers had not presented their leaf to best advantage, Captain Hutchings conducted a "grading school" before the sale. At eleven o'clock, a bronze bell high in the belfry began to ring. Captain Hutchings stepped forward, offered some "appropriate remarks," and began the auction. The farmers, whose frame of reference was six-cent cotton, were amazed to see their produce bring twelve cents, sixteen cents, even twenty-two cents a pound. A few lots of fine wrapper brought as much as seventy-five cents a pound.[95]

The tobacco market had an enormous impact on Mullins. According to the *News and Courier,* farmers and merchants alike were in high spirits. As the days passed, tobacco growers continued to stream into Mullins to convert their crop into cash. Because Mullins had no bank, William Henry Daniel had money sent by train from Marion. Daniel cashed farmers' tobacco checks in his store, deducting their accounts from the proceeds. Greenbacks flowed into the town's economy like cool water over parched ground. Indeed, several Mullins merchants happily reported being "paid up" by farmers they had been "carrying over from year to year."[96] Within days, Mullins became the market of choice for Marion County farmers and was drawing heavily from Horry as well. Truly, in 1895 Pee Dee farmers embraced Bright Leaf as their salvation.

The success of Mullins prompted other Pee Dee towns to establish tobacco markets. Sometimes communities pooled resources of capital, energy, and entrepreneurship to join the Bright Leaf boom. The founding of the Conway tobacco market offers an excellent example of small-town boosterism. By the late 1890s, scores of Horry farmers were growing tobacco and hauling it to markets in Mullins and Fair Bluff, North Carolina. Watching Horry produce enrich rival towns rankled Conway elites. Determined to recapture the valuable trade, Conway merchants launched a "Tobacco Campaign." The business community proposed a covenant with farmers: "We furnish the MARKET and you supply the TOBACCO."

Doc Allen Spivey, a Conway banker, led a stock subscription to raise capital for the enterprise. Merchants distributed free seeds and production guides to farmers. Tobacco instructors were recruited to advise and encourage novices. The warehouse was built, complete with stalls for customers' mules. The local bank agreed to cash tobacco checks at par. John E. Coles, an experienced warehouseman from Winston, North Carolina, joined the firm as general manager. Once again, "The Great" Garland E. Webb, also of Winston, presided over the inaugural sale at a Pee Dee warehouse.[97]

For Conway elites, the new tobacco market was more than a commercial undertaking; the very honor of the community was at stake. On opening day, the boosters reminded Horry farmers:

> So long as we allow ourselves to be used . . . in patronizing other markets and building up other towns at the expense of our own, just so long will we continue to be designated the "tail end" of South Carolina. . . . We have the House and the prospect of a fine Market. It only remains for us to ALL PULL TOGETHER and each carry out his part to maintain the market here for the advancement of Horry and the betterment of her citizens.[98]

The boosters were not disappointed. When the Horry Warehouse held its first sale on 27 July 1899, the local press boasted that "six thousand dollars handed out to tobacco planters in the middle of our dull season was something nice." The editor continued, "Our merchants have never had such broad grins before at this season of the year. . . . We will all plant tobacco next year."[99] As sales continued, leaf prices were described as "very gratifying" and citizens as "jubilant." Conway boosters were eager to spread the good news. They affixed banners to the sides of outbound trains proclaiming Conway's new status as a tobacco market.[100]

As local markets proliferated in the 1890s, flue-cured tobacco truly became a rising star in the economic firmament of South Carolina. The cumulative effect of boosterism, home markets, and the desperate cotton situation began to tell, and the trickle of farmers entering the new culture became a torrent. During the 1890s, the state's tobacco production increased one hundred–fold from 200,000 pounds per year to 20 million. The expansion of Bright Leaf culture in Marion County was nothing short of phenomenal. From a negligible 9,000 pounds in 1890, production in Marion County soared to 6,145,000 pounds in 1899, a 688–fold increase.[101]

While farmers throughout South Carolina continued to experiment with tobacco in the 1890s, the geographical focus of Bright Leaf culture clearly justified the *State* christening the crop "the Pearl of the Pee Dee."[102] By the century's end, the region accounted for about 93 percent of the state's tobacco production (see Table 5).

A key development in the rise of flue-cured tobacco was the acceptance of the new crop as a basis of credit. For decades, merchants had extended credit only on well-established cash crops, usually cotton or naval stores. At issue was tobacco's suitability as collateral. Liquidity was essential. Creditors required a dependable local market where debtors could sell their crop and pay up. As tobacco markets opened across the Pee Dee, the convenience and permanence of the Bright Leaf culture persuaded merchants that the new crop could provide a satisfactory basis of credit. Moreover, merchants liked the timing of Bright Leaf. Because tobacco came to market earlier than cotton, accounts could be settled sooner. Pee Dee businessmen found this aspect of tobacco culture especially endearing.[103]

It did not happen all at once, however. Predictably, merchants were more willing to do business with tobacco growers in communities where the new crop was better established. For example, Smilie A. Gregg extended credit to tobacco growers around Mars Bluff as early as 1890. At Galivants Ferry, Joseph William Holliday willingly backed his customers'

TABLE 5
Bright Leaf Tobacco Production in South Carolina, 1899,
Counties Producing More Than 100,000 Pounds

Chesterfield[a]	166,070	Kershaw	112,220
Clarendon[a]	1,355,280	Marion[a]	6,145,000
Darlington[a]	5,083,150	Marlboro[a]	146,610
Florence[a]	2,995,410	Orangeburg	332,150
Horry[a]	1,631,930	Sumter	840,950
		Williamsburg[a]	904,330

[a] Pee Dee counties.

ABSTRACT:

Pee Dee region	18,427,780	92.80%
non–Pee Dee	+ 1,348,320	7.20%
Total	19,776,100	100.00%

Source: *Twelfth Census of the United States* (1900), Vol. 6, *Agriculture*, 449.

Bright Leaf experiments.[104] Others, like William Henry Daniel in Mullins, hastened the transition to Bright Leaf by establishing a local market. Because their own capital was at risk in warehouse ventures, merchants were as committed to the new crop as were farmers. Some even distributed free tobacco seeds to their customers. At one dollar per acre, complementary seeds were an economical and practical means of building goodwill and assuring a bountiful crop.[105]

At first, small landowners tended to follow the tobacco movement from a safe distance. Because they had fewer resources of land, labor, and capital, yeomen were more likely to approach a change of staple crops with greater caution. Although cotton paid little, at least it was familiar. Moreover, cotton's infrastructure of gins, compresses, markets, and credit was well established. As a parallel tobacco infrastructure arose in the 1890s, however, yeomen gradually felt more comfortable with the new staple. With the means to grow and sell the new crop came wider acceptance among the plain folk of the Pee Dee.

Sharecroppers and tenants had fewer choices. Dependent on others for land and credit, they entered the new culture when landlords and merchants thought the time was right. By the mid-1890s, sharecrop and tenantry agreements based on tobacco were commonplace in the Pee Dee.

Sometimes both parties were landowners who agreed to share the risks of learning a new crop culture. Frank Mandeville Rogers was interested in several tobacco crops around Mars Bluff as early as 1889.[106] Typically, however, the traditional pattern of landlord and landless tenant was the rule. In tobacco tenancies, landlords furnished curing barns in addition to cropland. Sometimes landlords and tenants shared the cost of fertilizer and divided the crop. Others might pay cash rent. Tenants furnished all labor including woodcutting for curing and transporting the crop to market.[107]

The labor-intensive nature of tobacco culture tended to increase tenantry in the Pee Dee. Moreover, because Bright Leaf was typically more profitable than other crops, tobacco tenantry was more attractive to landless farmers. But while the evidence is compelling, it is not conclusive. In counties with strong commitments to tobacco, tenantry rates tended to rise, but some of these counties also produced significant amounts of cotton, which could also increase tenantry. To confuse the matter further, tenantry was increasing in areas of South Carolina where no tobacco was grown. Probably the most compelling case for the rise of tenantry in tobacco areas is Horry County. Historically, Horry produced far less cotton than other Pee Dee counties, yet tenantry rates in Horry nearly tripled in the years concurrent with the rise of Bright Leaf. Because Horry's small cotton acreage could not possibly account for such an increase, only the vigorous expansion of a labor-intensive crop like flue-cured tobacco will answer.[108] In her study of the Bright Leaf culture in the Old Belt, Nannie May Tilley found that tenantry grew substantially in the Bright Leaf areas of North Carolina and Virginia during the same period.[109]

Virtually from the time it opened its doors in 1893, Clemson College provided important leadership and support for the tobacco movement. Aware of the state's need for another cash crop, Clemson faculty and students joined their pens and voices in urging diversification. Faculty contributed articles to the popular press and submitted student monographs to the commissioner of agriculture for distribution to farmers throughout the state.[110] In 1912, Clemson established the Pee Dee Experiment Station near Florence to conduct agricultural research and advance tobacco crop science. The college hired Robert Eugene Currin, who assisted Frank Mandeville Rogers in his initial tobacco venture, to manage the station.[111]

The impact of the tobacco boom was not limited to growers. Indeed, some Pee Dee market towns experienced nothing short of a bo-

TABLE 6

Population of Selected Pee Dee Tobacco Market Towns,
1900 and 1910

Town	1900	1910	Percent change
Darlington	3,028	3,789	25.1
Dillon	1,015	1,757	73.1
Kingstree	766	1,372	79.1
Lake City	375	1,074	286.4
Marion	1,831	3,844	209.9
Mullins	828	1,832	221.2
Timmonsville	861	1,706	198.1
South Carolina	1,340,316	1,515,400	13.1

Sources: U.S. Department of Commerce, Bureau of the Census, *Thirteenth Census, 1910*, vol. 3, Population, 649–50; Julian J. Petty, *The Growth and Distribution of Population in South Carolina* (1943; rpt. Spartanburg: Reprint Company, 1975), 228–29.

nanta. The *Florence Times* called tobacco's effect on that city's economy "remarkable." When leaf sales began in late summer, Florence merchants were "as busy as Christmas time."[112] In smaller market towns, the Bright Leaf boom multiplied populations and payrolls. For example, the 1890 census counted only 242 inhabitants in Mullins. Ten years later, 828 people were living there, an increase of almost 350 percent. By 1904, more people were employed in tobacco-related jobs in Mullins than had lived there ten years earlier.[113] In the twentieth century's first decade, Marion grew sixteen times faster than the state as a whole, Mullins seventeen times faster, and Lake City twenty-two times faster. Darlington, whose growth was less dramatic, doubled the rate of South Carolina (see Table 6).

The South Carolina press credited Bright Leaf with the growth of Mullins, Lake City, and other Pee Dee market towns. In 1895, the *State* concluded: "It is a noteworthy fact . . . that a town that is a tobacco market quickly increases in population, and when it becomes the market of a section, the population quickly doubles."[114]

The growth of banking in Pee Dee market towns marched in step with that of Bright Leaf tobacco. "The amount of money that is put in circulation here each day through the cashing of tobacco checks has put our banks back on the lending list!" proclaimed the *Florence Times*.[115] Not only were well-established banks flush with tobacco money, but new banks were being chartered in market towns. For forty years, Mullins was judged too small to support a bank. With the coming of the tobacco market, however, Mullins merchants joined William Henry Daniel in founding the Bank of Mullins in 1899. A second bank, the Merchants and Planters, was chartered three years later. Thus Mullins acquired two banks in four years.[116]

Pee Dee tobacco communities also experienced a real estate boom. The *State* declared that when Bright Leaf took hold in Darlington County land values skyrocketed. Vacant lots in Darlington worth $200 in 1896 were bringing "$800 to $1200" ten years later. Residential properties there were showing impressive gains as well. R. K. Dargan paid $4,500 for his home in 1902 and sold it for $7,750 four years later, taking a profit of 72 percent. Commercial real estate was also in demand. Store buildings valued at $2,000 in 1900 were changing hands for "$10,000 to $12,000" in 1906.[117]

Predictably, Pee Dee farmlands made splendid gains during the tobacco boom. Indeed, the commissioner of agriculture observed that the profit per acre of growing tobacco was greater than the average selling price of farmland in South Carolina.[118] A farm in the Lydia community that brought $10,000 in 1902 fetched $25,000 in 1906. Tracts assessed at $20 per acre in 1900 were finding buyers six years later at $100 per acre. Ironically, the issue of the *State* that carried this story advertised farmlands in Greenwood County for $5 per acre.[119]

Commerce thrived as tobacco money circulated, confirming the adage that when the tide comes in, all boats rise. New businesses, schools, churches, banks, and homes were built in Pee Dee market towns. Busy main streets and quiet residential neighborhoods were transformed as merchants invested their profits in new stores and homes. Sometimes newly prosperous farmers built homes in town to enjoy their success in an urban setting. Along Wine Street in Mullins, Willcox Avenue in Marion, and West Broad Street in Darlington, the new prosperity was manifested in broad verandas and fancy millwork. A century later, many of these late Victorian structures bear elegant witness to the tobacco boom and continue to lend dignity and charm to their neighborhoods.

Reports from Florence, Darlington, Mullins, and Timmonsville cited the phenomenal growth of those communities. Contemporary accounts speak of "marvelous growth," "complete change," and "blessings innumerable." From Darlington came reports of "buildings going up all the time." Five new stores on Pearl Street were rented "before the walls were up." Sometimes, however, enthusiasm gave way to exaggeration. Seeing Timmonsville as "a young Atlanta" must have required uncommon vision.[120]

But even the soberest observers noticed the impact of the Bright Leaf boom in Pee Dee market towns. In 1896, the *State* told its readers: "Today large and rapidly increasing figures tell their own story. Tobacco farms, barns, packhouses, prizeries, warehouses, buyers, and factories are becoming a strong and representative part of our liveliest towns."[121] The pace of economic growth in the Pee Dee seems all the more remarkable because the United States was suffering a general recession in the mid-1890s.

By the early 1900s, railroads began probing their steel fingers into the region, joining South Carolina fields with North Carolina factories. A prime example is the Seaboard Railway extension of 1909–11, an ambitious plan to link the Seaboard's nexus at Hamlet, North Carolina, with Savannah, Georgia. Plans called for the main line to join the Georgetown and Western Railway at the Pee Dee River in lower Florence County. Entering the region from North Carolina, the tracks reached Dillon in February 1909. From Dillon, the fastest, most direct route lay due south through Marion. Instead, planners sent the road southeast to Mullins, then southwest to Centenary, adding several costly miles to the route. Obviously, only compelling commercial reasons could justify the expense of the Mullins detour.[122]

By 1910, Mullins was emerging as South Carolina's leading tobacco market, and most of the leaf changing hands there went to manufacturing centers in North Carolina for processing. Because there was no direct line north, the heavy wooden hogsheads of flue-cured tobacco traveled a roundabout route that added days and dollars to the journey. Clearly, Mullins needed better rail connections, and the town's lucrative freight business offered a powerful incentive to Seaboard's planners. The Mullins detour may have lengthened the route to Savannah, but it shortened the distance from Mullins to manufacturing centers in Durham and Winston. The road became an important asset to the Pee Dee, as well as to Seaboard Railway, and was still in service in the 1990s.

The first and second decades of the twentieth century were a time of prosperity in the Pee Dee and the state as a whole. Between 1900 and 1920, deposits in South Carolina banks grew from $44 million to $187 million, an increase of 425 percent.[123] In 1910, the commissioner of agriculture proclaimed the state's prosperity: "Never in the agricultural, industrial, and commercial history of South Carolina have conditions been so good and so full of promise for the future."[124] And Bright Leaf tobacco was playing an important role in the state's prosperity. Events both at home and abroad helped make the years 1911–20 prosperous ones for Pee Dee Bright Leaf growers. In 1911, the federal government successfully invoked the Sherman Antitrust Act against the Tobacco Trust. Resulting competition among the successor companies (and their common desire to avoid further litigation) raised leaf prices, at least for a while.[125]

World War I had a massive impact on American agriculture, and no crop benefited more than Bright Leaf tobacco. At first, the threat to exports posed by the belligerent navies added to general uncertainty in the market, and leaf prices fell in 1914 and 1915.[126] Soon, however, demand for American produce caused by disruptions of European agriculture and the Allied war effort pushed commodity prices to record levels. Wheat prices rose 175 percent, sugar 170 percent, cotton 175 percent, and tobacco 220 percent.[127]

The war made cigarette smoking more popular than ever. Allied soldiers, trapped in their trenches amid the horrors of the Western Front, smoked prodigiously. Hundreds of tons of American cigarettes were eagerly smoked by Belgian, French, and English troops. When America entered the war in 1917, getting smokes to American servicemen assumed greater urgency. General John J. Pershing called tobacco "as indispensable as the daily ration." Asked what the army needed to win the war, Pershing replied, "tobacco, as much as bullets."[128] Americans responded generously to Pershing's appeal, sending millions of cigarettes to the front. Many communities held "cigarette drives" to purchase smokes for the troops. At home and "over there," the American Red Cross and Young Men's Christian Association handed out free cigarettes along with coffee and doughnuts. This patriotic connection helped give cigarette smoking a new respectability among Americans. Millions started smoking during the war and continued for a lifetime. Between 1914 and 1919, cigarette production tripled and leaf prices more than doubled.[129]

As leaf prices soared, growers bent to the task of meeting demand. Between 1909 and 1919, tobacco production in South Carolina increased more than threefold as the number of farms producing Bright Leaf jumped from about eight thousand to more than twenty-five thousand. Counties that had never raised a leaf before the war invested labor and capital in tobacco production. For example, Dorchester County went from zero to 206,000 pounds by the war's end. The Pee Dee poured out a veritable torrent of leaf, boosting output nearly 400 percent in Chesterfield, 300 percent in Clarendon, 360 percent in Williamsburg, and a tremendous 660 percent in Lee County.[130] Warehouses and aftermarket services expanded to handle the trade. By 1920, seventy-seven warehouses were selling Bright Leaf in South Carolina, a number unequaled since. Towns without a tobacco warehouse before the war boasted as many as three when the armistice was signed.[131]

As Bright Leaf culture spread through the Pee Dee in the 1890s and 1900s, the region showed great enthusiasm for the new crop. The excitement was justified; flue-cured tobacco easily outperformed the region's traditional staples: cotton, rice, and naval stores. Indeed, Bright Leaf was the most profitable enterprise the region's farmers had known since the 1850s. Within a generation, technology, mass marketing, boosterism, and war had combined to bring a highly profitable cash crop to the Pee Dee. The $600 Bright Leaf added to the Pee Dee economy in 1885 had grown to $19 million by 1918. And the Pee Dee landscape was literally transformed. Thousands of curing barns, their furnaces winking in the black August night, bore witness to the change, as did scores of warehouses, a dozen new banks, hundreds of new stores and homes, and thousands of new jobs in the fields and towns of the region.

The Pee Dee Bright Leaf boom offered stark contrast to the overall condition of American agriculture in those years. Low commodity prices, unregulated business practices, deflationary monetary policy, and lingering depressions beginning in the 1870s and 1890s created widespread dissatisfaction in the nation's agricultural sector. Farmers throughout the United States responded by establishing self-help organizations in an attempt to improve their circumstances, and the Gilded Age saw a wave of agrarian activism unrivaled in American history.[132] But Pee Dee Bright Leaf growers, enjoying the success of their new crop, were too busy clearing fields and building barns to give the agrarian movement much notice. As newcomers to the tobacco business, they were not yet aware of some longstanding problems veteran growers in older tobacco regions were grappling with. Their ignorance—and their bliss—did not last long.

Before I'd give my 'baccer to Reynolds, R. J.,
I'd walk all night and sleep all day.
I'd walk all night to keep from sleepin'
and sleep all day to keep from eatin'.
ANONYMOUS FARMER, 1923

 Reform and Reaction, 1918–1926

IN THE EARLY 1920S, Pee Dee tobacco and cotton farm-
ers suffered from the correction of inflated wartime commodity prices.
But falling prices were only part of the problem. Many tobacco growers
throughout the Carolinas and Virginia believed they were being victimized
by a biased marketing system that prevented them from receiving a fair
price. Seeking reform, thousands of growers in the three states organized
a marketing cooperative they hoped would restore equity to the tobacco
business. Although the co-op held great promise for tobacco farmers, opponents of reform mounted a vigorous and highly effective counterattack.
The struggle for cooperative marketing was the most important—and

most dramatic—event in the Bright Leaf culture from the 1880s to the 1930s, and it deserves careful analysis.

Before turning to those events, however, some understanding of the tobacco marketing system is necessary. By the 1920s, the three-tier system of production, marketing, and manufacturing was firmly entrenched. Growers produced and cured the crop, carried it to an auction warehouse in a nearby town, and sold it to buyers representing cigarette manufacturers. Although warehouses added no value to the product, they provided a convenient place for buyers and sellers to meet and the crop to change hands. Unlike the state-chartered inspection stations of the colonial period, however, Bright Leaf warehouses of the 1920s were privately owned commercial businesses with no official sanction.

In the 1920s, tobacco warehouses essentially functioned as sales facilities. Once delivered to the warehouse, the farmers' leaf was divided into piles of about two hundred pounds, weighed, and placed on flat wooden baskets. The weight and grower's name were recorded on a card placed on each pile. The piles were then arranged in long rows a few feet apart. When the sale started, the auctioneer and buyers gathered on both sides of the row and slowly walked the length of it, bidding as they went. The auctioneer set the pace. As the group passed each pile, esoteric hand signals, nods, and winks from the buyers were rapidly processed by the auctioneer. The pile was then "knocked" to the highest bidder. A clerk recorded the buyer's name and bid on the card. The auction party continued this pace for the length of the row. So fast was this process that more than three hundred piles were often sold in an hour. Clerks in the warehouse office computed the value of the sale and paid the growers. The warehouse took a commission from the proceeds of each pile. It was customary to add an extra charge for weighing and auctioneering.[1]

By 1920, all Pee Dee market towns boasted at least two warehouses, and most had three or four.[2] Warehouses competed for patronage, and farmers often benefited from this competition by receiving efficient service. Sometimes warehouses even made loans to customers during the planting and harvesting seasons that were later repaid from sales proceeds.[3] But conflicts of interest often resulted from leaf speculation by warehousemen. Not content with their income from sales commissions, many warehousemen purchased leaf directly from their customers for resale. Warehousemen, with inside knowledge farmers often lacked, sometimes persuaded growers to sell to them directly without going through the auction. They then re-sold the tobacco to manufacturers for higher prices.

Another difference between the inspection warehouses of the 1770s and 1780s and Bright Leaf warehouses of the 1920s was the lack of a state-sanctioned grading system. In the earlier period of tobacco culture, impartial government officials inspected the farmers' leaf and assigned it a recognized grade. In the 1920s, however, consistent with the laissez-faire attitudes of the time, government considered marketing issues outside its purview. In fact, South Carolina had more laws regulating tobacco marketing in the eighteenth century than in the twentieth.

Manufacturers filled the void by developing proprietary grading systems slanted very much to their advantage. These secret "house grades" were known within the company but concealed from growers and competitors. Since South Carolina had no marketwide grades, companies commonly assigned buyers' bidding limits based on the secret grades. Predictably, bidding limits on South Carolina markets were often lower than for the same grades in North Carolina. In 1914, the South Carolina Department of Agriculture, Commerce, and Industries estimated the price disparity between the two Carolinas at three to five cents a pound, a margin of considerable importance when prices were low.[4]

The lack of a uniform grading system multiplied opportunities for exploitation. Manufacturers preferred to buy leaf already sorted by size and color. But many farmers, either through ignorance or desire to lower costs, simply piled their leaf together and carried it to market. Alert warehousemen bought the tobacco cheaply, sorted it themselves, and resold it for a tidy profit. Sometimes warehousemen shipped the leaf to North Carolina markets where prices were usually higher.

Warehousemen defended the practice, arguing that farmers were free to decline their offers and auction their leaf. But many observers saw leaf speculation as unethical exploitation of the warehouses' customers. Reformers insisted that warehousemen should protect their customers' interests and confine their efforts to securing them the highest possible prices. Warehousemen could take their just profits from the higher commissions and volume thus generated. In 1919, the Sumter Chamber of Commerce roundly condemned "speculators [with] absolutely no interest in Sumter or our tobacco producers [who] have been more interested in buying tobacco at the lowest possible prices and reselling it to the tobacco trust than in getting for the farmers what tobacco was worth."[5]

"Pinhookers" were another source of exploitation. They were pure speculators, who added no value and served no purpose except to profit from the trade. The pinhooker of 1920 was an individual buying on his own account with a few thousand dollars of capital. He would approach a farmer who might be persuaded to sell a few piles directly for cash. And, as the pinhooker was sure to tell the uncertain farmer, there was risk in waiting for the next auction because prices might well decline in the meantime. The pinhooker then repacked and resold the tobacco at a profit—every dollar siphoned from the grower. Pinhookers were rightly considered to be parasites. As a further mark of contempt, growers began calling them "snipers" during World War I.[6]

The absence of industry-wide grading standards confused buyers as well as sellers and often resulted in erratic price swings that dramatically exposed the defects of the auction system. To prove the point, reformers sometimes moved a pile of tobacco around a warehouse floor and auctioned it several times for widely varying prices. One growers' advocate related an incident in a South Carolina warehouse: "Some of the growers agreed to sell their tobacco in the first row, then change the tags and move it to the second and third rows. One farmer sold the same basket of tobacco ten times, with prices ranging from 8 to 28 cents per pound. The same buyer who bought it for 28 cents had also bought it for 11 cents."[7]

But not all abuses were on the same side of the transaction. Some dishonest growers attempted to cheat purchasers by "nesting" poor-quality leaf deep in piles of good tobacco. A few even "salted" piles with bricks and scrap iron to augment the weight of their crop. Others disguised moldy or discolored tobacco by sprinkling snuff in the pile. Often, the deception was not discovered until later, and the warehouse was compelled to cover the loss.[8]

Attempts at reform began in the Old Belt in the 1870s. A decade before Bright Leaf culture entered the Pee Dee, growers in the Old Belt collided with warehousemen over marketing practices that many believed robbed them of satisfactory returns for their crop. Farmers objected to excessive sales commissions and extra fees for weighing and auctioneering. The presence of several warehouses in a given market did not always enhance competition either. Indeed, warehousemen routinely formed "boards of trade" to facilitate collusion, and rate fixing was a persistent problem.

But farmers were also learning that strength lay in numbers. As early as 1874, active chapters of the Patrons of Husbandry (also called the Grange) forced warehouses in Danville to lower commission rates from 3 to 2.5 percent. Warehouses in other market towns soon followed suit, and the 2.5 percent rate soon became standard throughout the Old Belt.[9] In the 1880s, a vigorous agrarian reform movement called the Farmers' Alliance sought to eliminate middlemen altogether. For a few years, Alliancemen operated warehouses in several Old Belt markets. An Alliance-owned tobacco factory in Oxford, North Carolina, even manufactured smoking tobacco and shipped it to Alliance chapters and sympathetic merchants nationwide.[10]

Pee Dee tobacco growers took the first tentative steps toward reform in the 1890s. Florence and Darlington farmers established the region's first tobacco growers' organization in 1895. Predictably, some of the region's Bright Leaf pioneers helped to launch the Florence Tobacco Growers Association. Charter members included John C. Calhoun Brunson, Robert Eugene Currin, Eugene F. Douglas, and Thomas Ashby. From the minutes of their meetings it is apparent that most of the members were substantial planters. Besides the evidence of the rolls, the minutes complain that members "were mostly those who could impart information, while the learners were few."[11]

At first, these meetings served little purpose than to share knowledge of cultivation and curing methods. Soon, however, Pee Dee Bright Leaf growers became politically active. As in the Old Belt, the focus of concern was the auction system. In some Pee Dee markets, warehousemen charged higher than standard fees. In 1898, South Carolina tobacco growers asked the legislature to regulate warehouse charges to the standard Old Belt rate. The effort failed, but the following year legislators passed a watered-down version of the bill.[12]

Growers became more active in the early twentieth century. When the 1914 crop averaged less than ten cents a pound in South Carolina, Bright Leaf growers called a meeting in Mullins to discuss reform. Growers and businessmen from Horry, Dillon, and Marion Counties as well as agents of the Farmers' Union poured into Mullins to voice concerns and consider strategies. As a result of the meeting, tobacco growers again looked to government for relief. In 1915, supported by the Farmers' Union, they urged establishment of a state-approved standard grading system. A second feature of the bill asked that warehouse charges be lowered "to the North Carolina basis." In both cases, however, warehouse interests lobbied successfully to defeat the reforms.[13]

Speculation and grading issues aside, perhaps the growers' greatest handicap was their fundamentally weak marketing position. The technical definition is oligopsony: a market with few buyers and many sellers. That the buyers were large corporations and the sellers mostly small farmers compounded the inequity. In the 1920s, six firms dominated the tobacco industry: the "Big Four" domestic companies and two foreign firms. American Tobacco Company, Liggett & Myers, Pierre Lorillard, and R. J. Reynolds produced more than 90 percent of the nation's cigarettes. British-owned Imperial Tobacco Company had a virtual tobacco monopoly on the British Empire, and Export Tobacco Company had a lock on the Asian market.[14] Independent leaf dealers such as Dibrell Brothers bought on order for the six major companies and thus did little to support the market. Reformers considered them but another pocket in the same pin-striped suit.[15]

Worse, there was a general absence of competition among the cigarette companies in purchasing tobacco. Although the auction was theoretically competitive, manufacturers tended to concentrate purchases in different types and grades of leaf. R. J. Reynolds, for example, bought middle-grade Bright Leaf for its Camel brand. American's sales leader Lucky Strike used much Burley in its popular blend. Imperial's buyers wanted top-grade Bright Leaf (known in Britain as "Virginia") for their stable of brands, and Export Tobacco Company purchased lower-grade leaf for its Asian customers. By segmenting the market, therefore, tobacco companies minimized competition among themselves, and, intentional or not, this tended to depress leaf prices.[16]

Manufacturers' large leaf inventories also worked against the farmer. Cigarette makers typically kept two to three years' supply of raw material on hand. The American Tobacco Company commonly held enormous stocks totaling several hundred million pounds. Such inventories gave manufacturers considerable discretion with respect to leaf purchases and provided an effective buffer against price swings.[17]

Finally, manufacturers were well aware of their favorable marketing position and were determined to protect it. These giant companies could use their vast wealth and influence against a potential threat by making a few telephone calls. At the local level, tobacco warehouses were lucrative enterprises that nurtured powerful vested interests highly resistant to reform. Besides the professional warehouse managers, merchants and bankers commonly invested in warehouse partnerships.[18]

Another disadvantage for growers was the seasonal nature of staple agriculture. Making a crop required the grower to invest in a series of production costs. Once begun, the grower was committed. He could not reduce expenses in mid-season to accommodate market swings as merchants and manufacturers could sometimes do. Moreover, unlike cotton and grain, cured tobacco did not keep well on the farm. After curing, tobacco is perishable and must be redried and packed into hogsheads within a few weeks or risk deterioration. Redrying and packing facilities were expensive and beyond the means of individual growers.[19] Therefore, holding a crop in hopes of higher prices could backfire.

Farmers often compounded their own problems as well. Typically, tobacco growers responded to higher leaf prices with increased production. Therefore, favorable market swings were soon answered by the planting of thousands of additional acres. This tragic tendency to overproduce depressed prices and enabled manufacturers to augment their leaf inventories at bargain rates. An additional problem was the general lack of formal education and business acumen among Pee Dee farmers. Illiteracy, ignorance, and suspicion often hindered tobacco growers from helping themselves.[20]

The tobacco marketing system of the 1920s was thus a highly prejudiced environment. The paucity of buyers, the large number of small producers, manufacturers' leaf inventories, lack of genuine competition in buying, the perishability of tobacco, overproduction, illiteracy, and the hostility of vested interests to reform added to the cumulative burden crushing the tobacco farmer.

Events in Europe soon distracted farmers, warehousemen, and manufacturers from their squabbling. With the onset of World War I, fear of German submarines initially softened the export market and leaf prices plunged. But by 1916 the economics of war began to work for farmers, and commodity prices soared to record levels (see Table 7).

Pee Dee tobacco growers took full advantage of the situation. In 1916, tobacco prices doubled. Encouraged by a good year and the promise of

TABLE 7

Bright Leaf Tobacco Production in South Carolina, 1910–1919

Year	Poundage (1,000s)	Price (in cents per lb.) current	(1900)[a]	Value ($1,000s) current	(1900)
1910	19,750	8.5	(7.5)	1,698	(1,481)
1911	15,750	12.6	(11.1)	1,984	(1,748)
1912	27,650	10.9	(9.3)	3,014	(2,571)
1913	36,900	13.8	(11.6)	5,092	(4,280)
1914	35,250	9.7	(8.1)	3,419	(2,855)
1915	46,620	7.0	(5.8)	3,263	(2,704)
1916	27,300	14.1	(10.9)	3,822	(2,948)
1917	56,160	23.1	(15.1)	12,972	(8,480)
1918	64,240	31.1	(17.3)	19,914	(11,050)
1919	78,860	20.1	(9.7)	15,811	(7,650)

Source: Agricultural Statistics Service, United States Department of Agriculture, Columbia, South Carolina, 1992.

[a] Prices are reported in constant values to correct for inflation and deflation in tracking price movements over time. The year 1900 was selected as the base because it centered a seven-year period of stable prices and has the further advantage of being the first year of the century. The Brady-David-Solar index has been applied. See John J. McCusker, *How Much Is That in Real Money?: A Historical Price Index for Use as a Deflator of Money Values in the Economy of the United States* (Worcester, Mass.: American Antiquarian Society, 1992), 316–31.

still better, South Carolina leaf growers doubled their tobacco acreage in 1917. Despite this huge increase in supply, wartime demand boosted prices 64 percent to twenty-three cents. The 1917 leaf crop returned almost $13 million to the Pee Dee, a sum greater than the total for the three previous years combined.[21]

The crop of 1918 surpassed even that record, as sixty-four million pounds of tobacco—four times the total of the 1911 crop—were urged from South Carolina soils. The price was up again, passing thirty-one cents a pound, yielding nearly $20 million. The tobacco crop of 1918 was a major economic event in the Pee Dee. Cotton prices were also high, and the region experienced prosperity unknown since the 1850s. The significance of the 1918 leaf crop can best be appreciated by comparing it with returns for earlier years. Even corrected for inflation, the Pee Dee tobacco crop of 1918 grossed more than the combined totals of the four crops of 1910–13.

Sadly, some Pee Dee farmers mismanaged their wartime windfall. In too many instances, simple people unaccustomed to discretionary income over-indulged themselves. More prudent observers deplored the farmers' ex-travagance and lamented the lost opportunity for financial independence. David R. Coker, the Pee Dee's leading agriculturist, scolded improvident farmers: "Our people have made enormous profits during the past three years. If they had held on to a fair portion of their profits, they would be completely free from outside financial dictation." Coker continued, "Many, however, never having seen a hundred dollar bill before, had no training in thrift and spent their money without any thought of the morrow." [22]

Farmers' judgment did not improve much over time. The armistice of 11 November 1918 ended the fighting in Europe, but Pee Dee tobacco growers, ecstatic over the success of the 1918 crop, gambled on even greater acreage in 1919. That year, they produced a tobacco crop of unprecedented size, approaching eighty million pounds. But with the war over and market conditions returning to normal, prices fell before the huge quantity of leaf. Still, the average price of twenty cents a pound was higher than for any crop before 1916 and should have afforded good profits. But Pee Dee to-bacco growers were learning that inflation was a two-edged sword. If leaf prices had risen, so had costs of production. Corrected for inflation, their twenty-cent tobacco was worth less than the fourteen-cent crop of 1916. Reckoned in constant dollars, tobacco prices actually dropped 44 percent in 1919.

Historically, farmers have short memories. As often happened when prices rose, farmers forgot about reform and concentrated on short-term profits. Theoretically, of course, the injustices of the marketplace were still present when prices were high, and growers should have been no less con-cerned. But enthusiasm for reform seemed to wane during the years of record profits, and growers set aside their quarrel for the duration. The activism that characterized Pee Dee tobacco growers before the war was lulled to sleep by the song of the auctioneer.

The crop of 1919 jolted them awake. The arithmetic of overproduction was painfully clear: South Carolina tobacco growers received four million fewer dollars for fourteen million more pounds of tobacco than in 1918. The outrage of receiving less for more might seem illogical, but it was no less real. And the source of the problem was just as obvious. While the abuses of the auction system might rest with manufacturers and warehousemen, farmers could fault no one but themselves for overproduction.

Another matter of concern just then was the relentless march of the boll weevil. In 1919, the dreaded pest crossed the Savannah River and infested the lower part of the state. Fear of the insect added urgency to the tobacco dilemma. Clearly, one reason for tobacco's rapid rise as a cash crop in South Carolina was the steady advance of the scourge of the Cotton Kingdom. The *State* declared in October 1919: "Farmers, particularly in the Pee Dee section of South Carolina, have in tobacco an effective weapon with which to beat down the tide of economic losses incident to the invasion of the boll weevil. . . . Considerable agitation is being manifested in the lower section of the State, already invaded by the boll weevil, for the cultivation of tobacco as a substitute crop." [23]

Now that the boll weevil was finally upon them, however, and cotton farmers were seeking another cash crop, tobacco was showing signs of weakness.[24] The irony was not lost on the state's agricultural leadership. Commissioner of Agriculture Bonneau Harris attacked the problem of low tobacco prices head-on. Having long recommended tobacco production to reduce the state's dependence on cotton, Harris strongly urged tobacco farmers to organize and protect their interests.[25]

Harris's call struck a responsive chord in the Pee Dee. In July 1919, more than one hundred growers from seventeen counties met in Florence. In his message to the delegates, Harris warned that buyers would likely offer higher bids late in the season to placate anxious farmers after "the bulk of the crop was almost confiscated." Harris urged the farmers not to be appeased by higher prices but to insist on fair policies as well.[26]

Pee Dee tobacco growers heeded Harris and in June 1920 reorganized the convention of the previous year into the South Carolina Tobacco Association. N. A. McMillan of Mullins, Bright Williamson of Darlington, and J. W. McCown and Thomas B. Young of Florence were elected to lead the group. Williamson reported to Harris that changes would soon be made in the marketing system and spoke of tobacco growers joining together in vigorous pursuit of reform.[27] Both the tone and the content of Williamson's remarks portended the activism that soon characterized Pee Dee tobacco growers. The Great War—and great profits—were over, and the struggle for equity was resuming.

The South Carolinians realized they could do little without the cooperation of the other Bright Leaf states, and Bright Williamson contacted
growers' organizations in North Carolina and Virginia. Old Belt growers
had more experience with warehousemen and manufacturers and understood only too well the need for solidarity. They welcomed the South
Carolinians as allies. Early in 1921, representatives from the three states met
in Raleigh to bring the energies and assets of all into common cause. N. A.
McMillan headed the South Carolina delegation. Six Pee Dee counties
sent delegates, with W. W. Long representing Clemson College. North
Carolina growers were represented by James Yadkin Joyner, a tobacco
grower and a former superintendent of education in that state.[28]

The guest of honor at the Raleigh meeting was Aaron Sapiro, a California attorney who specialized in organizing marketing cooperatives for
western fruit growers.[29] Sapiro was touring the South, bringing the co-op
message to the tobacco country. Simply put, the co-op could hold the crop
to force up prices. Tobacco was an excellent commodity for cooperative
marketing, Sapiro told the growers, because, unlike fresh fruit, properly
packed tobacco could be stored indefinitely. Sapiro also reminded listeners
of the special character of their product: "If one thinks the price of apricots
or prunes is too high, he can eat something else. [But] there is no substitute for tobacco. The world must have it." And, he added with a smile, "I
never smoked an orange in my life." [30]

At the Raleigh meeting, the Pee Dee delegates joined with North Carolinians and Virginians to form the Tri-State Tobacco Growers Cooperative
Marketing Association. The co-op was open to flue-cured, fire-cured, and
sun-cured tobacco growers in the three states. Their avowed purpose was
to reform the basic marketing structure of the Bright Belt. Bright Williamson of Darlington, E. C. Epps of Kingstree, and Thomas B. Young of
Florence were chosen to represent the Pee Dee on the co-op's board of
directors.[31]

Clarence Hamilton Poe, editor and publisher of the *Progressive Farmer*,
played a leading role in launching the Tri-State Co-op.[32] Himself a tobacco
grower on his farm near Raleigh, Poe was a zealous advocate of cooperatives. In the 1910s, Poe had traveled the world observing farmers buying
and selling in partnership. In 1915, Poe published his observations and phi-
losophy in a book that became the manifesto of the cooperative movement,
How Farmers Cooperate and Double Profits.[33]

Poe also used the *Progressive Farmer* as a bully pulpit to champion the co-op plan. Published in three regional editions, the *Progressive Farmer* was the most popular journal in rural America, reaching more than two hundred thousand homes each week. Virtually every issue carried at least one article promoting rural cooperation. A regular column entitled "Questions and Answers About Cooperatives" explained the marketing plan and frequent editorials expounded the co-op message. A successful farmer known to practice what he preached, Clarence Poe was a highly respected and influential figure in rural America. Poe's enthusiasm for cooperative marketing was cited by supporters and damned by opponents.[34]

The cooperative plan was simple: producers of a given commodity formed a cooperative to sell their crops in concert. Pooling their individual holdings enhanced the growers' bargaining position. The cooperative, controlling the bulk of the crop, negotiated directly with manufacturers, exacting higher prices. One advantage was timing: the co-op could sell produce gradually rather than dump it all at harvest time. Stubborn buyers could be softened by depriving them of product altogether. Moreover, selling directly to manufacturers would eliminate the costly auction system with its attendant abuses of pinhooking and speculation. Another reform expected to accompany cooperative marketing was a uniform system of grading.

Farmers were heartened by the many examples of successful co-ops. Through the *Progressive Farmer,* Clarence Poe reminded readers of flourishing co-ops in Ireland, France, and Denmark as well as the United States.[35] A prime example was the Sun Maid Raisin Growers Association. Under the leadership of Aaron Sapiro, Sun Maid had bargained its control of the raisin crop into impressive price gains. In another Sapiro-led co-op, prune producers had increased their share of the consumers' dollar from eight cents to forty-eight cents. Sapiro also helped Canadian farmers launch the highly successful Canadian Wheat Pool.

Closer to home, co-op activists pointed to Kentucky, where tobacco farmers had organized the Burley Tobacco Growers' Cooperative Marketing Association with very satisfactory results. Led by Louisville editor Robert Bingham, a champion of the co-op creed, the Burley co-op was off to a roaring start. By 1922, member-growers controlled 117 of 132 warehouses on the Burley Belt.[36]

Hoping to duplicate these successes in the Bright Belt, the Tri-State

Co-op hired Aaron Sapiro as director and legal counsel. Sapiro organized the Tri-State Co-op along the lines of his other successful cooperatives.[37] Members were asked to sign "iron-clad" contracts pledging their tobacco to the co-op for five years. Upon delivery, the leaf would be weighed and graded by experts licensed by the U.S. Department of Agriculture (USDA). The grower received a certificate showing the amount and grade of each deposit.

At the time of delivery, the grower would also receive an advance payment. The amount was based on the size and grade of the leaf deposit. Growers could also borrow against their tobacco from banks. The co-op could sell some tobacco directly from the receiving floor, but most of the crop would be redried and stored in bonded warehouses. Meanwhile, co-op officials would negotiate with manufacturers and exporters for an overall price on a grade-by-grade basis. When the leaf was sold, members would be paid according to the amounts of each grade deposited.[38]

To succeed, however, the co-op needed to control a majority of the tobacco crop. In South Carolina, the agricultural establishment was solidly behind the co-op and urged farmers to join.[39] In March 1921, the General Assembly provided the necessary legal framework by passing the Cooperative Marketing Act. Besides setting operational guidelines, the law made it a misdemeanor to entice a co-op member to break the marketing contract or "knowingly spread false reports" against the co-op.[40]

At first, Pee Dee farmers were lukewarm to the idea of cooperative marketing. Tobacco prices in South Carolina had advanced a little in 1920, and growers lacked the sense of urgency of their counterparts in North Carolina and Virginia. Even the leadership was uncertain how Pee Dee tobacco growers would respond.[41] Despite a vigorous enrollment campaign and the support of a sympathetic press, fewer than half the state's leaf growers had signed by the spring of 1921. Acknowledging that "much missionary work remains to be done in South Carolina," co-op leaders decided not to attempt marketing the 1921 crop.[42]

South Carolina tobacco growers learned a hard lesson in 1921. Tobacco prices fell catastrophically, dropping from twenty-four cents to eleven cents a pound. Compared to 1920, the crop lost 70 percent of its value, returning less than $5 million instead of nearly $16 million. At first, farmers were dumbfounded. Abundant supply could not have caused the collapse, they reasoned, since the 1921 crop was one-third smaller than the 1920 crop.

TABLE 8

Bright Leaf Tobacco Production in South Carolina, 1919–1925

Year	Poundage (1,000s)	Price (in cents per lb.) current	Price (in cents per lb.) (1900)[a]	Value ($1,000s) current	Value ($1,000s) (1900)
1919	78,860	20.1	(9.7)	15,811	(7,650)
1920	66,150	23.8	(9.9)	15,744	(6,549)
1921	43,230	11.2	(5.2)	4,842	(2,248)
1922	42,560	20.5	(10.3)	8,930	(4,182)
1923	77,214	20.9	(10.3)	16,138	(7,953)
1924	47,530	16.6	(8.2)	7,700	(3,755)
1925	72,750	16.5	(7.9)	12,004	(5,747)

Source: Agricultural Statistics Service, United States Department of Agriculture, Columbia, South Carolina, 1992.

[a] Prices are reported in current and constant values with 1900 as the base year.

As the magnitude of the disaster began to sink in, bewilderment turned to anger. At Kingstree, sales were halted after two hours and farmers gathered at the courthouse for a mass protest. Faced with offers of five cents a pound, Dillon farmers reclaimed their tobacco from the warehouse floors and carried it home. At Mullins, farmers vowed never to plant another crop "to give away."[43] In Manning, observers were afraid of "what might happen" following sales there for four cents. Manning was not alone in its apprehension. Pee Dee press reports spoke of "bad feelings in this section" and "very keen feelings against bankers and warehousemen." Reckoned in constant dollars, it was the cheapest crop in ten years (see Table 8).[44]

Striking while the iron was hot, the co-op capitalized on tobacco farmers' dissatisfaction and motivation for change. Activists quickly channeled growers' discontent into an enrollment campaign of unprecedented energy and scope. A mass meeting was held in Florence to encourage growers to commit their 1922 crop to the program. In attendance were many nonmembers eager to join. A petition was presented from farmers and business leaders in Kingstree declaring themselves ready to organize and urging other Pee Dee counties to "take similar action."[45]

Respected agricultural leaders toured the Pee Dee urging tobacco growers to embrace cooperative marketing. Clarence Poe joined North Carolina's J. Y. Joyner and Clemson's W. W. Long on summer and fall excursions through the Pee Dee. Poe told an excited crowd in Marion to "stop asking 'How much?' but rather *tell them* how much through cooperative marketing!"[46] Tobacco growers from the Burley and dark-fired co-ops of Kentucky and Virginia brought their message of success to South Carolina. Co-op organizers hosted picnics for Conway and Loris farmers, and recruiters were on hand to serve up the co-op gospel along with the barbecue.[47]

Even a cursory glance at regional newspapers revealed whose side the press was on. Pee Dee journals wrote movingly of the farmers' plight and pleaded with growers to join the cooperative. A front-page editorial in the *Horry Herald* reminded readers: "Everybody in the business has made a real profit off of your tobacco excepting you—the one man who takes all the risk—the one man who keeps himself close to the soil—the one man who sweats and worries all year and wonders how he will come out in the end—the one man who does all the real labor—he is the only fellow who fails to make a profit."[48]

Pee Dee editors searched their vocabularies for words strong enough to persuade reluctant farmers to sign contracts. One can almost see sparks flying from the presses of the *Marion Star* as the editor thundered: "If you are Red-Blooded Men, stand up for your rights, South Carolina *will* put the Campaign across!"[49] The press monitored the enrollment crusade and reported notable successes. Recruitment of prominent farmers was publicized in hopes that others might follow their examples. When George J. Holliday, a leading merchant and tobacco grower at Galivants Ferry, signed, the *Horry Herald* devoted a column to the story. A. M. Dusenbury, a prominent grower in Toddville, made news when he joined in July. The weeklies also printed endorsements from famous individuals in neighboring states, including former secretary of the navy Josephus Daniels of North Carolina.[50]

Despite the enthusiasm of the enrollment campaign and support of the local press, the co-op faced serious obstacles in convincing growers to join. Holding a crop meant growers must wait for payment, and many were concerned about the advances promised them. Most were indebted to banks or merchants and could ill afford to wait for their money. Indeed, more than a few were under mortgages with short maturities, and delay could well cost them their land. The advance payment was intended to meet the grower's most pressing obligations until he or she received final settlement. But many growers were skeptical about where the co-op could lay its hands on enough money to fund the advances.

To obtain needed cash, the co-op floated a $30 million loan with the War Finance Corporation pledging the tobacco stored under bond as collateral.[51] Moreover, members in every community solicited local banks not only to arrange additional financing for co-op activities but to encourage them to offer member-customers later maturities. In most cases banks cooperated. Altruism aside, Pee Dee bankers could easily identify their interests with the general prosperity better tobacco prices would bring.[52]

The co-op also needed facilities to receive, process, and store tobacco. The logical places for these tasks were the tobacco warehouses and redrying plants located in market towns. But since the co-op planned to eliminate the auction system and sell directly to manufacturers, many warehousemen were understandably hostile to the co-op. In every market town, however, members convinced some warehousemen that a new and rewarding role could be found for them. Offers were made to lease warehouse facilities and employ warehousemen as operators. Lease income and salaries could yield a good return on their investment, they reasoned, without assuming the risks of entrepreneurship. Whether by lease or outright purchase, forty South Carolina warehouses were under contract by the spring of 1922. Several more were on line by June, including some in North Carolina border markets at Fair Bluff, Tabor City, and Rowland.[53]

The 1922 marketing season began on 7 August, when Pee Dee member-growers made their first deliveries to co-op warehouses. Nearly two million pounds of flue-cured leaf were received at co-op warehouses. The *State* reported that "a golden stream moved continuously today from wagons to graders, from graders to weighers, and on to the ever-accumulating piles of weed in the storage rooms of the association." Growers were "especially pleased" with the experienced graders who "expertly and uniformly" graded the various types of tobacco.[54]

Growers were also pleased with prices. Before the market opened, expectations were high that the cooperative would raise tobacco prices. They were not disappointed. Opening day prices averaged 20.5 cents, an impressive 83 percent above those of 1921. Co-op members were advanced as much as 15 cents a pound for their first delivery. Some commented that the advance exceeded the entire proceeds from their first 1921 sale. Observers were quick to credit the co-op for raising prices. Before the season was three weeks old, reports from Lake City, Mullins, Darlington, Marion, and other Pee Dee market towns agreed that "the public generally recognizes [that] the organization has brought prices of tobacco to higher levels." At Kingstree, the local editor called the co-op there "a revelation." Even non-members admitted cooperative marketing made tobacco "bring a fancy price" and that without the co-op prices would have been much lower.[55]

In August, Aaron Sapiro visited Mullins and addressed a throng of growers there. Sapiro told the crowd, "The Association has accomplished its first great purpose. It has given you fair grading, [and] it has doubled the price of tobacco." Sapiro reminded growers that higher leaf prices meant better homes, schools, and roads. He urged members to stick with the co-op and nonmembers to join for the coming year. During the next few days, Sapiro met with tobacco growers in Timmonsville, Kingstree, and other Pee Dee market towns.[56]

The momentum continued into September. Co-op growers delivered between three and four million pounds of leaf per week to Pee Dee receiving stations. Throughout the region, enthusiastic members spoke glowingly of the new marketing plan. W. R. Coker, a prominent tobacco grower in Kingstree, spoke for many when he compared the past and present: "The tobacco companies are our friends and customers. The reason they have taken our tobacco for low prices is that we have dumped it down and begged them to pay us what they would instead of merchandising it like businessmen as the cooperative association is now beginning to do."[57]

The co-op's directors were optimistic as well. Responding to rising tobacco prices throughout the flue-cured belts, the directors approved an increase in the advance payments made to members upon delivery. By November 1922, enough co-op leaf had been sold to fund a second payment to all member-growers.[58]

Not all was sweetness and light, however. There were some whose interests were gravely threatened by the success of cooperative marketing. At the industry's lowest level, pinhookers were reading the handwriting on the wall. Realizing that their place in the trade was exactly the kind of abuse the co-op meant to eliminate, pinhookers lined up squarely against the reformers. Of like mind were a minority of warehousemen. While many Pee Dee warehousemen leased floor space to the co-op and some were salaried managers, other warehousemen were reluctant to abandon the profitable speculation they had long enjoyed. Faced with the success of coopera-tive marketing, warehousemen escalated their opposition to the co-op.

Of course, manufacturers stood to lose most from higher tobacco prices, but some employees were more exposed than others. Tobacco buyers were especially worried. The threat to their livelihood was clear. If the new marketing plan succeeded and tobacco companies began purchasing di-rectly from the co-op, leaf buyers and auctioneers would quickly become superfluous. In the summer of 1922, all who stood to lose from reform began collaborating to oppose the co-op. From the mansions of Durham to dollar-a-day boardinghouses in Mullins, the enemy plotted a counter-attack.

It was not long in coming. The strategy was to divide and conquer. In August, mysterious leaflets began to appear. Early one morning, residents of Pee Dee market towns awoke to find handbills lying in the streets and posted on trees and fences. Experienced newspapermen who examined the leaflets commented on their crudeness, reporting that they were "printed in misfitting type with partially wrong fonts." The content was equally crude, denouncing the co-op as "a set of smart, slick-tongued, fancy dressed sports who came from Kentucky telling slick tales." In some of the leaflets, an unidentified co-op member was quoted as saying he had sold tobacco in a noncooperative warehouse for much more than he received from the co-op.[59] Of course, when the handbills were circulating in Au-gust, all any member had received from the co-op was the first advance payment. This obvious discrepancy was not mentioned, however.

The leaflets sought to encourage members to defect and bring their leaf to auction, and a few did break their contracts and sell tobacco in nonco-operative warehouses. The defectors' motives varied, but the most com-mon was an idea being promoted by area warehousemen. Full-page ads in Pee Dee newspapers asked farmers, "Why wait for your money?" and went on to say auction prices were as high as the co-op's, and the grower could receive full settlement immediately instead of "waiting till Christmas."[60]

Clearly, the co-op's very existence was the reason leaf prices rose at all in 1922. If thousands of co-op farmers had not been willing to wait for their money, prices would have been lower for all. That manufacturers paid the same at auction for "outside" tobacco as for co-op leaf was to be expected. Although manufacturers could have bought outside tobacco cheaply in 1922, doing so would have driven more farmers into the co-op and strengthened the resolve of sustaining members.

Manufacturers, warehousemen, and pinhookers wanted growers to believe their crop would bring just as much on the auction market and that the co-op was a needless complication. In fact, it was common practice for warehousemen to overpay for tobacco belonging to a few talkative farmers who would then eagerly broadcast the news of their "good sale" at such and such a warehouse. The object, of course, was to encourage co-op members to break their contracts, abandon the cooperative, and bring their crop to the generous warehousemen. Plainly, the vested interests paid the same for outside tobacco as for co-op leaf in 1922 — and advertised it — in hopes that member-growers would desert the co-op.[61]

Co-op leaders took the threat seriously. Defections were a mortal danger to the movement, and the Tri-State Co-op was grimly determined to maintain discipline in the ranks. Without the solidarity of member-growers, the co-op's bargaining position would be fatally weakened. Throughout the enrollment campaign, co-op officials had stressed that membership was voluntary, but once a grower placed himself under contract, the co-op was determined to enforce the covenant. Co-op leaders intended to make an example of turncoats as a warning to the faithless. As soon as hard evidence of desertions was in hand, the co-op's legal department began prosecuting those who broke faith.

Enforcement could be pursued in several ways. First, the co-op could sue the offender for breach of contract. Second, litigation could be brought against anyone who aided or abetted the offender under Article 24 of South Carolina's Cooperative Marketing Act. Since the Tri-State Co-op was an interstate organization, it could sue in federal courts as well. The co-op's legal department was well prepared. Complaint forms were printed in advance with blank spaces for the date, jurisdiction, and name of the defendant. The forms were signed for the co-op by Aaron Sapiro and countersigned by local law firms. The Florence firm of Willcox and Willcox represented the co-op in the Pee Dee.[62]

Court decisions generally supported the co-op. The North Carolina Supreme Court gave important sanction to the movement in April 1923 in a unanimous decision upholding the legality of the marketing contract. The court endorsed the association as "the most hopeful movement ever inaugurated to obtain justice for and improve the financial condition of farmers and laborers."[63] Writing for the court, Chief Justice Walter Clark expressed a viewpoint widely held in the Bright Belt: "Individual fortunes, aggregating many hundreds of millions of dollars in a few hands, have been created by the sale of the tobacco crop at prices fixed, as is well known, by a 'gentlemens' agreement' among manufacturers, who are few in number and strong financially, who at the same time have kept up, by similar agreement, the price of the manufactured article to the public."[64]

In the Pee Dee, the co-op vigorously enforced the marketing contract, and numerous suits for breach were filed in South Carolina's Fourth and Fifth Judicial Circuits. Although a few cases were dismissed, Pee Dee judges typically granted injunctions against deserters. For example, Florence judge S. W. G. Shipp enjoined W. M. Venters of Johnsonville from selling his tobacco "outside" although Venters claimed he had rented his crop to his son, who was not a member.[65] Members attempting to break their contracts tried other tricks. A popular maneuver was the so-called petticoat defense wherein a deserter claimed he had turned over his crop to his wife who was not a member. The Florence County court tried a petticoat case against a Mr. Bowen that resulted in a mistrial.[66] Judge John S. Wilson later sentenced C. C. Rogers, a Mullins grower, to thirty days or a $250 fine for violating an injunction not to sell his leaf at auction.[67]

The co-op's success in 1922 helped recruiting efforts in 1923. During the spring membership drive, the co-op touted its record of service to Pee Dee growers, and area newspapers featured stories comparing auction prices with those the co-op received. The *Kingstree County Record* reported that a Williamsburg County share-tenant sold his half of a tobacco crop at auction for $230 while his landlord was advanced $250 on his half by the co-op with another installment still payable.[68]

The co-op's recruiting efforts crossed racial lines as leaders actively recruited black members and invited blacks to attend meetings along with whites. Clarence Poe argued the case for black membership from the pages of the *Progressive Farmer*. Poe's argument for admitting blacks included altruistic as well as practical motives. "Not only should we wish to help Negro farmers," Poe argued, but, if excluded, black growers would continue to dump their crop on the auction market "and break prices for themselves and us."[69]

In light of the pervasive racism of the 1920s, especially in the rural South, the co-op's open door policy was extraordinary. For example, in July 1923, several hundred black tobacco growers joined whites at a co-op rally in Kingstree. The crowd ate barbecue—the races dined separately—and heard several speakers, including Senator Ellison D. "Cotton Ed" Smith and Ransom Westberry of Sumter, president of the National Negro Farmers' Association.[70] In August, tobacco growers of both races met in Florence to hear state senator N. B. Dial, Congressman J. J. McSwain, and Wofford College president H. N. Snyder praise cooperative marketing as "a new Declaration of Independence for South Carolina farmers."[71]

Throughout 1923, the reformers and their opponents waged a war of words in area newspapers. The co-op sought endorsements from local businesses. Because some growers questioned the willingness of merchants to await co-op payments to receive settlement, businessmen reassured their customers with declarations like the following:

> After the past year's experience we are thoroughly convinced of the soundness of the new plan of marketing, and believe the method one by which the farmers can be assured a fair and profitable price for their products each year. Our dealings with the members of these associations were entirely satisfactory for 1922, and we are willing to show our further confidence by extending aid to members worthy of credit, as far as we are able, in 1923. We are taking this position now in order that the members may work with the assurance that they can do business with us and still deliver their crops to their respective associations.[72]

In Conway's *Horry Herald,* the notice was underwritten by 93 merchants: grocers, furniture dealers, pharmacies, automobile dealers, banks, physicians, the telephone company, and the postmaster. An identical statement in the *Marion Star* was sponsored by 125 businesses and professionals, including the sheriff and other county officials.[73] But if local business was backing the co-op, warehousemen had other allies. A piece by the Phoenix Warehouse declared:

MR. FARMER, WHY NOT BE INDEPENDENT?
BIG COMPANIES ARE INTERESTED WITH US—YES!
Never lose sight of the fact that the big companies are with us in this fight. They want a strong independent market at Marion and have furnished us with buyers who have limits that will make you sit up and take notice. The big companies

want your crop and stand ready to go on our floor and bid in competition for it
—in the good old fashioned way!

PHOENIX WAREHOUSE

Marion, S.C.[74]

A few weeks later, the same warehouse was boasting:

> WE HAVE PUT OLD MARION BACK ON THE TOBACCO MAP
> They—you know who they is!—well, they said it would be impossible for us to
> re-establish Marion as a tobacco market. . . . Then we took the matter up with
> the big companies.[75]

Perhaps the greatest irony of these advertisements is the warehousemen's outright flaunting of their collusion with tobacco companies, as if manufacturers were opposing the co-op with the farmers' interests in mind instead of their own. One wonders why more farmers did not see through this transparent assault on their interests.

Warehousemen also used their financial leverage to pry members out of the co-op. For years, many warehousemen had made short-term production loans to customers. This practice was usually good business for the warehouse. Not only did the lender receive interest, but the borrower was compelled to sell his crop in the lender's warehouse, which also assessed a commission. Since the Tri-State Co-op was in no position to provide such loans to its members, noncooperative warehousemen eagerly exploited this advantage to maintain the loyalty of their customers. Doubtless some customers also exploited it.[76]

Higher prices prompted a massive increase in tobacco plantings in 1923, and Pee Dee Bright Leaf growers cured about seventy-seven million pounds, nearly equaling the record crop of 1919. Normally, such an increase in supply would have been punished by a steep decline in prices. But manufacturers were determined to undermine the co-op, and they held prices steady at 1922 levels.[77] The crop of 1923 sold at an average of twenty-one cents a pound and returned $16 million to Pee Dee growers, twice the value of the 1922 crop. Co-op receiving stations opened two weeks before the auction market, and members were pleasantly surprised with the larger advances they received for their first leaf deposit. Most grades were up nearly 50 percent over 1922.[78]

The Tri-State Co-op was costing manufacturers millions, and every conceivable means of resistance was mounted against the reformers. Propaganda remained the weapon of choice. One rumor that gained wide circulation charged that co-op executives were milking the association through high salaries. The co-op countered that its executives' salaries were comparable to those of noncooperative warehousemen who handled far less tobacco. In fact, during 1923, the co-op's peak year of operation, only four employees earned more than $15,000.[79]

When the truth failed to serve them, co-op opponents did not hesitate to lie. For example, rumors were circulated that the co-op secretary, M. O. Wilson, was paid $40,000 per year, when, in fact, he received only $7,500.[80] J. Y. Joyner, outraged by the insinuations, declined any salary at all and thereafter served without compensation. In a press release accompanying the announcement, Joyner blasted those "whose low ideals prevent them from ascribing to others any higher motives than their own mercenary ones."[81]

Opposition forces dipped their arrows in venom, employing slander, anti-Semitism, and racism against the reformers. Seeking to capitalize on the Red Scare then sweeping the nation, anti-co-op propaganda referred to Aaron Sapiro as a "bolshy" and likened co-op vice-president Oliver Sands to Leon Trotsky.[82] Trade publications heavily dependent on tobacco advertising joined the fray. Editorials in the *Southern Tobacco Journal,* sandwiched between ads for the Imperial Tobacco Company and the Wilson Warehouse Board, openly referred to Aaron Sapiro as the "California Jew." Some critics even suggested that Sapiro was part of a Jewish plot "to seize control over the agricultural and horticultural resources of the United States." Not content with attacks on his religion, they mocked Sapiro's Italian ancestry with sneering references to the "Co-Wop." Opponents also damned the association for admitting black farmers into membership.[83]

Assaults on the co-op were not always limited to words. After 1924, South Carolina law required that tobacco be sold under the owner's true name. Contract breakers attempting to sell their tobacco at auction sometimes hid behind false names as well as petticoats. Warehousemen abetted this illegal dodge by assigning fictitious names to their piles of tobacco. In Dillon, warehouseman Paul Hardy fired a pistol at co-op executives, attorneys, and the county sheriff while the group was searching his warehouse for illegal tobacco. The bullets missed, and Hardy was charged with assault.[84]

Despite the co-op's success in raising leaf prices, the growers' natural conservatism buttressed by the antireform campaign was beginning to tell. Perhaps the co-op's greatest problem was its inability to control at least half the tobacco crop. At its peak, the association handled less than 40 percent. Although the majority of growers enrolled during the co-op's initial sign-up campaign in 1922, actual deliveries amounted to only 36 percent of the crop. Hedging their bets, some growers pledged only a portion of their tobacco to the co-op, believing delivery of the amount pledged fulfilled their obligation and they were free to sell the balance of their crop on the open market. Obviously, such policies led co-op officials to overestimate the amount of tobacco under contract and inflated their expectations.[85]

Growers' participation did not improve with time. The co-op received roughly the same percentage of the 1923 crop as it handled in 1922.[86] In 1924, however, the co-op's market share dropped sharply; deliveries to co-op receiving stations fell to only 23 percent of the tobacco crop. Therein lay the greatest threat to reform: with the bulk of the crop outside the association, manufacturers could meet their leaf requirements without coming to terms with the co-op. Indeed, the availability of outside tobacco allowed major buyers to boycott co-op leaf.[87]

The American Tobacco Company, the strongest buyer in the market, routinely purchased 25 percent of the flue-cured crop. Yet American bought only 3 percent of co-op holdings in 1922 and not a single pound in 1923. The Imperial Tobacco Company of Great Britain, which customarily bought about 20 percent of the crop, purchased less than one-half of 1 percent of co-op holdings in 1923. Although R. J. Reynolds and Liggett & Myers made substantial purchases of co-op leaf, the boycott by the two largest tobacco companies ultimately doomed the reform movement.[88]

In May 1924, the co-op sent a delegation to Great Britain in an attempt to persuade Imperial to buy co-op leaf. Bright Williamson represented Pee Dee growers. The group met with Imperial's directors at their corporate headquarters in Bristol. They presented letters of recommendation from President Calvin Coolidge, Secretary of Commerce Herbert Hoover, and the governors of South Carolina and Virginia. They also furnished testimonials from R. J. Reynolds and Liggett & Myers attesting to the co-op's satisfactory performance.

The meeting lasted two hours. Imperial's directors were polite but repeatedly evaded the main question, whether Imperial would abandon the boycott and buy co-op tobacco. Though they showed "studied and careful courtesy," the British did not budge. They offered nothing and agreed to nothing. Hoping to salvage something from the meeting, Bright Williamson asked Imperial's directors to state, at the very least, that they were not hostile to the co-op. Imperial politely declined. The directors then invited the Americans to tea. The Americans politely declined. The trip was a complete waste of time. Of 150 million pounds of Bright Leaf tobacco handled by the co-op in 1924, Imperial refused to buy a single leaf.[89]

Not content with the passive resistance expressed through the boycott, Imperial went to extraordinary lengths to encourage tobacco production in southern Georgia. For example, Georgia farmers were allowed to sell "loose leaf," thus avoiding the costly steps of grading and tying required of Carolina and Virginia growers. But to enjoy this advantage, Imperial required growers to sell only in noncooperative warehouses.[90]

Imperial's hostility to the co-op kindled smoldering resentment among South Carolina farmers and political leaders. British hostility to American farmers in the wake of U.S. participation in World War I roused Governor Thomas G. McLeod to fury. McLeod spoke for many when he reminded a Mullins audience: "When Britain's back was to the wall and France was bled white, if it had not been for our American boys who went over there, there would be no Imperial Tobacco Company of Great Britain; it would be a Hun company!"[91]

Senator "Cotton Ed" Smith lashed the English firm in his flamboyant style before a crowd of two thousand tobacco growers at Kingstree:

We fought England because we had taxation without representation. We fought and won. Yet when it comes to selling the product your children depend on, you haven't any more to say about it than a Hottentot in Africa. We sit down here like dumb driven beasts and allow others to dictate what we sell it for. . . . Why isn't tobacco tobacco? Why would not any tobacco-buying corporation buy from you? You are not fixing the price. Why do they fight it? They know that if the farmers ever get this cooperative marketing started, the happy days of skinning you alive are gone![92]

Perhaps the most eloquent judgment of the opposition was made by James Y. Joyner. Evoking the imagery of the late war, he issued a stirring call to arms at the beginning of the 1925 season. "We are standing at the Marne," he told his comrades, "and arrayed against us are powerful forces, strongly entrenched, perfectly organized, powerfully financed, and determined in their own interest to destroy us this year if they can. . . . Let us recruit our ranks, increase our deliveries, and standing in unbroken columns with locked shields swear, 'They shall not pass!' "[93]

One reason the propaganda campaign against the cooperatives was so effective was because it did not need to invent issues to exploit but only exaggerated existing ones. The association had genuine and persistent internal problems. A continuing source of discontent among members was the size of advances paid on delivery. The cooperative's valuation committee—composed mainly of bankers and leaf dealers—set the amount of advance payments. The War Finance Corporation and the Intermediate Credit Bank, the co-op's financiers, appointed several members to this committee as well. Before the season began, the panel gathered information on the quality, size, and probable price of the tobacco crop. Taking all factors into account, they estimated a market price for each grade and based the advances on these projections.

In 1922, about 40 percent of the committee's estimate was advanced to growers.[94] When the market opened in 1923 with higher prices, advances were raised.[95] Furthermore, during the four marketing seasons the co-op was in existence, advances increased every year. The average for 1924 was about 50 percent, and advances in 1925 averaged about 65 percent.[96] But two-thirds was not enough for some farmers when they could get all their money at once by selling at auction. Of course, all tobacco growers, members and nonmembers alike, benefited from the higher prices generated by the co-op, but too few could maintain the discipline needed to make cooperative marketing a success.

Some farmers' lack of patience can be better understood when the co-op's record of slow payments is taken into account. The final payment for the 1922 crop, for example, was not remitted until 1 April 1924, nearly nineteen months after delivery. This long delay was fairly typical for co-op operations, since the average time from delivery to final settlement over the life span of the association was 19.4 months.[97] Of course, the boycott of co-op leaf by the American Tobacco Company and Imperial doubtless lengthened settlement times, but the organization held some of the blame for delayed payments. More timely payments to member-growers would have boosted morale and denied the opposition a lethal propaganda weapon. Tardy payment was a major source of discontent among loyal members and put a bludgeon into the hands of their enemies.[98]

Pee Dee member-growers fared somewhat better in this respect than their counterparts in North Carolina and Virginia. For example, South Carolina leaf was the first sold and settled for from the 1922 crop. Indeed, Pee Dee growers received 105 percent of the committees' valuation for their 1922 leaf. The South Carolinians were also at the front of the line in 1923, receiving settlement well ahead of growers in eastern North Carolina and the Old Belt.[99] Tobacco was planted earlier and ripened faster in South Carolina, and Pee Dee growers benefited from this seasonal advantage.

The association was also losing warehouses. South Carolina members made deliveries to forty co-op warehouses in 1922 and 1923. By October 1924, however, declining grower participation forced the association to reduce salaries, lay off employees, and close warehouses. Throughout the Bright Belt, 236 workers left the payrolls and hundreds more accepted pay cuts. In the Pee Dee, the co-op closed warehouses in peripheral markets at Georgetown, Lake View, and Moncks Corner. By 1925, only thirty warehouses were receiving and processing members' tobacco.[100] The loss of floor space limited the association's ability to serve the membership and further eroded confidence in the co-op.

By the end of 1925, members at the grass-roots level were concerned about the future of the organization. During November and December, local chapters held meetings to discuss reform and policy changes to be implemented in 1926 when the five-year contract expired. Although details remained to be worked out, there was a consensus that the next contract must address the legitimate concerns of the membership. High on their agenda was receiving prompt payment for the fruits of their labor. Serious questions were also being raised about the competence of management at various levels.[101]

These concerns were sharply intensified when a report on the Tri-State Tobacco Cooperative was released by the Federal Trade Commission (FTC) in January 1926. Among other things, the FTC discovered that two co-op executives were investors in a redrying plant contracted by the association to process members' tobacco. Apparently, the two had profited substantially from fees paid for this service. That their redrying plant charged the co-op $1.75 per hundred pounds rather than the $2.00 charged by independents did not excuse the breach of trust. Many loyal co-op members and a friendly press recoiled from the revelation of this unethical profiteering. Although the two directors agreed to return their profits to the association, the damage was done.[102]

A series of lawsuits followed, brought mostly by disgruntled members seeking to liquidate the co-op. In the spring of 1926 the association was still technically solvent, but the adverse publicity of the report so demoralized the membership that the association could not expect to receive much tobacco the following season. Responding to demands for relief, federal courts released the members from their marketing contracts and ordered the co-op into receivership. In the words of Clarence Poe, the loyal growers had reached the end of the trail.[103]

In analyzing the rise and fall of the Tri-State Co-op, more must be considered than the obvious issues of imperfect management and determined opposition. The co-op was not so grossly mismanaged that a resolute housecleaning would not have set it right. In fact, most co-op leaders appear to have been men of character and dedication. The Pee Dee's Thomas Benton Young and Bright Williamson and North Carolina's James Yadkin Joyner and Clarence Poe were reputable men who lent credibility to the organization by their association with it. It is unlikely that men of their stature would have failed to perfect the association if given time.

The Tri-State Co-op was also undermined by the persistent problem of overproduction. Tobacco growers were very sensitive to price increases and typically responded to higher prices with greater production. Ironically, the cooperative was ultimately weakened by the better prices it helped to achieve. This served notice on agrarian reformers that any attempt to raise crop prices would be self-defeating unless closely linked to production controls. Of course, controls work only if virtually all growers abide by them. Even at its peak, the Tri-State Co-op came nowhere near that level of grower confidence.[104]

Although vested interests played their part in defeating the co-op, the greatest burden of guilt for the failure of reform rests with the farmers themselves. Their reluctance to join and haste to defect proved fatal. Manufacturers and warehousemen could not have defeated the co-op without the aid, conscious or not, of the growers. Ironically, Clarence Poe had foreseen this problem years earlier in his guidebook for rural cooperation, *How Farmers Co-Operate and Double Profits:* "There will come bitter days

when the very men you yearn to help will judge you wrongly and misinter-
pret your motives and you will weary of the struggle . . . even as Moses
grew sick at heart when the Canaan-bound Hebrews mutinied because he
had not let them alone in their bondage." [105]

Clearly, many tobacco growers entered the co-op with unrealistic expectations. Many farmers based their hopes on the abnormally high prices of
the war years. Of course, not even the strongest cooperative could have
kept prices so high after the war, but some naively viewed war profits not
as a temporary windfall but as a permanent change in their living standard.
Indeed, contemporary observers censured the folly of farmers who had
borrowed, expecting to repay long-term debt with short-term profits.[106]
Another unrealistic demand was that some members expected the co-op
to solve their problems too quickly. The Tri-State Co-op could not resolve
in three years the entrenched injustice and exploitation of decades of tobacco marketing.[107]

Another critical factor that hobbled the co-op at every turn was the abys-
mal educational level of the Pee Dee. Of the five counties in South Carolina with the lowest literacy rates, four were in the Pee Dee. In other
Pee Dee counties that were not among the bottom five, the literacy rate of
farmers was lower than for the population as a whole.[108] Although it is
difficult to determine the precise extent to which farmers' ignorance placed
a stumbling block in the path of their interests, it is important that contemporaries considered this a primary factor in the failure of the reform movement. It is a tragedy of the human condition that those who could profit
most from guidance are often the least receptive to it. One warehouseman
who traveled the Bright Belt in those years summed up the failure of the
co-op in two words: "damn ignorance." [109]

The cooperative movement was the farmers' best hope to reform the
tobacco marketing system. It raised prices for a few years by exerting both
direct and indirect influences on the market. Prices rose in part because of
the inherent advantages of cooperative marketing, a direct influence reformers sought to establish and maintain. But prices also rose because
manufacturers and warehousemen deliberately inflated auction prices to
subvert the co-op and undermine the loyalty of member-growers. Thus
farmers who did not join benefited from higher prices in much the same
way nonunion workers sometimes benefit from union activity they do not

support. The sorry spectacle of member-growers deserting the co-op in 1923 to sell at auction bears a tragic likeness to another greedy farmer butchering the goose to get all the golden eggs at once.[110]

After the collapse of the Tri-State Co-op in 1926, both direct and indirect influences were lost, and prices began to slide. When the bottom fell out in 1928, farmers were defenseless. By the late 1920s, forces were gathering that would soon plunge the Pee Dee region to the depths of despair. Night was falling.

Our President, who art in Washington,
Hoover be thy name.
You took away our Chesterfields
And gave us Golden Grain.
SMOKERS' LAMENT, 1931

5 The Abyss, 1926–1932

OBSERVERS of southern agriculture had long predicted that flue-cured tobacco growers were headed for disaster. By the late 1920s, the handwriting was clearly on the wall. Efforts to reform the highly prejudiced marketing system had failed. Besides the inherent bias of few buyers and many sellers, growers were victimized by secret grading systems and predatory speculators who sought to profit at their expense. To make matters worse, farmers reduced their already weak bargaining position to groveling impotence by their chronic tendency to overproduce. This devastating practice eventually swamped the market with surplus tobacco, drove prices below the cost of production, and undermined the solvency of the Pee Dee region.

Saddest of all was the unwillingness of farmers to work together for their mutual advantage. Indeed, everyone in the tobacco industry was organized *except* growers. Manufacturers collaborated to advance their interests, and warehousemen had their "boards of trade." Only growers remained disorganized. Increasing demand for flue-cured tobacco relieved only slightly the growers' predicament and merely postponed the inevitable. Knowledgeable people in the tobacco belts knew the situation was ripe for catastrophe and only a nudge was needed to bring the whole rotten system crashing down. In the late 1920s, the threat became fact. It is to that grim tale that we now turn.

Since colonial times, tobacco growers had suffered when supply exceeded demand. As early as 1623, tobacco factors in London complained that "tobacco will yield now no price, the markets being overlaid." [1] Though the ailment was correctly diagnosed, the cure proved elusive. The failure of farmers to match supply with demand has been a persistent problem in southern agriculture. While farmers have understood (on a theoretical level, at least) the law of supply and demand, voluntary attempts to regulate production have always failed.

The greatest obstacle to effective production limits had always been lack of discipline among growers. Voluntary crop limits work only if everyone abides by them. Attempts to raise prices through voluntary production limits were typically undermined by greedy noncooperators seeking to profit from the restraint of their neighbors. Only government intervention or outright terrorism ever succeeded in maintaining discipline.

Government efforts to regulate tobacco production predate the republic. In 1639, with tobacco "sinking every day to a baser price," the governor of Virginia ordered half the colony's crop burned. Sometimes, however, government refused to intervene in an overproduction crisis, and angry growers took matters into their own hands. For example, in 1682, when leaf prices fell below a penny a pound, Virginia growers asked the House of Burgesses to forbid tobacco planting for a year. Enraged by government's refusal, tobacco growers rioted, destroying ten thousand hogsheads of leaf. [2]

The tobacco regions of Kentucky saw the worst crop-related violence in American history during the infamous Black Patch War of 1905–9. Commensurate with the rampant capitalism of the Gilded Age, cigarette manufacturers had consolidated their buying power into a "tobacco trust." Their purpose, of course, was to eliminate competition, including the competition for leaf tobacco. By 1906, prices for Burley and dark-fired tobacco had sunk to absurdly low levels. Indeed, contemporary estimates placed per capita income in the Kentucky tobacco belt at thirty cents per day. Kentucky Burley and dark-fired growers struck back at the trust's buying monopoly by creating a selling monopoly. Grower-activists organized marketing pools, declared a boycott against the trust, and called on members to reduce tobacco acreage.[3]

To enforce the boycott, Kentucky activists carried out organized terrorism on a scale unknown since the Civil War. Night riders burned tobacco barns, uprooted plants, shot livestock, and physically assaulted noncooperators. They attacked railroad yards and burned freight cars filled with tobacco. Riders swept into market towns, setting warehouses afire and rolling thousand-pound hogsheads of leaf into the Cumberland River. In 1908, grower-activists absolutely forbade tobacco planting in the Black Patch, and production fell an astonishing 70 percent. While some growers doubtless cooperated willingly, others did so out of fear. Finally, tobacco prices began to rise. By November 1908, the trust was paying seventeen cents for leaf it had refused at eight cents two years earlier.[4] It is a commentary on the conditions of American agriculture in those years that farmers viewed this reign of terror as a successful reform movement.

In the laissez-faire environment that characterized American agriculture in the 1920s, tobacco farmers had helped to create a vicious cycle. Higher prices tended to stimulate increased production, and growers planted to the windowsills to reap fat profits. But as supplies increased, prices fell. To compensate for lower prices, farmers often produced still greater quantities, hoping to offset slim profit margins with sheer volume. But greater acreage meant greater outlays for seed, labor, fertilizer, and draft animals. Thus overproduction not only lowered selling prices but raised the growers' total investment in the crop. Profit margins were squeezed from both sides, and farmers soon felt the pinch. Only natural calamities such as drought or disease exercised any "crop control" in the tobacco country.

But what of the other side of the supply/demand equation? Did not demand for tobacco products influence the farm price of the raw material? In fact, long-term demand and farm price were almost unrelated. Observing demand indexed by consumption for the period is revealing. Although tobacco was consumed in several forms, by far the most reliable measure of tobacco use in the United States is cigarette sales.[5] Between 1926 and 1930, leaf tobacco production in the United States rose 27 percent. At the same time, however, cigarette sales increased 34 percent. In an unbiased market, therefore, leaf prices could be expected to hold steady or, perhaps, advance a little. Yet between 1926 and 1930, leaf tobacco lost half its value. Clearly, other forces were at work.[6]

Manufacturers carried leaf inventories equal to about three years' requirements, and these stocks tended to depress farm prices (see chapter 4). In fact, leaf inventories formed the basis of another demand index. While consumption is the most obvious measure of demand, disappearance is the most comprehensive. Disappearance is computed by adding purchases of the current crop with stocks on hand, then subtracting the amount of stock on hand a year later. Thus disappearance accounts for inventory fluctuations as well as current consumption.

In 1930, University of North Carolina economists under the direction of Howard W. Odum found that over time the rate of disappearance had no observable correlation to farm prices of leaf tobacco. Further, they found the rate of production to be running ahead of the rate of disappearance. Consequently, tobacco prices responded to changes in supply but were far less sensitive to changes in demand. Under these conditions, manufacturers needed to pay tobacco growers only enough to keep them from switching to another crop.[7]

To make matters worse, as demand increased, tobacco cultivation expanded into new areas. Within a generation, Bright Leaf had spread from its native Old Belt into eastern North Carolina, the Pee Dee region of South Carolina, southern Georgia, and northern Florida. By the late 1920s, Bright Leaf was being produced in a much larger area by many more growers than in 1900. Thus the supply of flue-cured tobacco was expanding in two dimensions: the crop was entering new culture areas, and individual growers were producing more. Both dynamics tended to keep the market soft and profits low. Rising demand, therefore, served only to allow more farmers to produce the crop at smaller profits rather than raise the incomes of veteran producers.

The Pee Dee's agricultural and business elite understood full well the nature and magnitude of the problem. They also knew how difficult it would be to solve. Successful crop control required virtually unanimous grower participation sustained by a high level of organization and discipline. Regrettably, tobacco farmers had shown little affinity for either. For example, the ill-fated Tri-State Co-op had failed to evoke even the relatively mild commitment required for cooperative selling. This did not bode well for the much tighter discipline needed to sustain crop controls.

Another obstacle to a successful crop reduction campaign was the sheer number of growers involved. Bright Leaf tobacco was produced by thousands of mostly small landowners and tenants of both races. Convincing such a large, diverse, and inherently conservative group to embrace radical change while exposing themselves to considerable risk was a daunting prospect. Again, the recent collapse of the Tri-State Co-op furnishes an example. At its peak, the Tri-State Co-op represented only about half of flue-cured tobacco growers. This level of participation in a cooperative selling venture was enough to raise prices, but it would have been far too low for successful crop control.

Farmers had good reason to approach crop reduction schemes with caution. To begin with, voluntary plans were inherently vulnerable. As a chain is only as strong as its weakest link, so a voluntary plan is only as strong as its weakest member. Growers knew that even a few noncooperators profiteering from the sacrifices of their neighbors could destroy the movement in a single season. Growers also knew that crop controls placed them at considerable risk, and their suspicion of controls arose from their natural desire to avoid risk. Cooperative selling involved comparatively less risk. Many growers had joined the Tri-State Co-op knowing that if it collapsed (as it ultimately did), they could sell their remaining tobacco at auction. But crop controls required faith of a higher order. If a grower agreed to reduce his crop and the control movement foundered later in the season, he faced serious hardship. He could not turn back the calendar and plant more tobacco to recover his shortfall. In the 1920s, no individual or organization in the tobacco states could justify that level of confidence.

Government offered little help. Reformers had long lobbied state governments to impose limits on tobacco production. But flue-cured tobacco was grown in several states, and laws regulating its production in one state were meaningless without corresponding legislation in the others. North Carolina was by far the largest leaf-producing state, and reformers knew that any interstate crop reduction movement must have the enthusiastic support of North Carolinians.

But North Carolina was also home to the American Tobacco Company, R. J. Reynolds, and P. Lorillard. These wealthy corporations had powerful allies ready to oppose any policy likely to raise tobacco prices. North Carolina governor O. Max Gardner supported the idea of voluntary crop controls but balked at any law that could make controls workable. Gardner promised to oppose "any law which makes a North Carolina farmer a criminal for growing anything on his land he wants to."[8] Many Tarheel farmers scoffed at Gardner's sentiments and spoke bitterly of his "protecting their rights" to be paupers. Later, when Congress debated crop controls, North Carolina senator Josiah Bailey harangued the Senate about "tyranny" and "socialistic communism" and called Secretary of Agriculture Henry A. Wallace the "commissar of agriculture."[9] If tobacco growers were underrepresented in the halls of power, apparently manufacturers were not.

The mid-1920s were prosperous years for most Americans. It was a time of confidence and well-being during which incomes and living standards improved for much of the nation. Like most of their countrymen, Pee Dee Bright Leaf growers had reason for optimism. Demand for their product had never been greater. Indeed, tobacco growers enjoyed a banner season in 1926. The Mullins market opened strong, and newspapers boasted that "the days of prosperity have returned." Kingstree reported the highest first day averages in its history, and Timmonsville growers were "satisfied and optimistic."[10] The Pee Dee's leaf crop averaged almost twenty-four cents in 1926, the highest in six years, and tobacco growers were delighted. Ironically, their very optimism was their undoing.

During the next three years, Bright Leaf growers again succumbed to their tragic tendency to smother rising prices under massive production. South Carolina growers were equally guilty. Basing their expectations on the uncommonly high prices of 1926, Pee Dee farmers raised a quarter-billion pounds of tobacco over the next three years (see Table 9). This massive output exceeded anything the state had ever produced, and even a strong marketing cooperative would have been challenged to keep prices steady in the face of such tremendous volume.[11] As it was, the weak, disorganized leaf growers plunged into the highly prejudiced marketing environment like lambs rushing to the slaughter. The outcome was predictable. Pee Dee farmers glutted the market with a record seventy-nine

TABLE 9

Bright Leaf Tobacco Production in South Carolina,
1926–1932

Year	Poundage (1,000s)	Price (in cents per lb.)		Value ($1,000s)	
		current	(1900)[a]	current	(1900)
1926	57,915	23.6	(11.2)	13,668	(6,486)
1927	79,083	20.2	(9.7)	16,275	(7,671)
1928	84,360	12.7	(6.2)	10,714	(5,230)
1929	87,320	15.5	(7.6)	13,535	(6,636)
1930	98,600	12.0	(6.0)	11,832	(5,916)
1931	69,870	9.2	(5.1)	6,428	(3,563)
1932	39,440	11.4	(6.9)	4,457	(2,721)

Source: U.S. Department of Agriculture, Bureau of Agricultural Economics,
Tobaccos of the United States: Acreage, Yield per Acre, Production, Price and
Value by States, 1866–1945, and by Types and Classes, 1919–1945 (Washington,
D.C.: U.S. Government Printing Office, 1948), 74.
[a] Prices are reported in current and constant values with 1900 as the base year.

million pounds of Bright Leaf in 1927, and prices fell 13 percent. It would
get worse.

After the shock of 1927, concerned growers and their allies appraised the
situation and considered how best to approach the problem of overproduction. A friendly press sought to awaken farmers to their peril. Through
the winter, editors monitored signs of trouble. Conway's *Horry Herald*
noted with concern the many new curing barns being built for the 1928
season. The editor told farmers it was "the greatest of folly" to increase
tobacco acreage again after the drubbing they had taken in 1927. The editor
urged self-sufficiency and diversification.[12] He might have saved his ink.
Horry farmers, like those everywhere in the Bright Belt, intended to use
their curing barns to the fullest in 1928.

A generation of Americans remembered the Wall Street crash of October
1929 as the beginning of the Great Depression. For Pee Dee tobacco growers, however, the Great Depression began fourteen months earlier in the
summer of 1928. Ominously, it arrived amid thunder and lightning. In July,
as the tobacco crop entered its final stage of maturity, heavy thunderstorms

lashed South Carolina, dumping twenty-one inches of rain on the Pee Dee in eight days. The deluge drowned much tobacco and caused the rest to ripen quickly and cure badly.[13] A tobacco company spokesman raised the black flag even before the market opened, predicting that "there would be some disappointment among farmers as to prices."[14]

Events soon proved him right. The first offerings of the largest leaf crop yet produced in South Carolina sold sharply lower than the previous year, averaging about eleven cents.[15] Hopes that prices would rise as the season advanced proved vain. The 1928 crop averaged only 12.7 cents a pound, about half the 1926 average. Ironically, this amount equaled the estimated cost of producing a pound of Bright Leaf tobacco in South Carolina, assuming labor costs at one dollar per day (see Appendix table "Costs of Producing One Acre of Tobacco").[16] Pee Dee Bright Leaf farmers again found themselves in the irrational position of receiving less money for more tobacco. As Table 9 reveals, the crop of 1928 returned six million fewer dollars for five million more pounds than the crop of 1927.

Growers' profit margins were shaved on both sides at once. Not only were revenues cut by one-third, but the cost of producing five million extra pounds of tobacco had to be covered from these smaller receipts as well. After paying expenses, many growers kept almost nothing for their year's toil. Landowners fared little better than share-tenants in this respect. One cheerless farmer reckoned that "all of nothing is no better than half of nothing."[17] Writing in September 1928, David R. Coker observed, "I have never known a worse condition of discouragement and depression among our farmers."[18]

The dramatic plunge in farm income made it difficult for landowners to pay property taxes and service mortgages. The extent of the calamity was known in Conway as early as October. Lengthening delinquency lists prompted the *Horry Herald* to report that more Horry County land was in danger of being sold for taxes than ever before.[19] Debtors were also being dispossessed. Many who had borrowed when tobacco prices and profits were high now found mortgage payments impossible to meet. Landlords and tenants alike were displaced as delinquencies soared and farms went under the auctioneer's hammer.

Worse followed as foreclosures triggered a falling-domino sequence of commercial bankruptcies and bank failures. As tobacco prices and profits dwindled, many farmers were unable to repay merchants for advances of seed and fertilizer. Merchants, in turn, defaulted on loans they had floated to purchase the supplies advanced to customers. A few banks with sufficient reserves weathered the storm, but many did not. Within a five-week period in 1928, sixteen banks in the Pee Dee region closed their doors.[20]

Bank failures and merchant bankruptcies squeezed the already tight credit situation in the Pee Dee. Farmers who had relied on these now defunct capital sources faced the chilling prospect of being without the wherewithal to make another crop. Without short-term production credit, many farmers laboring under mortgages faced foreclosure and ruin. David Coker described conditions at Hartsville to W. W. Long at Clemson: "Good, intelligent, industrious farmers—dozens of them—do not know how or where to turn." [21]

Throughout the winter of 1928–29, surviving bankers and merchants were besieged by pathetic farmers begging them to "take them on" for the 1929 crop season. Most were turned away. Indeed, many surviving merchants were themselves dangerously overextended and kept their doors open only through the forbearance of their own creditors. The losses of 1928 had drained the region's reserves, and barely solvent Pee Dee merchants were hard-pressed to carry their old customers, let alone new ones.

The credit crunch was felt hardest by sharecroppers and tenants. With prices and profits low, some merchants feared that even creditworthy landowners would be unable to settle at season's end. Understandably, many balked at financing landless tenants who stood even less chance of breaking even.[22] Traditional tenure arrangements between landlords and tenants were also subject to closer scrutiny. Thin profit margins made landowners less willing to retain cropper families whose upkeep could exceed the value of their labor. Even so, most landlords were loath to turn families off in the dead of winter and allowed them to stay on in their crude little houses until spring. Others feared losing their labor force permanently. A warehouseman later recalled: "There never was a time when more work was done for so little. I personally know of several [tenants] who hopped a freight and never looked back." Meanwhile, unemployed tenants roamed Pee Dee communities looking for whatever work they could find.[23]

In September 1928, some Pee Dee tobacco growers sought to establish another marketing cooperative to replace the defunct Tri-State Co-op. Although the Tri-State's collapse had soured many on the idea of cooperative marketing, even critics admitted that the co-op had raised leaf prices during the few years of its existence.[24] Consequently, there was still a nucleus of growers who believed that an ethically and competently managed co-operative was still the farmers' best hope. Determined to seek reform, a cadre of tobacco growers and their allies met in Florence in September 1928 and resolved to launch a new marketing pool for South Carolina tobacco growers under "vital and fundamental principles."[25]

Florence businessmen were eager for their city to become the permanent headquarters of the new co-op and perhaps the center of an important commodity trade as well. They offered substantial support to get the new co-op off the ground. The Chamber of Commerce voted to underwrite the co-op's start-up expenses and authorized Chamber officers to borrow the funds if necessary. Dr. M. D. Nesmith of Lake City was appointed chairman of the organizing committee. Nesmith was joined by prominent growers from other Pee Dee communities to form a board of directors: W. C. Edwards of Darlington, J. B. Britton of Sumter, J. G. McCullough of Kingstree, and A. B. Jordan of Dillon.[26]

While the new co-op was being organized in Florence, growers were meeting in Conway, Loris, Marion, and Mullins in hopes of reducing the size of the next tobacco crop. Even before the 1928 season ended, thoughtful people feared growers would attempt to recoup their losses by planting still greater acreage in 1929. Hoping to avoid such a disaster, some prominent farmers and businessmen suggested a voluntary quota scheme to reduce production. According to the plan, quotas would be based on the number of draft animals employed on each farm. Growers were asked to plant no more than four acres for the first horse or mule and two acres for each additional horse or mule. Thus a "one-horse" farm would have a four-acre quota, a "two-horse" farm six acres, and so on. Signers pledged by their "honor and manhood" to abide by the agreement.[27]

Although the group's frustration and activism are understandable, what they could realistically hope to accomplish is less certain. Skeptics pointed out that Bright Leaf was produced in several states, and because the market was already softened by overproduction, manufacturers could boycott South Carolina leaf altogether and still meet their requirements. Some growers bitterly recalled that the Tri-State Co-op was partly undermined by manufacturers' encouragement of tobacco culture in Georgia and Florida. How a crop control campaign limited to one state could hope to succeed, therefore, was more a rhetorical question than a practical one.

The futility of attempting crop reduction in only one state was demonstrated the following season. Although Pee Dee tobacco growers planted 30,000 fewer acres in 1929, other Bright Leaf regions actually increased their tobacco acreage. The result of the "horse and mule" reduction plan of 1929 was a net gain of 116,000 acres throughout the tobacco states.[28] While the idealism of such an undertaking is laudable, one can only marvel at the naïveté of a plan to reduce production in a single state.[29]

The following spring, the crop of 1929 gave Pee Dee tobacco growers cause for optimism. Throughout the region, all who saw the magnificent fields of broad, green leaf commented on its uncommon quality. As the harvesting and curing seasons advanced, the crop ripened perfectly and came from the curing barns with the finest color and texture many growers had ever seen. When tobacco began arriving at the warehouses in late July, its excellence was confirmed by the trade. Warehousemen remarked on its "sweet aroma" and stated that "tobacco never looked better." A Mullins buyer called the first day's offerings "a beautiful break of tobacco." The presale consensus was that the 1929 crop would bring "a vast deal more money" than that of 1928, and Pee Dee tobacco interests spoke confidently of breaking sales records. When the Georgia market opened with higher prices, a profitable season was seen as a near certainty. This year, the farmers hoped, this year for sure.[30]

But the finest crop in living memory opened at fifteen cents, only slightly higher than the waterlogged crop of 1928. No doubt some farmers were thankful for any increase at all, but many voiced surprise and disappointment. Prices were no better in North Carolina. Opening day averages at Wilson, Goldsboro, and Rocky Mount hovered around thirteen cents, well below what farmers expected. As the days passed, incredulity turned to outrage. Throughout the Bright Belt, exasperated growers removed their tobacco from warehouse floors and went home.[31] In characteristic support of South Carolina farmers, the *State* printed letters from frustrated tobacco growers on its front page. One called for a suspension of leaf sales "until there could be some kind of understanding with the tobacco companies as to whether they intend paying anything near a fair price." The consequences of overproduction had made an impression on one Dillon County farmer: "I use ten barns for curing," wrote Charles Taylor of Fork, "and I would prefer to burn down every barn I have if such drastic action would guarantee a reduction of the 1930 crop." [32]

Much discontent focused on the discrepancy between the acknowledged excellence of the 1929 crop and its low selling price. In past seasons, manufacturers had often blamed low prices on poor quality. But the 1929 crop was universally regarded as outstanding, and growers could not understand why bids were still so low. Farmers and warehousemen were stunned to hear company representatives blithely resolve the paradox, stating that they were now "showing preference for low-grade leaf." [33]

As the crisis deepened, frantic tobacco growers turned to Washington for relief. Prompted by complaints from Pee Dee constituents, South Carolina congressmen joined representatives from grain and cotton regions (who had their own problems) in urging federal intervention in the agricultural crisis. Government responded with the most ambitious attempt yet made to redress the grievances of American farmers.

The centerpiece of the Hoover administration's farm policy was the Agricultural Marketing Act of June 1929. [34] It was a sincere attempt to resolve some long-standing problems in American agriculture, and it was backed by serious money. The act established the Federal Farm Board with a purse of $500 million to buttress the commodity markets. The Farm Board set up "stabilization corporations" to raise commodity prices by aggressive buying and, it was hoped, bring supply and demand into better balance. A revolving fund was established to finance purchases. Congress intended that commodities bought under the plan would be resold and the proceeds recycled into other purchases.

But while policymakers knew overproduction imperiled the program, they imposed no production controls. President Hoover insisted—somewhat naively, it turned out—that farmers must be willing to cooperate voluntarily with programs designed to benefit them. [35] Thus the Farm Board's policy was to support crop prices above market levels with no limits on supply. Good intentions notwithstanding, not even the United States government could repeal fundamental laws of economics. Although termed a revolving fund, "dissolving fund" ultimately proved a more accurate description of the Farm Board. [36]

Believing that grass-roots organizations were needed to coordinate an orderly and effective policy, the Marketing Act required that Farm Board aid be channeled only through grower-owned marketing cooperatives. Aid would take the form of loans made to cooperatives to fund cash advances paid on delivery of produce. When the produce was sold, the loans would be repaid. Lawmakers knew cooperatives could maintain a measure of discipline over the crop and carry out an intelligent marketing strategy. Cooperatives could feed a crop onto the market gradually, make deals with buyers for specific grades of produce, or hold an entire crop if conditions warranted. Since marketing pools offered the best means of coordinating thousands of small producers, the law permitted the Farm Board to intervene only in commodity markets where grower-owned co-ops controlled a substantial percentage of the crop.[37]

In September 1929, hundreds of tobacco farmers representing the Carolinas and Virginia met in Raleigh to organize a marketing cooperative under Farm Board guidelines. James C. Stone, head of the Farm Board's tobacco section, explained the government's plan to the anxious delegates. Himself a tobacco grower and former manager of the Kentucky Burley co-op, Stone was a good choice to head the tobacco section and assist growers in forming cooperatives.[38] Stone assured the anxious delegates that help was on the way if they cooperated with Uncle Sam.

Though heartened by the prospect of relief, the recent, bitter memory of the Tri-State debacle hung over the Raleigh meeting like a dark cloud. Wisely, the delegates agreed not to resurrect the Tri-State Co-op. Instead of a large, multistate organization, they opted for state associations "with a greater degree of local responsibility." Since the state associations would operate under federal auspices, the delegates reasoned, state organizations would serve equally well and be easier to manage.[39]

The Pee Dee delegation promptly placed their fledgling co-op under Farm Board guidelines, and the South Carolina Tobacco Growers' Cooperative received a federal charter in November 1929. Joining the board of directors were W. W. Long, head of Clemson's Cooperative Extension Service, and Jefferson Boone Aiken, a prominent Florence banker and entrepreneur. Boone's appointment added balance and prestige to the board. The association hired J. T. Lazar, an agent for Clemson's Agricultural Extension Service, to manage the new co-op.[40]

The Federal Farm Board required the cooperatives to achieve a certain level of grower participation before operations could begin, so in the spring of 1930 the new South Carolina Tobacco Growers Cooperative vigorously sought members. Recruiters and officials adopted a comprehensive strategy to earn the confidence of growers, merchants, and bankers. Local supporters stressed that the federal government was backing the new co-op with substantial resources and portrayed the organization as "a partnership with Uncle Sam."[41]

Eager to overcome the bitter memory of the Tri-State disaster, recruiters stressed that the new co-op's management and operating policies must meet federal guidelines and would be audited regularly. Moreover, the directors sought to address specific issues that had caused problems for the defunct Tri-State Co-op. For example, growers complained that a five-year commitment was too long, so the new marketing agreement permitted members to withdraw after two years. To allay the concerns of bankers and merchants, the directors promised that the co-op would apply the sales proceeds of any mortgaged tobacco against the debt with the remainder going to the producer.[42]

Despite the obvious need for a growers' organization, co-op recruiters encountered opposition. The failure of the Tri-State Co-op had disillusioned many growers. They recalled the long intervals between payments and the charges of profiteering leveled at some directors. Furthermore, four years after the Tri-State Co-op was forced into receivership, some members had yet to be paid for their final deliveries. Understandably, some growers felt they had been burned by the Tri-State, and, like Mark Twain's cat, were loath to sit on any more stoves.[43]

That the Tri-State's failure was largely caused by the opposition of manufacturing and warehouse interests was a subtlety lost on many growers. Adding insult to injury, propaganda spread by enemies of reform had tainted the idea of cooperative marketing in the minds of many. Thus many bewildered Pee Dee farmers seemed to accept their plight with dumb resignation, skeptical that anything could rescue them from their misery. Still others preferred to "wait and see" if the new co-op would succeed before joining. This attitude presented organizers with a "catch-22": the co-op could not succeed unless it controlled a substantial amount of the crop, yet growers were unwilling to join until the co-op proved successful. Thus the new cooperative's greatest challenge was overcoming the fears and prejudices of those whose interests it wished to advance.[44]

Reformers considered such self-imposed handicaps to be the economic and moral equivalent of suicide. Growers' advocates groped for images powerful enough to shake stubborn farmers from their ignorance and lethargy. One editor asserted that "so long as the farmer . . . stands aloof from movements that tend to lift him as a class, so long will he remain the mudsill." The same editor later mocked farmers who "fawn upon their knees, begging for 'the best you can do, Mister,'" and asked "How long will this antiquated system crush them into the ground and keep them in slavery?"[45]

Pee Dee merchants posed similar questions from the pages of local newspapers: "Uncle Sam wants you to succeed. Will you refuse to help yourselves?"[46] As if in reply, one Galivants Ferry farmer wrote in despair, "We are all so ignorant, selfish, and lack business acumen." He went on to suggest a remedy: "The first thing to do . . . is to buy augers—not ordinary ones, but those shipbuilding augers that will bore into a fat lightwood stump. Then bore a hole into each farmer's head, take out the mud, and put in some gray matter. Then we'll cooperate."[47]

Many concurred with the diagnosis if they stopped short of endorsing the remedy. Newton Bright, commissioner of agriculture for the commonwealth of Kentucky, explained in a widely read news release how success had spoiled the Kentucky Burley Growers' Co-op. Even after the co-op had achieved six years of high prices, Bright explained, jealous members refused to renew marketing contracts because "outside" growers were receiving equally high prices at auction. When only 5 percent of the crop had been pledged, Bright related, the Kentucky co-op was forced to suspend operations. Burley prices promptly collapsed.[48]

In the Pee Dee, growers' advocates, exasperated by the blindness of farmers to their own interests, vented their frustrations. Palmer W. Johnson, editor of the *Marion Star*, wearied by months of effort on the growers' behalf, declared that anyone else encouraged by the federal government to organize under its auspices for their own protection would quickly do so. At the very least, Johnson asked his readers, could the Farm Board's plan be any worse than what they now had?[49]

Gradually, the message began to sink in, though some communities proved more resistant than others. Although growers' commitments were below what the Farm Board considered desirable, they allowed the South

Carolina Tobacco Growers' Cooperative to operate in 1930 and approved loans to fund advances to members.[50] Although the co-op was a much needed step toward restoring balance to the marketplace, it left untouched the ancient and persistent problem of overproduction.

The tobacco regions of the Carolinas awaited the 1930 marketing season with a sense of foreboding.[51] As July turned to August, all eyes focused on Georgia. The news was bad. Opening day bids below ten cents a pound brought Georgia farmers to the brink of insurrection. Angry farmers at Cairo took matters into their own hands and closed the market there. Georgia senator Walter George and congressmen from tobacco districts accused cigarette makers of "combining to buy Georgia's tobacco crop below the cost of production." Senator George further charged that manufacturers were "taking advantage of general [depression] conditions when actual conditions in their industry did not justify it."[52] Congressman Charles C. Edwards labeled manufacturers "heartless thieves" and accused them of "robbing, ruining, and impoverishing Georgia farmers." Further, Edwards asked the Federal Farm Board to purchase "at least $5,000,000 worth" of leaf to support the market.[53]

In the days that followed, Justice Department agents hurried to south Georgia to investigate charges of collusion, and Farm Board representatives met with state officials in Atlanta. James C. Stone, chief of the Farm Board's tobacco section, likened the Georgia crisis to the events of 1920 that convinced Kentucky Burley growers to form their first co-op. Stone reminded Georgia farmers that they had placed themselves at the manufacturers' mercy by increasing production against the advice of experts and counter to good judgment. Despite warnings of probable "marketing difficulties," Georgia and Florida Bright Leaf growers had enlarged their 1930 crop by 11,500 acres. As tactfully as possible, Stone clearly laid much of the blame for the farmers' troubles at their own doorsteps.[54]

As low prices continued, a sympathetic press rolled out the familiar indictment against the tobacco marketing system for a fresh airing on the front pages. One Pee Dee editor called the auction process "a miserable farce" and reported how a farmer in a Mullins warehouse moved a pile of tobacco to the next row and resold it ten minutes later for a 70 percent increase in price.[55] Underscoring the need for a universal and "scientific" grading system, the *Progressive Farmer*'s editor Clarence Poe related selling seven piles of the same curing on the same sale, and every pile of this identical tobacco brought a different price.[56] Editors fired broadsides at the fundamental injustice of the tobacco industry and roundly condemned the brevity of the marketing season as further evidence of exploitation.

Editorial rhetoric aside, the tobacco auction system was the very essence of a buyers' market. The selling season opened when company buyers came to town and closed when they departed. Thus the timing and duration of the marketing season rested with those who dispatched and recalled buyers. Growers had little choice of when to market their leaf. Tobacco companies had condensed the selling season to six weeks, and Georgia producers had no choice but to rush their leaf to market or risk not selling it at all. Though prices were subject to short-term fluctuations, the general effect of the short selling season tended to depress them. Warehousemen suffered along with producers. Not only were warehouse commissions reduced by lower prices, but many warehouses could have easily sold greater quantities if given time.[57]

Perhaps the beleaguered farmers enjoyed seeing manufacturers pilloried in the press. If so, that is the only benefit they got. Appeals to the Federal Farm Board to intervene on behalf of Georgia and Florida tobacco growers proved fruitless. Incredibly, more than a year after the Farm Board announced that grower cooperatives must be established to coordinate aid, Georgia farmers had neglected to start one. Faced with the worst marketing crisis in a generation, Georgia growers were ineligible for federal aid.

Now facing disaster, Georgia growers searched frantically for any cooperative to serve as a conduit for aid. Finding none in their own state, the hapless Georgians sought to join the South Carolina cooperative. Officials concluded that while legal obstacles might be overcome by joining the South Carolina co-op, Georgia growers lacked the facilities and staff to handle several million pounds of tobacco. Moreover, the selling season was already under way, and there was no time to sign growers, rent facilities, and hire and train staff. A consensus emerged that selling the Georgia-Florida tobacco crop through a cooperative in 1930 was "practically impossible."[58] Though forewarned of their vulnerability, Georgia growers did not act until it was too late. One warehouseman remarked, "They are like the man who don't think about fire insurance 'til his britches are burning."

Without the necessary marketing vehicle, all the Farm Board could offer was sympathy.[59]

The first day of tobacco season was traditionally a happy event in the Pee Dee. But as the opening break approached in August 1930, tobacco growers and state officials braced themselves for the worst. Although South Carolina growers had a marketing cooperative and were eligible for Farm Board assistance, the co-op represented only 25 percent of the crop. With the bulk of the state's leaf outside the co-op, observers knew South Carolina's marketing position was little better than Georgia's.

Before the first leaf was sold, Commissioner of Agriculture J. W. Shealy toured the Pee Dee and satisfied himself that the 1930 crop was sound. He then asked the Federal Farm Board to be ready to intervene on South Carolina markets when the season opened. Some officials urged farmers to ignore the auctions altogether and bring their tobacco to state-owned, bonded warehouses for redrying and storage "to await more advantageous prices." Others expressed the hope that the crop's high quality could somehow make up for part of the loss.[60] Their optimism did not prove justified.

Within days, Georgia's mournful chorus was joined by lamentations in Carolina. Opening day bids for the crop of 1930 averaged nine cents, the lowest in fourteen years. Observers said quality did not seem to be a consideration as buyers were offering uniformly low bids for virtually everything. Others reported that about the same prices were being paid for South Carolina's high-grade crop as for Georgia's poor one. Pee Dee tobacco interests were well aware of the situation in Georgia, and low prices surprised no one. In some places grim-faced farmers began removing their leaf from the warehouse floors even before the auction party reached it.[61]

The day's only good news came from the South Carolina Tobacco Growers' Cooperative. Initial payments advanced to members upon delivery of tobacco, estimated at 75 percent of its value, were often greater than the full prices paid by manufacturers on auction markets.[62] This liberal policy was not without risk, however. Since the co-op had borrowed the money it was advancing and repayment depended on eventual sale of members' leaf to manufacturers, the co-op was clearly betting on the draw.

Desperate tobacco growers reacted to the calamity in a variety of ways.

Many farmers refused to sell their leaf at all, and market activity slowed to a crawl. The Mullins market, which often sold six hundred thousand pounds in a single day, auctioned a minuscule fifty thousand pounds on the third day of the season. The *Mullins Enterprise* reported that area farmers "were firm in their determination to hold their weed until prices advance."[63] Warehousemen were frantic. The combination of low prices and low sales volume had depressed warehouse revenues severely. It was more than some warehousemen could stand. Between 1928 and 1930, the number of warehouses in South Carolina fell from fifty-nine to thirty-seven, and six Pee Dee towns ceased to have tobacco markets at all (see Appendix table "Tobacco Markets and Warehouses in South Carolina").

Seeking to reassure his customers, and possibly himself, Mullins warehouseman V. P. Paullette declared that tobacco prices were "very satisfactory" and angrily blamed the crisis on "newspaper agitation and politicians." How an openly sympathetic press and government had forced down tobacco prices—or why they would wish to—Paullette did not reveal. Nor did his indictment mention manufacturers, who, after all, ultimately set tobacco prices. Palmer W. Johnson, editor of the *Marion Star* and staunch ally of tobacco farmers, mocked Paullette in a scorching editorial. After proving that tobacco growers were losing twenty-five dollars an acre at prevailing prices, Johnson concluded: "According to Mr. Paullette, tobacco prices are satisfactory; and white is black, and hot is cold, and north is south!"[64]

The Pee Dee's tobacco crop averaged twelve cents a pound in 1930, down 23 percent from 1929 and nearly a whole cent below the cost of production. Despite ruinously low prices, growers were ultimately forced to market their leaf, even at a loss. By mid-September, many farmers were facing mortgage payments with very short maturities. They had a pressing need for cash to meet these obligations and no other source for it but the fragrant bundles in the packhouse. When they could hold out no longer, growers began bringing tobacco to the warehouses, though most of them lost money on every pound. The *Horry Herald* commented on the "poor unfortunates" and noted that the bustle common to Conway in past tobacco seasons was conspicuously absent in 1930. Merchants complained that farmers "had all they could do" to pay debts and had nothing left to spend.[65] Everyone was hurting.

Manufacturers' profits, however, were enormous. In fact, the cigarette business had never been better. The prosperity of the 1920s funded large increases in cigarette sales every year of the decade. Moreover, as social constraints relaxed, women began smoking in greater numbers. Of course, tobacco executives helped foster this particular phase of women's liberation by hiring attractive female models to smoke cigarettes in public. The strong, unfiltered brands of the 1920s were highly addictive, and casual smokers were soon regular customers. Profits increased apace. Between 1926 and 1931—years of rock bottom leaf prices—annual earnings of the five largest tobacco companies advanced from $74 million to $115 million (see Figure 1). Tobacco growers were outraged at being denied a greater share of the ultimate value of their own produce even as others profited from it on an enormous scale.[66]

The extent of tobacco company profits was neatly summarized by American Tobacco Company president George Washington Hill in 1929. Hill boasted to the *New York Journal of Commerce* that a single share of American's common stock, worth $142 in 1918, had, by 1928, returned $287 in cash dividends and risen to a market value of $862 through stock dividends and appreciation. Thus, Hill explained, the shareholders' investment was repaid eightfold in ten years.[67] But tobacco companies were not content with even this rate of return. On 24 June 1931, when material costs were at a record low and the nation was sliding deeper into the Depression, the Big Four raised cigarette prices.[68]

The Hill salary scandal of 1931 furnishes another example of profiteering. The bylaws of the American Tobacco Company provided that 10 percent of the firm's profits above its 1910 earnings be paid to top-level managers.[69] Lower leaf costs and higher cigarette prices propelled American's profits and, consequently, the salaries of top executives to stratospheric levels. Between 1926 and 1931, Hill's compensation rose from $191,000 to $892,000 per year. The vastness of such a sum can be best appreciated when placed in context. The per capita income of South Carolinians was about $300 per year, so Hill could have supported a fair-sized town in the Pee Dee.[70]

Farmers throughout the Bright Belt believed, with some justification, that Hill's fantastic salary was being squeezed out of them, and they bitterly resented it. So did many of American's shareholders. Hill's personal arrogance only fueled their resentment. Dismissing shareholders' complaints as "chatter," Hill boycotted the company's annual meeting, refusing to face the irate investors.[71] American exorcised Hill's ghost twenty

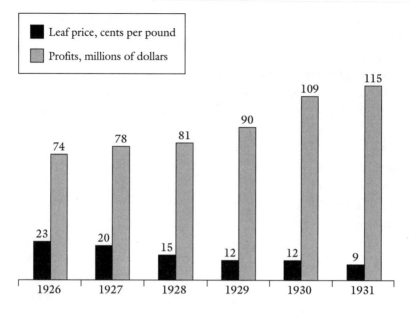

FIGURE I

Combined Earnings of Five Largest Tobacco Manufacturers Compared to Prices of Flue-Cured Tobacco, 1926–1931

Source: Nannie May Tilley, *The R. J. Reynolds Tobacco Company* (Chapel Hill: University of North Carolina Press, 1985), 575.

years later, acknowledging in a company publication that the period "reflected bitter, biting hardship among thousands of small farmers."[72]

Another example of the fabulous wealth amassed by tobacco barons during the Depression is Graylyn Mansion, the home of Bowman Gray Sr., president of R. J. Reynolds. The forty-six-thousand-square-foot house was built between 1928 and 1932 in the style of a Norman chateau. It boasted thirty-five bedrooms (each with a private bath), fifty telephones, a heated indoor swimming pool, a photography room, a flower-arranging room, and a walk-in vault for the silverware. Entire paneled rooms were removed from European palaces and installed in the Winston-Salem house. Graylyn's library had once been the office of an English king, and its fireplaces were crowned with mantels carved by Renaissance masters. Graylyn's architecture paid homage to the source of the family's wealth. Limestone columns along the corridors were topped with carved tobacco blossoms, and bathroom tiles featured "Old Joe" the Camel and wreaths of smoke rings. The Grays even maintained a "farm" on the property complete with black laborers and a mule.[73]

Bright Leaf tobacco growers fell further behind in 1930. The crop was enormous. The flue-cured tobacco states harvested a record 1.14 million acres in 1930. South Carolina farmers also set a record that year, contributing almost 99 million pounds to the 1930 crop. They sold it for a loss. The state's leaf crop averaged twelve cents a pound, and with production costs of 12.7 cents, Pee Dee farmers fell about $700,000 short of breaking even. The South Carolina Tobacco Growers' Cooperative received 17 million pounds of tobacco—about 20 percent of the crop—and advanced about $2 million to members. The advances, based on 75 percent valuation, were often higher than full prices paid at auction. Co-op officials were therefore expecting a dramatic increase in membership for the 1931 season.[74] In September, Farm Board vice-chairman James C. Stone visited the Pee Dee and urged growers to join the co-op. He also renewed the plea for crop reduction, telling growers, "Nothing can save you from low prices if you continue to grow more than the market can absorb."[75]

Stone knew whereof he spoke. In fact, the Federal Farm Board was having its own problems absorbing great amounts of commodities, and the board's wheat and cotton sections were already staggering under a ponderous load. By paying artificially high prices without imposing production controls, the Farm Board was inadvertently putting itself out of business. As the worldwide economic slump dried up foreign demand, farmers merely dumped their surplus on the Farm Board. Reluctant to sell on an already glutted market, the Farm Board stored its vast holdings and gritted its teeth. As prices languished and storage costs mounted, the Farm Board's outlook was grim.[76]

Farm Board–sponsored cooperatives were also running into trouble. Many of them were taking on sizable inventories at above market prices and storing the produce for want of buyers.[77] The South Carolina co-op, following Farm Board policies, paid above the market for seventeen million pounds of the largest tobacco crop in history. Predictably, attempts to sell at break-even prices on a glutted market proved difficult, and well into 1931 the bulk of the co-op's 1930 holdings were still in storage. Co-op manager J. T. Lazar reported in February 1931 that only one-fourth of the 1930 receipts had been sold.[78]

As the 1931 season approached, the South Carolina co-op was going to extraordinary lengths to sell its 1930 tobacco. In March 1931, Jefferson Boone Aiken along with James C. Stone of the Farm Board went to New York and called on top executives of the major tobacco companies. Aiken found their demeanor "very satisfactory," even cordial in some cases. All promised to purchase leaf from the co-op, and Liggett & Myers even offered to raise its offer to reflect the savings of not having to employ buyers. At American, President George Washington Hill greeted Stone and Aiken but excused himself after "some facetious general remarks." Vice-Presidents Charles Penn and James Lipscomb frankly stated that it was not their duty to solve the farmers' problems and that they were content with the present system. As a gesture of goodwill, however, Lipscomb gave the co-op an order for "70-odd hogsheads" of tobacco. Executives at the Export Tobacco Company and Lorillard bought nothing but promised "to buy of us another year."[79]

Lazar held no delusions about the outlook for the coming season. "From a strictly business standpoint," he wrote to W. W. Long, "consider the tremendous production of tobacco last year."[80] Throughout the Bright Belt, agricultural leaders were analyzing the results of 1930 and appraising market conditions facing them in 1931. Earlier that year, the U.S. Department of Agriculture had estimated that the supply of flue-cured tobacco was approximately "one whole crop year ahead."[81] When the USDA's annual crop report confirmed the estimate, the peril facing tobacco growers became all too apparent. Not only did manufacturers have three years' leaf requirements on hand, but they had augmented their stocks by a further ninety million pounds at very low prices in 1930 (see Table 10). The avalanche was gaining momentum.

Throughout the fall and winter, agricultural and business leaders in the Carolinas urged farmers to retrench for the coming year. Experts predicted that the 1930 crop could depress prices for at least two years and warned growers not to expect to profit from tobacco in 1931 and 1932. Farmers were advised to cut tobacco acreage at least 25 percent to reduce overall supplies and minimize losses if it again sold below the cost of production. Moreover, the leadership counseled farmers to employ land and labor released from tobacco to grow their own food and fodder until the crisis had run its course. Of course, the "hog and hominy" plan had been preached since before the Civil War, but the need to heed it had never been greater. On

TABLE 10

Production, Disappearance, and
Stocks on Hand, Flue-Cured Tobacco, 1930[a]

Stocks on hand, 1 January 1930	926.5[b]
Production, current year	+ 865.2
Total available	1,791.7
Stocks on hand, 31 December 1930	−1,016.6
Disappearance	775.1
(exported 432.7)	
(domestic 342.4)	
Increase in stocks on hand	90.1

Memo: 31 December inventory = 2.97 years supply
             domestic consumption

Source: Compiled from United States Department of Agriculture, *Statistical Bulletin No. 58: First Annual Report on
Tobacco Statistics* (Washington, D.C.: U.S. Government
Printing Office, 1937), 7, 84, 109.
[a] This analysis does not take into account foreign stocks.
Information on inventories of leaf tobacco in many Asian
and European nations for the 1930s is unobtainable. Nevertheless, growth of foreign leaf stocks is strongly indicated
by growth of domestic stocks.
[b] Quantities in millions of pounds.

many Pee Dee farms, commercial agriculture had regressed to precapitalist
strategies of survival.[82]

North Carolina governor O. Max Gardner hammered the message home
in radio broadcasts heard throughout the Carolinas. The Tarheel governor
called the agricultural situation "an issue of life and death, financially
speaking." Recalling the mass protests in the fall of 1928 and 1929, Gardner
reminded growers that the Farm Board had urged them to reduce acreage
and join marketing co-ops. Most of them did neither, however, and were
now suffering the consequences. He went on to warn farmers "before a
single seed is planted" that markets for both cotton and tobacco were practically glutted in advance. "Therefore," the governor continued, "if relief
is to be obtained, it must be obtained now and not at indignation meetings
of distressed growers next fall." Gardner then pitched his "two-thirds"
plan. If growers limited cotton and tobacco production to two-thirds of

what they had planted in 1930, they would "make more money than three-thirds would bring." The governor concluded by suggesting that time and acreage thus saved be devoted to "growing food for farm folks and farm animals."[83]

Gardner's plan had much to recommend it. Reducing staple production could help to stabilize prices, and "living at home" could provide subsistence. Moreover, home production could improve the region's cash flow by reducing food purchases from outside the South. Doubtless Gardner's appeal made sense to many farmers. The number of rural families that survived on their vegetable gardens and henhouses in the early 1930s can never be known, but anecdotal evidence suggests there were many.[84]

There was another side to the coin, however. The advantages of subsistence agriculture tend to diminish in inverse proportion to farm size. Thus though Gardner's plan made sense to small farmers, it had limited appeal to larger landowners. Another obstacle was the lack of interstate cooperation. Gardner asked the governors of South Carolina, Georgia, and Virginia to join him in supporting the campaign—and they all endorsed it—but like all voluntary reduction plans, it was doomed from the start. The states simply lacked the policy vehicle to carry it out.

Of the four Bright Leaf states, only South Carolina had a viable growers' cooperative. Attempts to organize co-ops in North Carolina and Virginia had little success, and sign-up campaigns in both states had fallen short of the minimum grower participation considered necessary. James C. Stone informed co-op officials in Raleigh and Blacksburg that their respective associations were "without enough volume to make for a reasonable chance for success."[85] Thus neither Virginia nor North Carolina growers could expect government help in 1931. Gardner's "Live at Home" plan may have filled some stomachs, but it had no significant influence on tobacco prices.

In April 1931, the Pee Dee press again underscored the urgency of the problem. Seeking to reduce the size of the 1931 crop before it was planted, agricultural leaders and concerned business interests sponsored full-page advertisements in newspapers throughout the Bright Belt. The ads stressed that ever larger tobacco crops had yielded ever smaller profits. Growers were reminded that the 1922 crop returned $16 million more than the 1930 crop for half as much tobacco. One ad issued a call for farmers to "act wisely" and reduce their tobacco acreage.[86]

TOBACCO GROWERS
of Georgia, South Carolina, North Carolina, Virginia
ATTENTION
A TREMENDOUS SURPLUS OF TOBACCO IS NOW ON HAND—

The 1930 tobacco crop was the largest ever grown. Material reduction in acreage planted this year is absolutely necessary, otherwise, lower prices are inevitable and financial disaster will be the result next fall.

Tobacco grower, supply merchant, fertilizer dealer, banker—
ACT NOW AND AVERT CERTAIN FINANCIAL DISASTER AHEAD OF US

We earnestly urge a reduction in acreage of from 25 to 35 percent in all the bright tobacco growing states. Prosperity lies in smaller production with quality. Lower prices are certain with another large crop. The figures below are conclusive evidence of constantly lower prices with constantly increased production:

BRIGHT LEAF TOBACCO

Year	Production	Average
1922	408 million pounds	$28.95
1923	592 million pounds	$22.25
1927	715 million pounds	$21.30
1929	750 million pounds	$17.82
1930	858 million pounds	$11.86

The 1922 crop—408 million pounds—sold for $118,338,000.00

The 1930 crop—858 million pounds—sold for $101,758,800.00

COMPARE THESE FIGURES

In 1922 less than half as much tobacco sold for $16,000,000.00 more money.

FARMERS, ACT WISELY—REDUCE YOUR ACREAGE.

TOBACCO ASSOCIATION
of
Virginia, North Carolina, South Carolina, Georgia

Some growers heeded the call. Pee Dee farmers planted fourteen thousand fewer acres of tobacco in 1931 and applied less fertilizer. Doubtless some growers chose to use less fertilizer while others were constrained by limited credit. In any case, the size of the Pee Dee tobacco crop declined by 30 percent, precisely the reduction urged by the leadership. Production declined from 98.6 million pounds to 69.8 million pounds. But again displaying a self-defeating lack of judgment, discipline, and cooperation, the other tobacco states failed to follow South Carolina's example. In 1931, total production throughout the Bright Leaf culture was only 5 percent below the previous year's record.[87]

When the 1931 marketing season opened in Georgia, prices were euphemistically described as "somewhat weaker." A more accurate description would have been "catastrophic." Georgia markets averaged from nine cents a pound at Blackshear to a pathetic three cents at Bainbridge.[88] Growers in South Carolina greeted the news from Georgia with a grim resolve to hold their leaf as long as possible. Opening breaks on the South Carolina Belt in 1931 were even smaller than in 1930. Sales volume was off 50 percent, and several markets reported the lightest first sale in decades. Auction prices justified the growers' reluctance to sell. Bids for the 1931 crop were below those of 1930, ranging from six to eight cents on most markets.[89] Farmers who believed they had hit bottom in 1930 soon learned otherwise. Sixty years later, a Pee Dee warehouseman described the 1931 season as a leap from the frying pan into the fire.[90]

At first, the South Carolina co-op appeared to be holding its own. The directors had scraped together every cent they could raise from banks and the Farm Board, but most of the co-op's capital was still tied up in its stock of 1930 tobacco. Co-op officials reported that despite "an aggressive sales effort" and the cordial promises of the tobacco companies, manufacturers were "ignoring" co-op tobacco. Nevertheless, co-op stations continued to receive and process leaf and pay advances on it. In fact, auction prices were so low that co-op membership rolls were increasing at a brisk pace. As Pee Dee auction markets entered their third week of sluggish sales, observers remarked that efforts to educate growers to the advantages of cooperation coupled with the obvious failure of the auction system were finally beginning to tell.[91]

Events soon confirmed, however, that riches do not always come to men of understanding. Just as the co-op was beginning to show signs of strength, auction prices rose sharply. Within days, warehouses in several market towns were literally overwhelmed by anxious farmers eager to sell.[92]

The abrupt price increase caught the co-op by surprise, and with good reason. Manufacturers had politely but repeatedly declined to purchase stored co-op leaf already redried, prized, and packed for the same prices they were now paying at auction for raw tobacco. While co-op leaders were pleased that prices were higher, the increases caused an immediate problem. The sudden rise opened a substantial gap between auction prices and co-op advances, and the flow of leaf into co-op stations slowed to a trickle. Co-op leaders quickly raised the advances being paid to members, but because they were only partial payments, the advances fell short of the full prices being paid on auction markets.

The South Carolina co-op was soon facing a crisis of confidence. Members had yet to receive full payment for their 1930 tobacco and were now being asked to take a partial payment on their 1931 crop. Since they could not know when, if ever, last year's crop would be sold and final settlement made, many members opted for a bird in the hand. Within a week, so many growers deserted the co-op for the auction markets that the association's ability to function was seriously compromised.[93]

Hoping to stem the flood of defections, co-op directors sought help from the Federal Farm Board. Although it had other fish to fry, the Farm Board offered to lend the co-op enough to raise advances to 80 percent of valuation. But even this was not enough for most members. Pee Dee farmers had suffered four bad years in a row; their patience was exhausted, and their morale was broken. On 4 September, members voted to suspend operations for 1931. A separate resolution commended the officers and directors for their "zeal and integrity." In his eulogy for the South Carolina co-op, Palmer Johnson warned that with the co-op out of the way, prices on auction markets "could easily tumble to new lows."[94] The ink was hardly dry on Johnson's prediction before prices began to fall, and by month's end the bottom had dropped out.

There is compelling circumstantial evidence that these drastic market swings were not coincidental but rather a deliberate manipulation contrived to wreck the co-op and sink tobacco prices. The motives, at least, do not admit of a doubt. Because the co-op's cash advances set a price floor under each grade of leaf, manufacturers were forced to pay above the co-op rate to get any tobacco. With the co-op out of the way, however, the price floors would be gone and prices could fall unencumbered. While none can dispute that a healthy growers' cooperative, especially one sponsored by the federal government, was hostile to manufacturers' interests, did the tobacco companies intentionally destroy the co-op?

The South Carolina Tobacco Cooperative operated successfully in 1930 and earned the confidence of an increasing number of farmers. As late as August 1931 new members were still joining the organization. If manufacturers wished to weaken the co-op, boycotting its tobacco would serve this end in two important ways. First, a boycott would delay final settlement on the 1930 crop—a condition sure to undermine morale. Second, with its capital tied up in last year's crop, the co-op would be short of cash to advance on the current crop.

Addressing the discrepancy between the companies' words and deeds, co-op directors Nesmith and Aiken pressed the limits of polite discourse. Stating that while the co-op had received "the expressed good wishes and promises of cooperation from all of them [manufacturers], the fact remains that we have not been able, after an aggressive sales effort, to dispose of our stock, which naturally leads us to the conclusion that some of these companies are not genuine in their attitude."[95]

Another tactic sure to harm the co-op would be to begin the season with low prices, then raise prices abruptly while the lower grades were still being sold. Such a maneuver would encourage co-op members to defect at a critical point in the season. Furthermore, since it costs less to raise prices of low-grade leaf, the ploy would be cost-effective. Assuming the co-op failed midway through the season (which it did), manufacturers could then lower their bids on the better grades that came to market later in the season. By underpaying for good tobacco, manufacturers could easily recoup what they had overpaid for the lower grades. With the co-op's price list now only a memory, manufacturers could drop prices to absurdly low levels with impunity. Indeed, prices did decline just in time to exact deep discounts on high-quality tobacco.

The indictment of the manufacturers must rest on circumstantial evidence. But circumstantial or not, it is the only theory that fits the facts. Most damning of all, perhaps, is the anomaly of prices falling late in the season when the best tobacco was coming to market.[96] Sixty years later, old men and women remembered 1931 with glistening eyes and trembling voices. Edward Walden recalled buyers walking warehouse floors bidding "two cents, three cents," and now and then "one cent."[97]

Some farmers did not bother to market their tobacco at all but mixed it with stable compost and used it for fertilizer.[98] South Carolina tobacco averaged 9.2 cents in 1931, 3.5 cents below the cost of production. Pee Dee growers lost $2.4 million on what they sold in 1931. Losses on leaf that was not sold, of course, cannot be known. The crop returned only $6.4 million to the Pee Dee, the least in ten years. Valued in constant dollars, the 1931 crop was the cheapest in twenty-eight years. In Mullins, the Pee Dee's leading tobacco market, both of the town's banks closed on the same day.[99] In a touching attempt to find the silver lining in a very dark cloud, one official ventured that prices might improve in 1932 because so many farmers were bankrupt that supplies of leaf would likely be smaller.[100] If manufacturers conspired to wreck the South Carolina co-op in 1931, it was a strategy as vicious as it was successful.

The Bright Leaf tobacco culture reached rock bottom in 1932. True to predictions, the crop was much smaller. The Pee Dee crop declined by almost 45 percent, and other leaf belts had similar reductions. Prices improved a little but far less than the amount of the reduction. Averages on the South Carolina belt hovered around eleven cents in 1932. With short production and low prices, the crop grossed only $4.4 million, the lowest since 1916.

The Federal Farm Board was also breathing its last. The agency's attempt to support prices without production controls had bled it to death. By the end of 1932, the Farm Board held 100 million bushels of wheat and 1.3 million bales of cotton that were later disposed of at substantial losses. Critics sometimes assert that the Hoover administration did little to help farmers cope with the Depression. The truth is, however, that the Federal Farm Board put almost a half-billion dollars into farmers' hands. Moreover, by soaking up surpluses at higher than market prices, Farm Board purchases were essentially subsidies. But even this unprecedented largesse toward the nation's farmers was insufficient to withstand the pressures worldwide depression was placing on American agriculture.

By 1932, the need for viable crop control was obvious to all. Voluntary reduction campaigns had failed because growers feared their neighbors would not abide by them and that one's sacrifice would be another's windfall. The efforts of individual states to sponsor crop controls were also ineffective. For example, South Carolina farmers had voluntarily cut tobacco acreage in 1929 and 1931, only to see growers in other states produce more. Only an entity able to enforce policy in all the tobacco states and large enough to stand toe-to-toe with manufacturers could hope to solve the problem. Providing the necessary framework for this bilateral policy would be the work of the next administration.

Above left. Frank Mandeville Rogers (1857–1945) introduced Bright Leaf tobacco to South Carolina and founded the Florence tobacco market. *Courtesy the Rogers Family.*

Above right. Francis Warrington Dawson (1840–1889), editor and publisher of the *Charleston News and Courier. Courtesy Special Collections Library, Duke University.*

Left. William Henry Daniel (1841–1915) founded the Mullins tobacco market. *Courtesy the Daniel Family.*

Left. Joseph William Holliday (1827–1904), pioneer tobacco grower and merchant of Galivants Ferry. *Courtesy John Monroe J. Holliday.*

Below left. Bright Williamson (1861–1927), vice-president and director of the Tri-State Tobacco Growers Cooperative. *Courtesy Darlington County Historical Commission.*

Below right. Clarence Hamilton Poe (1881–1964), editor and publisher of the *Progressive Farmer* and director of the Tri-State Tobacco Growers Cooperative. *Courtesy North Carolina Division of Archives and History.*

Stalk harvesting Bright Leaf tobacco, B. F. Williamson farm, Darlington, about 1897.
Courtesy Darlington County Historical Commission.

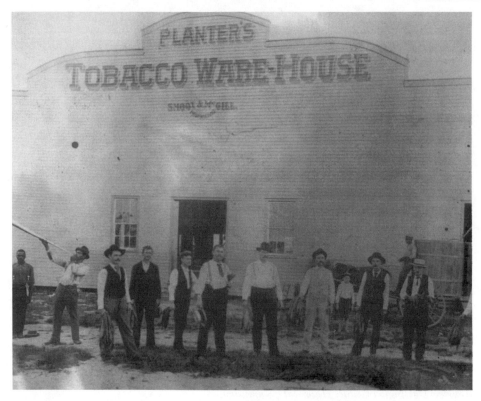

Planter's Warehouse, B. F. Smoot and E. E. McGill, proprietors, Darlington, August 1895. Note "Gabriel" at left. *Courtesy Darlington County Historical Commission.*

Barn raising, Horry County, about 1938. *Courtesy William Van Auken Green Collection, Horry County Museum.*

Rabon Family, Aynor, about 1939. *Courtesy William Van Auken Green Collection, Horry County Museum.*

Marketing tobacco in Conway, Laurel Street at Fourth Avenue, early 1920s.
Note bell on roof. *Courtesy South Caroliniana Library, University of
South Carolina, Columbia.*

Dixie Warehouse, Coit Street, Florence, about 1914. *Courtesy South Caroliniana Library,
University of South Carolina, Columbia.*

Agriculture cannot survive in a capitalist
society as a philanthropic enterprise.
HENRY A. WALLACE

6 The Lord, Mr. Roosevelt, and Bright Leaf Redemption, 1933–1935

SELDOM HAS AN EVENT drawn so bold a line across the page of history as did the New Deal in the chronicle of southern agriculture. The benevolent paternalism that came to characterize government's attitude toward farming began in the first hundred days of Franklin D. Roosevelt's presidency. The heart of the New Deal's farm program was the commitment to raise farmers' incomes by bringing supply in line with demand. The idea was not new. In the 1920s, southern and midwestern congressmen had twice pushed agricultural reform bills through Congress only to see them vetoed by President Coolidge. During the Hoover administration, the ill-fated Federal Farm Board was a compromise plan that failed largely because it attempted to support prices without regulating production. In the election of 1932, however, Americans expressed their readiness for sweeping economic and social reform and granted the new administration a clear mandate for change.[1]

Change came at a good time. After the well-intentioned calamity of the Federal Farm Board, farmers throughout the United States sank deeper into depression. But none, perhaps, sank lower than tobacco growers in the Pee Dee region of South Carolina. The Farm Board had been touted as the farmers' last, best hope. When it collapsed, dragging with it the Bright Belt's only cooperative, many farmers despaired of recovery. In fact, some viewed their reduced circumstances with grim fatalism as though their misery was somehow ordained by Providence. A Baptist preacher in Horry County voiced the silent supplications of many hearts when he offered a prayer for the 1933 crop season: "Lord," he said, "the night has been long. Send the light."[2]

The year 1933 was a watershed in the Pee Dee and much of the South. While the region reached a point of utter despair, reforms began that restored equity to the tobacco business and returned prosperity to the Pee Dee. The night was waning.

The fundamental problem in the tobacco country was the golden leaf's dramatic loss of purchasing power. In 1932, the Department of Agriculture estimated that the purchasing power of a pound of flue-cured tobacco had fallen to about half what it was in the 1920s.[3] Many Pee Dee tobacco farmers—landowners and tenants alike—had little to spare in the best of times, and the relentless erosion of buying power had long since exhausted their reserves.

There was general agreement on the causes of the problem. It was well known that the decline of leaf prices resulted from overproduction and the inherent prejudice of the marketing system. Moreover, given the enormous profits of the tobacco companies, it was obvious that growers were not receiving a fair share of the ultimate value of their produce. Everyone from the secretary of agriculture to high school "ag" teachers agreed that production must be controlled and manufacturers persuaded to pay higher prices. The question was how.

Meanwhile, not all Pee Dee tobacco growers were suffering in silence. From Galivants Ferry came an eloquent appeal for "mothers go[ing] from the curing barns late at night, their small children sleepy and pitiful," and for "strong men . . . [who] faint from overheat and [are] dragged from the field." The writer compared the meager returns of this brutal work routine to the wages of R. J. Reynolds factory workers and asked if the government might "do something for his [Reynolds's] slaves all over Virginia, the Carolinas, and Georgia who toil in the hot sun for him and produce the product on which the very life of his industry depends."[4] In the spring of 1933, Congress acted to restore equity to agriculture. But unlike the Baptist preacher, the lawmakers did not call upon heaven. They believed the growers' loss of equity had more worldly origins.

Government's response to the farm crisis was the Agricultural Adjustment Act of 12 May 1933. The act articulated an ambitious policy intended to correct inequities in American agriculture. In the act's opening paragraph, the Depression was blamed in part on the "severe and increasing disparity between the prices of agricultural and other commodities" that had undermined the living standard of rural America. It promised to restore the purchasing power of farm products by balancing production with consumption.[5]

Congress further resolved to redress the inequity by increasing the farmers' share of consumer expenditures rather than by simply raising prices. Although lawmakers included this clause to reassure consumers, it was a clear statement of purpose. The Agricultural Adjustment Act (or "Triple A," as it came to be known) not only gave government the means to implement crop control but empowered it to assist growers at the expense of manufacturers.[6]

The statute covered six agricultural commodities—wheat, cotton, dairy products, corn, swine, rice, and tobacco.[7] Initially, there was some question about including tobacco. Anthony Badger's outstanding treatment of the period credits Bright and Burley Belt congressmen with insisting that tobacco be included in exchange for their support. Although congressmen from leaf-growing districts were unsure how the AAA could help tobacco growers, they were eager to channel any potential benefits to their constituents. At the same time, the administration wanted to implement controls as soon as possible because spring planting was already under way. Tobacco was hastily included, and the bill gained important support in the Carolinas, Virginia, and Kentucky.[8]

Perhaps more was involved than politics, however. The federal government derived enormous revenues from tobacco products. Indeed, the treasury's share of the tobacco dollar was greater than that of growers and warehousemen combined. In 1932, the Department of Agriculture estimated the farm value of the tobacco in a package of cigarettes at about 1.5 cents. At the same time, however, federal excise taxes added 6 cents to the price of a pack. Thus the federal government received about four times the income from cigarettes that tobacco growers or warehousemen did. The desire to safeguard a very lucrative source of revenue probably influenced the administration's decision to include tobacco in the AAA.[9]

Once the bill was law, the Department of Agriculture hastily created a bureaucracy to oversee the program. The Agricultural Adjustment Administration was divided into production, finance, information, and marketing departments with specialists for each commodity. State AAA offices were set up to administer programs at the local level. Secretary of Agriculture Henry A. Wallace appointed John B. Hutson to head the tobacco section. Hutson hailed from a tobacco farm in the Kentucky Black Patch and remembered well the tobacco growers' uprising of the early 1900s.[10]

To establish parity guidelines, the act proposed "fair exchange value" objectives for each commodity. These were defined as "the price that will give the commodity the same purchasing power, with respect to articles that farmers buy, as . . . during the base period."[11] For purposes of the act, lawmakers chose base periods when each commodity's value was nearer that of selected industrial goods and growers had enjoyed a higher living standard. The years 1909–14 were the designated base period for the other five commodities, but Congress specified the 1920s, when leaf prices had been higher, as the valuation period for tobacco. AAA officials set the parity objective for flue-cured tobacco at 15.8 cents. Though below the inflated level of the war years, it was 40 percent above what Pee Dee farmers had received for their 1932 crop.[12]

In attempting to raise farm prices, John Hutson and his staff were determined to avoid the mistakes of the Federal Farm Board. Congressional leaders knew that production must be balanced with consumption and that practical crop control must be the centerpiece of the recovery program.[13] But in spite of the obvious benefits of balancing supply with demand, not all farmers could be counted on to perceive where their interests lay. Formulating a workable crop reduction plan, therefore, presented lawmakers with a dilemma.

AAA planners knew that successful crop control required virtually unanimous grower participation, but Congress had balked at making controls mandatory. Major constitutional issues were involved. Restricting land-owners' use of their property challenged traditions older than the republic. Another consideration was protecting consumers from sharp price increases. At the same time, however, policymakers were determined to apply crop controls as broadly as possible. Considerable debate followed, and several proposals were considered before a workable plan emerged.[14]

In the act, Congress provided for "rental or benefit payments" to encourage crop reductions and allotted $100 million to fund them. Hutson and his staff proposed that tobacco growers be offered cash incentives to reduce their acreage.[15] Since growers would participate voluntarily, non-compliers would not be fined or taxed but simply declared ineligible for AAA payments. Wallace and Hutson believed payments served two important ends: the promise of hard cash would ensure greater participation while enhancing growers' incomes. After all, they reasoned, income enhancement was the stated purpose of the act.[16]

This was a revolutionary approach to crop control. Before 1933, no growers' organization or government entity had the authority or resources to conceive of such a program. Heretofore, voluntary control campaigns had failed because the uncertain hope of price increases had not lured enough farmers into the fold. Other attempts had failed because there was no way to administer a program across several states or monitor compliance among thousands of growers.[17] The Agricultural Adjustment Act made crop control feasible for the first time. With a considerable budget and a writ that ran in every state, the AAA could offer growers a bird in the hand—immediate, tangible rewards for compliance.

As welcome as cash incentives were, the greatest benefit of crop control would be higher leaf prices. But prices do not rise by themselves; buyers must agree to pay them. Lawmakers did not expect the Big Four to pay parity prices without coercion, so they fitted the Agricultural Adjustment Act with a set of sharp teeth. The very language of the statute revealed the suspicions of lawmakers. Should manufacturers balk at paying parity prices, they could be required to purchase special licenses "as may be necessary to eliminate unfair practices" in the commerce of tobacco. The secretary of agriculture was empowered to suspend the licenses and impose fines of $1,000 per day for noncompliance.[18]

Hutson and his staff understood that balance of supply and demand alone would not correct the inherent bias of the marketing system. Their dominance of the industry would allow the Big Four to raise prices temporarily to assuage the situation only to force them down again in a few years. It had happened before. The AAA provided another means of compelling manufacturers to raise leaf prices. The act specified that a "processing tax," a surcharge equal to the difference between the market price and the parity price, could be levied against manufacturers. The taxes would fund benefit payments to producers. Thus manufacturers could be forced to pay parity prices either directly to growers in the normal course of business or indirectly through processing taxes.[19] It was expected that the tobacco companies would not absorb the tax but pass it along to consumers through price increases. As long as the percentage of the consumer dollar retained by manufacturers did not increase, this method of transferring income from smokers to growers was consistent with the act.[20]

In summary, the political and economic framework of the Agricultural Adjustment Act and its commodity programs differed from previous crop reduction plans in three critical ways. First, the federal auspices of the AAA made enforcement, especially interstate enforcement, genuinely possible for the first time. Second, the AAA was empowered to make cash payments to producers in exchange for acreage reductions. Congress backed its commitment to parity with $100 million of initial funding and empowered the secretary of agriculture to raise additional monies by levying processing taxes against manufacturers who obstructed parity objectives. When many counties in the Bright Belt were so broke they were paying schoolteachers in scrip, the power of the purse made a vital difference. Finally, the tax and licensing provisions of the act gave federal authorities a strong bargaining position in dealing with manufacturers. By the summer of 1933, the legal apparatus to redeem the Bright Leaf culture was in place. It awaited an opportunity.

Once again, the alarm sounded first in Georgia. Before the markets opened, experts predicted Georgia leaf would average fifteen cents a pound, but when the Georgia–Florida Belt opened on 1 August, bids were 25 percent below forecasts. Before the day was out, Secretary of Agriculture Henry A. Wallace was receiving telegrams from Georgia growers protesting low prices.[21]

As the days passed and prices stayed low, angry farmers met at Valdosta,

Douglas, and Adel and fired off telegrams to Atlanta and Washington. Growers went beyond complaining about low prices and urged Governor Eugene Talmadge to close Georgia markets. Talmadge openly sympathized with them and accused manufacturers of playing "the biggest skin game on the face of the earth."[22] But the Georgia governor also appreciated his state's minor status as a source of leaf tobacco and conceded that if Georgia markets closed, manufacturers would simply withdraw their buyers and fill their orders in the Carolinas and Virginia.[23] He did, however, wire President Roosevelt that "many farms would be sold under the hammer unless a living price was paid" for Georgia leaf.[24]

In the past, protests by growers had done little besides enrich Western Union. This time, however, Hutson and his staff saw their discontent as an opportunity to effect lasting change. To agricultural leaders, the real prize was crop control. Government largesse could bring temporary relief, but only balance of supply and demand could achieve permanent reform. By 1933 most producers were sold on the idea, but there were still some who objected on principle or doubted crop controls could succeed.

Because crop controls must be both voluntary and unanimous, AAA officials sought to convince reluctant tobacco growers to accept acreage restrictions. The Georgia crisis was Wallace and Hutson's first opportunity, and they capitalized on the widespread dissatisfaction to sell the AAA plan. Within days, AAA field agents were in Georgia meeting with growers and urging them to agree to reduce next year's crop in exchange for help now.[25] So vital were crop controls, the agents argued, that if producers tried the AAA plan for one season, they would never wish to abandon it.

Markets opened on the South Carolina–North Carolina Border Belt on 10 August. At first, farmers there were optimistic. Although bids for the first offerings were below parity levels, they were higher than the year before. Producers believed that when the better grades were sold later in the season, prices would surely rise.[26] But after ten days, averages were up only one cent, and well into the season's third week, prices remained static despite the fine tobacco that growers were bringing in. By now, many Pee Dee farmers believed they were being had. Lulled early in the season by small increases in the lower grades, producers realized their best tobacco was now being taken from them at "lug" prices.[27] Business leaders accused the Big Four of lowering leaf prices to offset higher operating costs brought on by the National Recovery Act (NRA). To support their accusation, they pointed out that foreign and export companies not subject to the NRA were paying higher prices.[28]

As the selling season advanced and prices remained low, sentiment for drastic action swept through the Border Belt. Hutson sent staffers into the Pee Dee to explain the AAA program and enlist the growers' support. USDA tobacco expert J. C. Lanier addressed ten thousand people at the Mullins Tobacco Festival on 25 August.[29] Later that week, anxious growers met in Florence and sent a committee to Governor Charles Blackwood urging that markets be closed for ten days pending AAA action to raise prices. "The people of the Pee Dee are being trampled upon," a spokesman from Dillon told the governor, adding that while "we have the best tobacco crop since 1919 . . . our farmers will be in the most deplorable condition in a generation." The spokesman added that should the governor fail to act, "five hundred men in Dillon County could close every market in South Carolina."[30]

Predictably, not everyone agreed. The question of closing tobacco markets was complicated by fears that the crop would soon deteriorate. Moreover, merchants who carried tobacco farmers were themselves indebted to banks and wholesalers and were understandably anxious to settle their accounts. Telegrams urging that markets remain open came from Timmonsville and elsewhere. Confused by conflicting opinions among Pee Dee tobacco interests, the governor dithered. On 31 August, Blackwood announced that he felt "favorably inclined" toward closing tobacco markets and "rather thought" he would "probably take some action tomorrow."[31]

But the pace of events soon overtook the hesitant Blackwood. North Carolina took the lead in responding to the crisis. North Carolina governor J. C. B. Ehringhaus seized command of the movement to close tobacco markets in both Carolinas. Two thousand North Carolina tobacco growers met in Raleigh on 31 August. Some speakers openly called on growers to close leaf markets by force and laced their rhetoric with ominous allusions to revolution.[32]

Governor Ehringhaus did not take the threats lightly. In the extreme conditions of the early 1930s, acts of agrarian terrorism were occurring throughout the United States. In the West, wheat producers were burning their grain, and dairy farmers were blocking highways and pouring milk into ditches. In Iowa, enraged farmers burned railroad bridges to stop trains from removing corn.[33] The spectacle of traditionally conservative landowners being radicalized startled Ehringhaus. He promptly gave warehousemen a day to sell the tobacco on their floors and then close. The delighted growers responded by drafting Ehringhaus to lead a delegation to Washington.

Tarheel warehousemen were not so pleased. Most were willing to cooperate with the governor but hesitated as long as markets in South Carolina remained open. Indeed, warehousemen in Rocky Mount and Kinston made their compliance conditional on market closings in South Carolina.[34] Since Virginia markets were not yet open, Ehringhaus was probably relieved to have only one other state to worry about. Before boarding the train for Washington, Ehringhaus wired Blackwood asking him to close leaf markets in South Carolina.[35]

The North Carolinian's bold action gave Blackwood a way out of his dilemma. Content to follow Ehringhaus's lead, Blackwood agreed to close South Carolina tobacco markets. Learning that he had no legal authority to do so, the governor quickly wired every warehouse in the state asking for cooperation. Warehousemen were hurting, too. Their income was based on sales commissions, and they were anxious to do anything that could raise prices. W. H. Daniel Jr. of Mullins, president of the South Carolina Warehousemen's Association, provided critical support by endorsing the governor's request and encouraging others to cooperate.[36]

After receiving pledges of support from warehousemen, Blackwood issued a proclamation closing the state's tobacco markets effective Saturday, 2 September 1933. He also appointed a blue-ribbon committee to "go to Washington and stay there" until the crisis was resolved. The South Carolina delegation was a Who's Who of Pee Dee tobacco interests: A. H. Buchan, W. H. Daniel Jr., Ransome Williams, and Charles Dixon of Mullins; McIver Williamson of Darlington, R. S. Rogers of Dillon, and Doc Allen Spivey of Conway. The delegation resolved to support "any just plan of acreage control that seems equitable to the Secretary of Agriculture."[37]

Holding conferences with tobacco growers, warehousemen, and politicians, Secretary Wallace and John Hutson had their hands full. Because markets were closed, everyone felt pressured to find a solution as soon as possible. As always, the issue turned on crop reduction. Earlier that summer, cotton farmers had voluntarily plowed under one-third of the cotton crop in exchange for AAA benefits.[38] But tobacco producers had no such option. It was late August, and most of the tobacco crop was already harvested and cured. Much of it, in fact, was already sold. The best that Bright Leaf growers could offer was to reduce next year's crop. Of course, the most pressing need was a higher price for the present crop. But with the 1933 crop locked in, officials hoped the promise of cutbacks in 1934 might induce manufacturers facing smaller supplies next year to pay more for the current crop.[39]

Predictably, manufacturers were skeptical. After all, they were being asked to buy a pig in a poke. Indeed, there was little reason to believe the government's crop control plan would succeed. Manufacturers knew well the sad history of crop reduction plans. Nothing short of terrorism had ever kept farmers in line for even a few months. If this latest scheme was like all the rest, the companies reasoned, they would spend millions anticipating a shortage that would never materialize.[40] In informal talks with tobacco company representatives, AAA officials had no luck selling them on the plan.

The Agricultural Adjustment Act empowered Secretary Wallace to compel manufacturers to comply with parity objectives. Rather than force their compliance, however, Wallace preferred to seek their willing cooperation. Hoping to reach an amicable settlement, Wallace met with Big Four representatives and asked them to suggest ways to raise leaf prices that were acceptable to them. R. J. Reynolds president S. Clay Williams proposed— with a straight face—that federal cigarette taxes be lowered to stimulate sales and thus increase demand for leaf tobacco. But Williams would not promise to lower cigarette prices or pass along tax savings to farmers in the form of higher leaf prices. Wallace quickly saw that such a plan would only increase manufacturers' profits at the treasury's expense and rejected the proposal.[41]

Secretary Wallace met with manufacturers again on 30 August and offered them another chance for input. Williams again spoke for the Big Four. He suggested that cigarette manufacturers establish a fund to underwrite the AAA crop reduction program for tobacco growers. When Wallace expressed interest in this proposal, Williams smoothly added that each manufacturer must contribute to the fund according to its unit sales volume. USDA economists pointed out that this funding formula would bankrupt smaller companies whose lower-priced goods and thinner profit margins made them vulnerable to volume-based contributions. Under questioning, it came out that two small companies, Axton-Fisher and Brown & Williamson, were cutting into the Big Four's market share.[42]

Faced with the Big Four's stonewalling and self-serving "policy recommendations," Wallace realized that the carrot had not worked, and he began to apply the stick. On 1 September, he announced that processing taxes of four cents a pound would be levied on all leaf tobacco acquired by manufacturers after 1 October. The tax rate would be the approximate difference between current leaf prices and the parity price set by USDA. Officials estimated that the tax could return $10 million to the treasury and would be used to "bring production of the 1934 flue-cured tobacco crop as much below the present level of consumption as the present crop is above it."[43]

Wallace and Hutson quickly called a meeting of all growers, warehousemen, and representatives currently in Washington. The delegations met with USDA and AAA staff on 4 and 5 September. At the meetings, Hutson reaffirmed the government's commitment to parity and outlined the plan to use pledges of future crop reduction as a basis for current benefits. To induce farmers to enroll, the contract offered "rental" payments of $17.50 for each acre of tobacco withdrawn from production. The size of the acreage cut was unspecified but was estimated to range from 25 to 33 percent of the current crop. Moreover, producers could receive "adjustment payments" to compensate for leaf already sold below parity. The delegation's response was favorable, and Hutson urged the Carolinians to return home and begin enrolling growers while the markets remained closed.[44]

South Carolina officials wasted no time. The full resources of federal, state, and county agricultural services were mobilized to distribute contracts and collect signatures. Clemson's Agricultural Extension Service director W. W. Long was asked to coordinate the campaign. By 7 September, 150,000 crop reduction contracts were en route to tobacco growers in the Pee Dee. The contracts bound growers to reduce next year's tobacco plantings by 25 percent of the previous three years' average.[45]

Governor Blackwood declared 11 and 12 September (Monday and Tuesday) as "general holidays" in tobacco-producing counties to facilitate the sign-up campaign. Meetings were held in every market town to explain the reduction plan and collect signatures. From Washington, John Hutson dispatched eleven tobacco specialists to aid in the local campaigns. Pee Dee businessmen also had a stake in the outcome, and shopkeepers in every town left their counters and drove through the countryside calling on farmers and asking them to sign. Thirty automobiles were dispatched from Kingstree to contact growers in remote areas of Williamsburg County.[46]

Compelled by desperation and urged on by front-page editorials in local newspapers, the farmers made an extraordinary response. More than half the tobacco producers in South Carolina signed in the first three days. Nearly fifteen hundred signed en masse at a Florence meeting led by J. C. Lanier. Marion County farmers were described as "flocking in" to sign reduction contracts.[47] Within a week, more than 95 percent of Horry County growers signed contracts. Growers in Dillon County were reported to be "pushing the campaign," and observers predicted that enrollment there would approach 100 percent. Georgetown County actually achieved unanimity when every tobacco grower in the county endorsed the plan. The Georgetown County extension agent reported that "the farmers here realize the government is fighting for them, and they are cooperating to the full extent of their ability."[48]

By 15 September, only nine days after the kickoff meeting in Washington, 95 percent of the tobacco acreage in the Carolinas, Georgia, and Virginia was under contract. Henry Wallace and John Hutson were delighted by the success of the enrollment campaign and promptly summoned manufacturers to a third meeting. The reasoning behind the AAA crop reduction plan rested on the assumption that prices for the current crop would rise when buyers faced the certainty of smaller supplies next year. Before the sign-up campaign, manufacturers doubted if significant numbers of farmers would go along. But now that acreage cuts were assured and processing taxes were scheduled to begin in two weeks, Wallace believed the growers' bargaining position was much stronger.

At the meeting, Wallace proposed that manufacturers agree to pay a minimum average price for leaf tobacco. Though unspecified in the formal proposal, the minimum was understood to be sixteen cents a pound. To protect consumers, Wallace reserved the extraordinary power to veto cigarette price increases he deemed unreasonable. Moreover, Wallace wanted access to manufacturers' books to monitor compliance. By now, tobacco companies were resigned to paying more for tobacco and entered the negotiations to get the best deal they could. But the consumer protection clauses Wallace proposed were anathema to the cigarette makers. Their representatives quickly asked for seven days to study the government's proposal.[49]

As the clock was ticking, leaf markets remained closed. For thousands of grower families it was a cruel wait. Pee Dee farmers and others in the Bright Belt were feeling serious financial pressure. For many, tobacco was their only source of income, and they had seen no cash in nearly a year. There were logistical problems as well. By the third week of September, many farmers had nowhere else to store tobacco. Barns and packhouses were full, and growers were moving tobacco into their homes and covering it with quilts. They were motivated by more than mere inconvenience. Some producers lacked the cash to harvest and handle the rest of their crop until they sold their early curings. Moreover, the leaf itself was beginning to suffer. In the humid Pee Dee summer, some tobacco was becoming moldy and might be permanently damaged if held much longer. As the days passed, more and more growers were reaching the end of their rope.

The market holiday, meant to last ten days, passed its sixteenth day on 17 September. After the highly successful sign-up campaign, growers felt the moratorium had served its purpose and were anxious to sell their tobacco for the higher prices they believed would be forthcoming. Pressure to reopen the markets began to mount in both Carolinas. Appeals from desperate farmers were arriving daily at the governor's office urging Blackwood to allow sales to resume as soon as possible.

As expected, there was widespread disagreement. Grower activists and AAA officials opposed ending the holiday before manufacturers agreed to pay higher prices. They predicted that if sales resumed before a price agreement was reached, manufacturers would deliberately postpone a decision while buying the crop as cheaply as possible. Much hard-won ground would thus be lost. North Carolina governor Ehringhaus agreed and extended the ban on leaf sales in that state until 25 September. He also asked Governor Blackwood to prolong the sales holiday on Pee Dee markets.[50]

Of course, since much of North Carolina's crop was unready for market, Governor Ehringhaus did not assume as great a political risk as he asked of his South Carolina colleague. Moreover, many substantial growers who urged continued delay had other income sources and felt less pressure to sell. Indeed, the agricultural professionals who advocated keeping the markets closed were salaried government employees. While their position on

extending the market holiday was theoretically sound, one wonders if having a thousand pounds of flue-cured tobacco in their living rooms—as
many growers did—might have influenced their attitude.

Faced with conflicting demands, Blackwood compromised. He lifted the
ban on tobacco sales in South Carolina effective 19 September 1933 but
added that warehouses could voluntarily remain closed to await the outcome of the negotiations.[51] The governor's action placed the initiative
with the state's warehousemen. Aware that negotiations were at a critical
stage, warehousemen agreed to give Secretary Wallace as much time as
possible. Within hours of Blackwood's statement, W. H. Daniel Jr. announced that South Carolina markets would conform with those in North
Carolina and remain closed until 25 September 1933.[52]

The Big Four were feeling some pressures also, and not only
from government. Since the Tobacco Trust was "busted" in 1911, the cigarette industry had been dominated by the flagship brands of the four successor companies. American's Lucky Strike, R. J. Reynolds's Camel, Liggett & Myers's Chesterfield, and P. Lorillard's Old Gold accounted for
93 percent of the nation's cigarette sales in 1929.[53] Had cigarette sales been
more evenly distributed among smaller companies, some makers would
doubtless have offered their products at lower prices to attract customers,
and cigarette prices would have tended toward a truly competitive level. As
it was, however, the dominance of the Big Four meant that each company
knew a reduction of its prices would be answered immediately with comparable cuts by the other three. Indeed, from 1923 to 1951, a span of twenty-
eight years, there were only fifteen days when the price lists of the Big Four
differed.[54] Price cuts to attract customers, therefore, were pointless because
they lowered profit margins to no purpose. The Big Four tolerated no price
competition among themselves.

In the early 1930s, however, competition hit the Big Four on their blind
side. The tobacco oligarchy was threatened from the very source that had
provided its profits so long—cheap tobacco. After the cigarette price increase of 1931, the Big Four's standard brands retailed for fifteen cents per
package of twenty cigarettes. This price level supported large advertising
budgets and afforded comfortable markups to manufacturers, distributors,
and retailers. But the combination of generous profit margins, rock-
bottom leaf prices, and depressed incomes opened a gap at the lower end

of the cigarette market. Minor players in the tobacco business rushed to fill that gap with a wave of discount cigarettes called, appropriately, "ten-centers."

The discount brands were an immediate success and a serious challenge to the Big Four. At a time when five cents would buy a loaf of bread, price made a difference to cost-conscious smokers. The dime brands were made by such second-tier companies as Brown & Williamson (Wings), Philip Morris (Paul Jones), and Axton-Fisher (Twenty Grand). Backed by a serious marketing effort, the ten-centers enticed millions of price-conscious smokers away from the more expensive standard brands. Between 1931 and 1933, the new economy brands multiplied sales volume twenty-fold as their market share rose from less than 0.5 percent to 9 percent.[55]

The Big Four fought back savagely, ordering deep price cuts, rebates, and so-called advertising allowances that were little more than bribes. Some important distributors received thousands of dollars to "merchandise" the standards against the dime brands.[56] In short, the Big Four realized they were under siege and carried out the twentieth-century commercial equivalent of pouring boiling oil over the battlements. The counterattack was only partly successful. Lured by "two-packs-for-a-quarter" pricing, some smokers returned to the standards, but not all. The discount brands dug deeply into Big Four profits. Their net earnings dropped to $57 million in 1933, about half the 1931 figure. The Big Four were hurting and looking for a way to squelch the low-price upstarts.

Higher leaf prices offered the Big Four just such an opportunity. The Big Four's ample profit margins could absorb higher material costs easier than the much narrower margins of the discount brands. As Reynolds's president Clay Williams later admitted, it did not matter how much he paid for tobacco as long as his competitors paid the same.[57] This sentiment may have been on the minds of company representatives when they returned to the bargaining table.

The negotiations resumed in Washington on 22 September with Williams again representing the Big Four and Hutson speaking for the government. Having mulled over Hutson's proposal for a week, Williams presented a counteroffer that came very close to meeting government demands. The tobacco companies agreed to buy at least as much of the current crop as they had bought in 1932. They also agreed to pay an average of seventeen cents a pound. On the matter of government access to their books, however, the companies were less accommodating. They agreed to turn over records relevant to leaf purchases but conceded no prerogative with respect to cigarette prices.

Hutson was pleased with the offer of seventeen cents, a cent above the understood minimum, and agreed that manufacturers could recover some of their increased costs with a modest rise in cigarette prices. But he refused to limit the government's inspection rights to only those records that the companies wanted them to see. Nor did he drop the demand for veto power over retail price hikes. Williams stressed that the offer to raise prices depended on manufacturers retaining the right "to manage, conduct, and operate their respective businesses . . . as heretofore." Both sides hardened on this point, and the negotiations stalled.[58] Despite the market holiday, there was still no purchasing agreement with manufacturers.

Tobacco markets reopened in the Carolinas the following Monday with near record sales volume. After the three-week holiday, many farmers were desperate for cash. The Darlington market was described as "completely swamped" with tobacco. At Lake City a record seven hundred thousand pounds changed hands, and Mullins sold more than one million pounds. Prices were well below parity levels. By the third day of sales, a few grades were up slightly, but the USDA Market News Service reported that prices were about the same as before the holiday.[59] Growers and warehousemen felt disappointment, outrage, and betrayal. Sixty years later, one warehouseman remembered: "We didn't know what else to do. We had gone along with the closing, and the farmers had all signed up. None of us understood what was going on in Washington, but we knew tobacco was still cheap. Everybody thought the companies were being stubborn and the government had let us down."[60] By week's end, the Market News Service reported that prices for most grades of flue-cured tobacco had actually declined, and some were even lower than last year.[61]

In Raleigh, Governor Ehringhaus was furious. On 30 September he appealed directly to President Roosevelt, reminding him that producers' enthusiastic and near unanimous acceptance of crop limits was founded on government promises of parity. Negotiations with producers and processors of other commodities were taking place, Ehringhaus continued, and failure to deliver for tobacco farmers could endanger the entire agricultural recovery program. He informed the president that even as manufacturers "haggle over details, their agents continue to acquire more of the crop." Ehringhaus charged that the government's "inability to cope with the great tobacco interests . . . [and its] hesitancy and inaction are increasingly demoralizing." The governor concluded that "the situation challenges the power of the national government." [62]

The next day, 1 October 1933, processing taxes went into effect, and John Hutson announced that implementation of the punitive licensing provisions of the Agricultural Adjustment Act were imminent. On 2 October, spokesmen for the Big Four stated that they were prepared to make concessions on every major point. President Roosevelt summoned both parties to the White House later that week. When the meetings got under way, it was apparent that the tobacco companies were ready to come to terms. Manufacturers began by offering to make any agreement the parties might reach retroactive to 25 September. Thus any leaf purchased since the markets reopened would be factored into parity averages and count toward the total amount the companies ultimately agreed to buy. This was an important concession. According to the parity formula, the purchases of all companies would be treated collectively, and the companies had until 31 March 1934 to bring averages to seventeen cents a pound. Since markets had reopened, however, prices were well below that. Thus manufacturers would have to pay proportionally more for tobacco purchased after the agreement took effect to achieve the seventeen-cent average.

Since cigarette makers had agreed to open their books, the last obstacle to a marketing agreement was the complex issue of cigarette price controls. Hutson wanted the right to overrule price hikes he considered excessive. Manufacturers insisted, with some justification, that current cigarette prices were abnormally low. Earlier that year, the Big Four had cut wholesale prices from $6.00 per thousand to $5.50 to counter the discount brands. Since they intended eventually to return cigarette prices to their former level, they did not want the temporary lower price locked in by government contract. The companies felt they were making a good faith effort and wished to avoid further punitive action, but they balked at conceding control of their price lists.

A final compromise broke the logjam. AAA legal counsel pointed out that it made no difference if the government's rights were spelled out in the marketing agreement. Government authority is derived from the Constitution and acts of Congress, not contracts with third parties. Therefore, the marketing agreement could be drafted without the controversial provision, and the AAA would retain any prerogatives granted under the act. The final draft of the marketing agreement contained no direct references to federal price controls, and the companies agreed not to raise prices above $6 per thousand. A codicil was appended stating that "no officer of the government can by agreement limit or curtail any authority vested in him by law."[63] The resolution of this technicality cut the Gordian knot that had bound the negotiations for months. The marketing agreement for flue-cured tobacco was signed on 6 October. Doubtless everyone concerned breathed a little easier.

When the marketing agreement took effect in October, most Pee Dee leaf had already been sold. Understandably, growers were eager to benefit from rising prices and felt left out since they had little tobacco left to sell. They remonstrated that Old Belt growers could take full advantage of higher prices because markets there opened later. Recognizing the validity of their concerns, AAA officials wrote a "price equalization" clause into growers' contracts to compensate Border Belt (as well as Georgia–Florida Belt) growers. Leaf sold in August qualified for a 20 percent "equalization payment," and September sales received a 10 percent bonus.[64]

Income received by Pee Dee tobacco growers for the 1933 crop was vastly greater than in 1932. As Table 11 reveals, sales proceeds alone were two and one-half times the 1932 figure with AAA rental payments and price equalization bonuses still payable. Although the selling price was only slightly higher, the huge size of the 1933 crop multiplied sales proceeds dramatically. Comparing production and sales data for 1932 and 1933 is revealing. Under normal market conditions such immense production would have been punished by lower prices. That prices rose at all in 1933 testifies to the importance of government intervention on behalf of producers.

Infusions of cash quickened the Pee Dee's sluggish economy and stimulated commerce throughout the region. "There is more money in Marion County just now than at any time within the past several years," boasted Palmer Johnson. "With tobacco prices greatly improved, cotton selling at ten cents, and the government payments, money is pouring into the hands of farmers . . . and this means the speeding up of business and financial conditions."[65] As Pee Dee farmers crowded into stores, merchants reported business activity double the previous year. Tobacco in-

TABLE II
Bright Leaf Tobacco Production in South Carolina,
1932–1938

Year	Poundage (1,000s)	Price (in cents per lb.) current	Price (in cents per lb.) (1900)[a]	Value ($1,000s) current	Value ($1,000s) (1900)
1932	39,440	11.3	(6.9)	4,457	(2,721)
1933	88,580	12.6	(8.1)	11,161	(7,175)
1934	56,880	21.6	(13.5)	12,286	(7,678)
1935	89,760	18.8	(11.5)	16,875	(10,322)
1936	73,350	19.9	(12.0)	14,597	(8,802)
1937	108,080	20.8	(12.1)	22,481	(13,078)
1938	98,800	22.2	(13.1)	21,934	(12,943)

Source: U.S. Department of Agriculture, Bureau of Agricultural Economics, Tobaccos of the United States: Acreage, Yield per Acre, Production, Price and Value by States, 1866–1945, and by Types and Classes, 1919–1945 (Washington, D.C.: U.S. Government Printing Office, 1948), 74.
[a] Prices are reported in current and constant values with 1900 as the base year.

come coupled with that from the AAA cotton program brought the region closer to prosperity than at any time since World War I.

Indeed, many looked upon the Agricultural Adjustment Act as deliverance on near biblical scale. Not since the Emancipation Proclamation had a single act of government affected the Pee Dee so profoundly. The state's commissioner of agriculture happily departed from a long series of gloomy annual reports and declared, "In 1933 the South Carolina farm situation presents a cheerful picture." Perhaps a Pee Dee tenant farmer put it best when he received his tobacco check in a Darlington warehouse. "Hallelujah," the man said. "Hallelujah." [66]

The following year, 1934, tobacco marketing proceeded smoothly and profitably for Pee Dee tobacco growers and warehousemen. The crop of 1934 was the first to be produced under the AAA plan, and the particulars of the new system were soon familiar to all concerned. Tobacco allotments were assigned based on the average production on each farm from 1929 to 1933 inclusive. Thus the average of five crop years became the farm's "historic base" by which future allotments were defined. For example, the 1934 allotment was specified as 70 percent of the historic base.[67] In every county of the Bright Belt, agricultural agents supervised allotment assignments and handled the inevitable complaints from growers. The tobacco allotment was deemed to reside in the land rather than with the grower, thus only landowners received allotments. USDA field agents physically measured tobacco fields to verify compliance, and each grower was issued a marketing card on which sales were recorded. In 1934, Pee Dee farmers and warehousemen witnessed the miraculous arithmetic of crop controls coupled with AAA incentives yield more money for less tobacco. Leaf prices averaged twenty-one cents in 1934, 70 percent above 1933 levels. Even with thirty million fewer pounds, South Carolina's gross income from tobacco surpassed that of the previous year by $1 million. Of course, producing a smaller crop entailed less expense and yielded greater profits. The stringency that had gripped the region since 1928 was loosening. One could walk into any dry goods store in the Pee Dee and see entire families being fitted with new clothes and shoes. Automobile dealers reported unprecedented sales. Pee Dee warehousemen earned larger commissions from higher tobacco prices and, like producers, were spared the expense of handling thirty million extra pounds of leaf. The recovery was felt in the region's labor market as wages rose in such aftermarket services as stemmeries and redrying plants. For many Pee Dee folks, it was their first decent job. For example, many black women left jobs as domestic servants for higher-paying tobacco-related work.[68]

Besides the greater profits afforded by higher sales prices, growers received payments for "rented" acres and parity adjustment payments as well. Furthermore, virtually all Pee Dee tobacco growers received a price equalization payment to compensate them for 1933 leaf sold before the marketing agreement went into effect. In addition, growers who failed to produce their entire quota received a "deficiency payment" of two cents per pound for the shortage. Such payments were essentially pure profit to tobacco growers. Congress further pressed manufacturers to fund its largesse. Besides the processing taxes, domestic inventories of tobacco products and tobacco imports were also assessed.[69] While higher sales prices were by far the most important gain, government benefit payments added materially to profit margins. Figure 2 illustrates the dramatic rise of sales

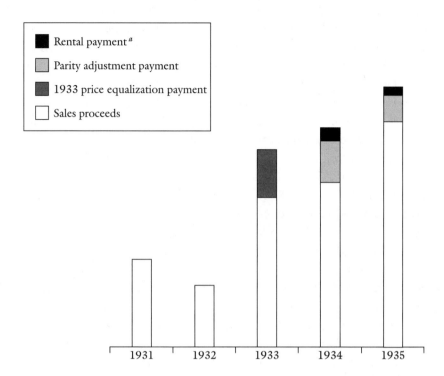

FIGURE 2

Total Cash Value of Tobacco Crops, Including Government Benefit Payments,
South Carolina, 1931–1935

Source: U.S. Department of Agriculture, Bureau of Economics, *Tobaccos: Acreage, Yields, and Value, 1866–1945* (Washington, D.C.: U.S. Government Printing Office, 1946), 47; Harold B. Rowe, *Tobacco Under the AAA* (Washington, D.C.: Brookings Institution, 1935), 294–96.
[a] Prices in millions of dollars.

proceeds and the relative value of benefit payments under the AAA tobacco marketing contract.

Much has been said about the impact of New Deal cotton programs on tenants and sharecroppers, and a consensus has emerged that crop controls often displaced tenants whose labor was made superfluous by acreage reductions.[70] Removal of tenants was less common in the tobacco country. Of course, some tobacco tenants lost their places as early as 1928, when leaf prices collapsed and landowners could no longer afford to keep them (see chapter 5). Although acreage cuts eventually caused some displacements on tobacco farms in the Pee Dee, evidence suggests that traditional tenure patterns persisted longer in Bright Leaf tobacco regions than in cotton areas. The labor-intensive character of tobacco culture as well as the smaller size of the average holding may account for this stability.

Hutson and his staff also protected tenants and sharecroppers in their long-range planning. Because the allotment resided in the land, only landowners could receive payments for diverted acres. But tenants did receive 1933 price equalization payments and adjustment payments in proportion to their share of the crop. Moreover, Hutson lowered the proposed $20 per acre rental payment to $17.50 so more funds could be allocated to benefits that tenants could receive. Hutson further protected the interests of tenants by insisting that landowners not reduce tenant populations because of acreage cuts. A tenant could be displaced only if the landowner replaced him with another tenant of like status.[71] To enforce this policy, field agents physically verified the tenant population on each farm when they came to measure the tobacco fields. The agents were also to see that tenants received their rightful share of AAA benefits.[72] Although the system was far from perfect, tobacco tenants generally fared better under AAA programs than their counterparts in the cotton country.

To say that Pee Dee tobacco farmers and warehousemen liked the AAA program risks understatement. The AAA marketing plan exceeded their highest expectations. They realized, however, that the crop control plan was vulnerable and must be protected. The continued success of the plan depended on the confidence of producers and their willingness to comply. Although the rate of compliance was very high, a handful of noncompliers could threaten the program and jeopardize the well-being of all. Many farmers feared that rising leaf prices would encourage profiteering among noncompliers. Under such pressures, the program—and the new prosperity—would last only one season. To forestall this eventuality, tobacco growers asked Congress to counter any potential advantages of noncompliance. The AAA legal section responded with a defense plan that became the Tobacco Control Act of 1934.

Essentially, the law applied a punitive tax on tobacco not grown under AAA contract. Since compliance with AAA commodity programs was voluntary, the act taxed all tobacco equally but issued tax exemption warrants to cooperating growers for the amount of their allotment. The act empowered the secretary of agriculture to levy a tax of from 25 to 33.3 percent of the selling price on noncontract tobacco. To give noncompliers a second chance, the bill provided a thirty-day grace period to allow them to join the program and receive an exemption.[73] Congressman John H. Kerr of North Carolina's Second District represented the nation's heaviest tobacco constituency and was a natural choice to sponsor the bill in the House of Representatives. South Carolina Senator "Cotton Ed" Smith, chairman of the Senate Agriculture Committee, steered the bill through the upper chamber. The law became known as the Kerr-Smith Act.[74]

The value of a deterrent lies in its ability to prevent something. Since it is impossible to measure accurately what does not happen, the effectiveness of a deterrent can be difficult to assess. Even so, the Kerr-Smith Act must be deemed successful. By countering the temptation to beat the system, the law helped deter dangerous profiteering by noncompliers. Throughout the Bright Leaf culture, total production exceeded allotments by only 4 percent. In South Carolina, "outside" tobacco accounted for only 1.5 percent of the crop, a truly astonishing level of compliance.[75]

The Bright Leaf crop of 1935 was the most profitable since the bonanza of World War I. Not since 1918 had income from tobacco been so high. Improving economic conditions in the United States spurred record cigarette sales, and AAA officials raised flue-cured tobacco allotments to 85 percent of the historic base. Since allotments were specified by acreage only, Pee Dee farmers applied their considerable farming skills—and no small amount of fertilizer—to achieving a record yield of 935 pounds per acre. In 1935 the Pee Dee crop approached ninety million pounds and averaged a healthy nineteen cents, pouring $17 million into the region's economy. This represented nearly four times the value of the 1932 crop.

For the first time in the history of southern agriculture, effective crop control was in place and running smoothly. Since both cotton and tobacco were under AAA commodity programs, the Pee Dee was twice blessed. As Pee Dee farm families sat by their hearthsides in December 1935, no doubt many reflected on how far they had come. The AAA recovery program was working, and their land and labor now provided them a decent living. The Great Depression finally seemed to be over, and they looked forward to 1936 with hope and confidence. They were in for a rude awakening.

7

War and Peace, 1936–1950

THE BLOW FELL in January 1936. The farm recovery program suffered a setback when the Supreme Court declared the Agricultural Adjustment Act unconstitutional. In a six-to-three decision, the Court ruled that government had no right to "regulate and control agriculture." Speaking for the majority, Justice Owen J. Roberts, a Hoover appointee, stated that policies intended to reduce acreage or limit production were "outside the range of proper governmental powers." Further, the processing taxes that forced manufacturers to pay parity prices and funded AAA benefits were "but a means to an unconstitutional end." The verdict was clear: the AAA, the Kerr-Smith Act, and all related programs were dead. In a single blow, the Supreme Court had smashed the centerpiece of the New Deal's farm program.[1]

A wave of disappointment and apprehension swept the tobacco country. Farmers were confused and frustrated by the spectacle of government seeming to work against itself and its citizens. Many were angry that millions in promised benefits would go unpaid. Most daunting of all, there was no longer any crop control. Though controls had been in place for only three seasons, they were already a cherished fixture of the tobacco culture. After decades of self-defeating overproduction, tobacco growers had finally achieved a place of equity in their industry. Farmers were further dismayed to see their hard-won progress threatened by the very source of their deliverance—the federal government.

Predictably, farmers felt betrayed and reacted with bitter denunciations of the Court and demands for redress. Dillon farmers wired Secretary Wallace, pleading that controls be restored and warning that a return of the Depression was imminent.[2] Outrage was not limited to tobacco growers or to the South. The national scope of the problem was underscored by angry protests throughout the United States. Some farmers called for a constitutional amendment covering agriculture; others suggested that tariff revenues be diverted to fund benefit payments canceled by the ruling. Despairing of federal intervention, some called on state governments to enact interlocking legislation to control tobacco production. As in the dark days of 1933, however, most looked to Washington to restore the balance of supply and demand.[3]

President Roosevelt and the congressional Farm Bloc were equally anxious to see production controls restored and the momentum of recovery preserved. Time was short. Tobacco growers in South Carolina and Georgia were already sowing seedbeds, and the planting season was only weeks away. Cotton farmers faced similar pressures. Working closely with representatives of major farm organizations, Secretary of Agriculture Henry A. Wallace hastily formulated an alternate plan to control commodity production. The broad strokes of the new program came into focus in a few days. By expanding conservation policies, a means was found to effect crop control in another form.[4]

Soil conservation had been on the agrarian reform agenda since the nineteenth century and was an important part of the USDA's long-range plans. During the economic crisis of the early 1930s, however, conservation issues had been temporarily subordinated to economic recovery. But the overthrow of the administration's crop control policies provided an opportunity to use conservation as a legal means of achieving the same end.[5]

The new plan, called the Soil Conservation and Domestic Allotment Act of 1936, sought to restore crop control by offering growers cash payments to reduce their acreage of certain soil-depleting crops. Since most of the crops covered under the defunct AAA were soil-depleting, payments to divert these crops were, in essence, incentives to curtail their production. Lawmakers officially designated tobacco, cotton, and a few others as soil-depleting and declared producers eligible for crop reduction incentives. Thus tobacco growers who agreed to limit their acreage qualified for conservation payments.[6]

The conservation program paid tobacco growers five cents for every pound they reduced their 1936 crop below their historic base. Since farmers made about five cents a pound when tobacco sold for the parity price, the payment offered a reasonable incentive to reduce production. Additional payments were offered producers who planted idle acres in soil-building legumes and grasses. Penalties for noncompliance were mild. If a noncomplying tobacco grower was enrolled in other government programs, he sacrificed five cents for each pound of tobacco he produced above his historic base from benefits due him from those programs. But if a grower chose not to participate in any conservation program, he paid no penalty whatever. In other words, the only penalty for noncompliance was the loss of possible benefits from other government programs.[7]

Some observers were openly skeptical that this indirect method of crop control would entice enough tobacco out of production to keep prices stable. One serious drawback was the lack of adequate funding. Under the AAA, payments to growers were financed by processing taxes levied on manufacturers and were, therefore, essentially self-funding. Now that this source of revenue was forbidden by the Supreme Court, however, Congress was forced to finance the program from the conservation budget. Many questioned whether Congress could afford crop control at all or if the smaller benefits it could afford—and the weaker penalties it could impose on noncompliers—could maintain discipline among growers.[8]

Doubts notwithstanding, the new program was soon under way. AAA facilities and personnel were reassigned to the Soil Conservation Service.

Offices and agents were soon operating in every county in the Bright Belt. In March and April 1936, agents met with growers, explained the conservation program, and encouraged them to enroll. As of old, area newspapers made common cause with government to sell the program. The press fairly represented the conservation campaign as the farmers' best hope until a more permanent program was in place or the composition of the Supreme Court changed.[9]

In 1936, four out of five flue-cured tobacco farmers participated in the new conservation/control program. It is not surprising that, having reaped the rewards of a balanced market, growers feared a return to the bad old days of large crops and low prices. Throughout the Bright Belt, grower participation was down slightly from 1935, but with 80 percent of the crop committed to the conservation plan and an unusually dry growing season, the tobacco crop of 1936 actually declined 10 percent from 1935 levels.

In the Pee Dee, the tobacco crop of 1936 was off a more substantial 18 percent, and prices reacted favorably to diminished supply. A sign of the times, Congressman Allard Gasque auctioned the first pile on the Darlington market with proceeds going to the Democratic Party. One million pounds changed hands in Mullins on opening day, and growers seemed satisfied with prices. Indeed, growers remained satisfied throughout the 1936 marketing season. Overall prices rose 6 percent in 1936, and market income was the second highest in fourteen years. Crop control was achieved in 1936 by masquerading as soil conservation.[10]

No permanent replacement for the lost and lamented AAA was in place by planting time 1937, and the situation was causing concern. Ironically, the very success of the interim conservation program was undermining growers' loyalty to the plan. The lure of higher prices was pulling farmers harder than modest conservation incentives, and many were tempted to increase plantings in 1937. Reformers rightly feared the consequences of greater acreage. They understood that prices had risen in 1936 in response to smaller supplies, the result, at least in part, of dry weather. But tobacco growers could not count on drought to enforce crop control every year. And without the firm hand of the Kerr-Smith Act to keep growers in line, discipline was beginning to break down. In fact, USDA economists estimated that the conservation program reduced the tobacco crop only 19 percent in 1936, far below the 30 percent diverted by the AAA in 1934.[11]

Pee Dee farmers increased their acreage in 1937 and, aided by excellent weather, urged a record 965 pounds per acre from their soils. The crop of 1937 exceeded 108 million pounds, by far the largest yet produced in South Carolina. Income from the crop also set a record. Valued in constant dollars, tobacco earnings surpassed even the banner year of 1918. Despite increased supply, real prices held at the 1936 level. Unprecedented demand for tobacco saved farmers in 1937. The nation was slowly climbing out of the Depression, and cigarette sales were growing apace, rising 21 percent in two years.[12] Although pleased with short-term profits, thoughtful tobacco growers feared—with good reason, it turned out—that weak conservation restraints would snap under the pressure of higher prices and the floodgates of overproduction would reopen with a vengeance.

Farmers breathed easier when President Roosevelt signed the revised Agricultural Adjustment Act in February 1938. Like the first AAA of 1933, the second AAA set marketing quotas for flue-cured tobacco and assigned allotments based on historic production. Although penalties could be assessed on noncooperators, Congress eliminated the processing tax that had been the Achilles' heel of the first AAA. To preserve the democratic character of crop controls, Congress required that growers endorse the new program. When the act's tobacco provisions were approved by 86 percent of tobacco growers in the March 1938 referendum, many reformers felt the age-old problem of overproduction was finally solved. Their optimism was premature.[13]

The second AAA had problems from the start. Marketing quotas that should have been announced well in advance of planting time—by January at the latest—were delayed until mid-March. Many growers thus planted too much or too little and were understandably resentful. The AAA "corrected" this problem by allowing farmers who had inadvertently planted above their quota to sell their extra leaf subject to a 50 percent penalty. Such a discount usually lowered sales receipts below the cost of production. Thus, through no fault of their own, some growers went to the trouble and expense of growing unauthorized tobacco only to sustain a loss on it.[14]

Another source of discontent with the second AAA was the imposition of poundage quotas. Unlike acreage restrictions, which allowed farmers to sell every leaf they could urge from their allotment, poundage quotas placed an absolute limit on production. Predictably, growers disliked poundage quotas from the outset. To make matters worse, some farmers were not informed of their poundage quotas until marketing time, which confused many growers and generated further resentment against the second AAA.[15]

Most serious of all, however, were the results of the 1938 marketing season. Instead of the substantially higher prices growers were expecting, bids for the 1938 crop were only one cent above those for 1937. Ultimately the 1938 crop, produced and marketed under AAA controls, returned less income than the uncontrolled crop of 1937. Some observers blamed the mediocre quality of the 1938 crop for its disappointing returns, but most growers scoffed at this excuse. After all, they argued, the fundamental purpose of crop control was to raise prices. North Carolina and Virginia prices were even lower, and growers there were keenly disappointed.[16]

Tobacco growers expressed their dissatisfaction with the second AAA in the referendum of December 1938. To confirm the democratic nature of crop controls, the law required tobacco growers to renew their commitment to the program periodically. Since 1933, controls had been extended year by year based on an annual grower referendum. Officials set the referendum on the 1939 crop for 10 December 1938. Weeks before the vote, agricultural leaders knew the program was in trouble. Growers' discontent aroused by delayed allotments, poundage quotas, and lower prices had accumulated throughout the Bright Belt. Fearful that irate growers would throw the baby out with the bathwater, Clarence Poe made an extraordinary radio address from Raleigh on 7 December. Acknowledging that the program was flawed, Poe nonetheless urged growers to support the principle of crop control while continuing to press for improvements in the program.[17]

Although a solid majority—57 percent—voted to continue crop controls in 1939, this fell short of the required two-thirds majority. Indeed, it was a far cry from the 95-plus percent who supported controls in the desperate autumn of 1933.[18] South Carolina was no exception. Returns from the Pee Dee were comparable with those from other Bright Leaf areas: 56 percent for continuing crop controls and 44 percent against. As Bright Leaf growers faced the 1939 season, there would be no marketing quotas, no acreage allotments, no government support. Growers were on their own again.[19]

Reformers' worst fears were realized in the spring of 1939 when a tobacco crop of two million acres—a record that still stands—was planted in the tobacco states. Favorable weather combined with improved cultivation techniques brought forth an unprecedented harvest of 1.8 billion pounds. The Pee Dee crop of 1939—133 million pounds—set a production record that stood for many years.[20] When markets opened sharply lower, no one was surprised. South Carolina leaf averaged fourteen cents on opening day, down 35 percent from the year before. Though disappointed by lower prices, growers took some comfort in the size of their crop, hoping to compensate for lower margins with sheer volume. Such speculations soon became moot, however, when events in Europe overtook the tobacco industry.

At the outbreak of World War II in September 1939, the British government ordered the Imperial Tobacco Company to suspend purchases of American leaf immediately. Imperial already held more than three years' supply of tobacco, and the British War Cabinet wisely ordered it to draw on this massive inventory and conserve foreign exchange. On 8 September 1939, a week after German divisions rolled into Poland, Imperial announced its withdrawal from American tobacco markets.[21]

This was a serious blow to tobacco growers. Not only was Imperial a major buyer, but by concentrating purchases in the expensive grades, it wielded even greater influence on leaf markets than its proportional share. Simply put, Bright Leaf growers and warehousemen were facing the terrifying prospect of selling the largest crop yet produced in a market bereft of its best customer. Moreover, Imperial's withdrawal occurred early in the marketing season when most of the crop was still in farmers' hands. A collapse of the tobacco market surpassing even the disaster of 1933 was all too likely under the circumstances.[22]

Imperial's Friday announcement gave tobacco interests the weekend to find a way out of their predicament. Warehousemen and growers along with state and federal agents hastily formed an ad hoc committee to face the crisis. Knowing a permanent solution would take time, their first priority was to give everyone some breathing space. Warehousemen prudently offered to conduct Monday sales to clear their floors and then close indefinitely. Meanwhile, harvesting and curing would continue. But with barns and packhouses filling, delay worked against the farmer.[23]

Everyone agreed that the problem was beyond the resources of the industry and only government could save the situation. The Department of

Agriculture stood ready to help, but without a marketing contract with growers there was no legal framework for federal intervention. USDA attorneys advised that only by reestablishing a formal relationship with government by approving a marketing agreement for the next year could growers expect help now. A second referendum, this time to revive crop controls, was set for three weeks later.[24]

Reformers mounted a vigorous campaign to persuade tobacco growers to save themselves by giving crop controls a second chance. Analysis of the December referendum confirmed Clarence Poe's judgment that dissenting growers were dissatisfied with some of the program's features, not with the principle of crop control itself. USDA attorneys began revising the troublesome sections. Meanwhile, everyone with a stake in the tobacco business—warehousemen, merchants, USDA officials, county agents, and agriculture teachers—joined in urging farmers to approve controls for the 1940 crop.[25]

The Clemson Extension Service and USDA agents sponsored grower meetings throughout the Pee Dee. Black farmers were invited and attended meetings along with whites. Speakers informed anxious growers that objectionable features of the 1938 program had been purged from the new plan. For example, the unpopular poundage quotas had been scrapped, and allotments would henceforth be specified by acreage only. A grower's marketing quota thus became the amount of tobacco he could grow on his allotment.[26]

Scheduling problems were also addressed. In the future, growers were told, they would receive their marketing quotas no later than December, allowing them ample time to prepare their plantings. Significantly, small growers were given modest increases in their allotments. This revision corrected some inequities in the allotment system and paid political dividends as well. Small growers outnumbered larger ones, and their support was critical. With these obstacles removed, growers' enthusiasm for reviving their partnership with the New Deal gained momentum.[27]

Although dissenting voices continued to be heard, they were fainter. Pee Dee newspapers urged farmers to revive their commitment to crop control. Palmer Johnson of the *Marion Star* warned his readers that "voting against control will be committing economic suicide."[28] Recognizing their own stake in the outcome, local businessmen joined the chorus urging control. The day before the referendum, Pee Dee newspapers carried a double-page advertisement urging Bright Leaf growers "for their own good and the common good" to restore crop controls. In the *Marion Star,* the advertisement was underwritten by thirty businesses including three banks, the Chevrolet dealer, and the Coca-Cola bottler. It concluded with the warning, "United we stand; divided we fall!"[29]

Given the grim prospects tobacco growers faced without government intervention, the forceful education campaign was probably unnecessary. Still, reformers knew from bitter experience that farmers were tragically prone to act against their own interests. In this case, however, the combination of dire circumstances, an improved program, and the comprehensive effort to sell it was overwhelming. The flue-cured tobacco states approved the new contract by far more than the necessary two-thirds majority. Eighty-nine percent of Pee Dee tobacco growers endorsed the new program. Ironically, many black farmers who had never seen the inside of a voting booth were encouraged by their white neighbors to participate in the 1939 grower referendum.[30]

As soon as Bright Leaf growers agreed to limit their 1940 crop in accordance with AAA guidelines, government moved swiftly to stabilize the market. Acting through the Commodity Credit Corporation (CCC), the federal government agreed to fund Imperial's leaf purchases for the 1939 season. The CCC held title to the tobacco, and the leaf was stored under USDA supervision. Imperial had the option to take delivery anytime at cost plus 1.5 percent. Under this plan, Imperial could stay on the market and purchase tobacco according to its requirements, and tobacco growers could receive their money in the usual way.[31]

Warehouses reopened and sales proceeded smoothly. There was still a huge crop on hand, and some tobacco had suffered during the month-long market holiday. Nevertheless, prices hovered around fifteen cents, and Pee Dee farmers received $19.5 million for their 1939 crop. Though less than 1938, it was more than anyone had dared hope for a crop of unprecedented size. Certainly, returns were greater than growers would have received had they not restored production limits and prudently allowed government to rescue them. For the second time in six years, direct federal intervention in a marketing crisis had saved tobacco growers.

Rejection of production controls on the 1939 crop was unique in the partnership of tobacco growers and government. Chastened by their brush with ruin in 1939 and heedful of balancing supply and demand, growers never again strayed from the fold. After the Court's disapproval of the first

AAA and growers' disapproval of the second one, farmers and their advocates were eager to demonstrate to manufacturers their commitment to crop controls. In July 1940, growers voted to extend the program for three years rather than the customary year-by-year renewal. The long-term commitment paid dividends. Heartened by the growers' acceptance of crop controls, congressmen from tobacco states, led by Senator Alben Barkley of Kentucky, redefined the parity base period for tobacco. Changing the base period from 1919–29 to 1934–38 (when leaf prices were higher) raised parity rates by 14 percent.[32]

New Deal policies protected tobacco growers from their tendency to overproduce and from the manufacturers' tendency to exploit them, but it was the popularity of cigarette smoking that sustained the entire industry. The growth of cigarette consumption in the United States from the 1880s through the 1940s was extraordinary. Clearly, economics played a part. The nation's spectacular economic growth in the twentieth century surpasses that of any other period in American history, and greater incomes helped to put Camels and Luckies into smokers' pockets. Sometimes, however, observing an economy in retrenchment provides keener insight than in periods of growth. Analysis of consumer spending in the early 1930s is revealing, therefore, since the severe economic pressures of those years forced Americans to make hard choices.

Examining components of the nation's living standard during the Great Depression reveals that while all sectors declined, some suffered less and recovered faster than others. Table 12 shows the tenacious grip cigarettes had on the American public. In fact, the Depression influenced tobacco products less than virtually any category of consumer spending. Some reflection here will repay the effort. Between 1929 and 1933, dollar sales of tobacco products declined less—in some cases, much less—than outlays for the basic necessities of life.

And there are witnesses yet to be called. Although cigarette sales declined in 1931, 1932, and 1933, sales of smoking tobacco and rolling papers soared. For example, American Tobacco Company's Bull Durham brand enjoyed a tremendous revival, leaping from about eight million pounds per year to eighteen million during this period. The venerable muslin bags of granulated tobacco sold for five cents and included a supply of rolling papers. With a little patience, a smoker need spend only half the cost of dime

TABLE 12

Personal Expenditures by Category, 1929 and 1933

Category	1929	1933	Change (%)
Food	19,544[a]	10,865	−44
Clothing	10,633	5,266	−50
Housing	11,530	7,907	−31
Medical care	2,937	1,983	−32
Transportation	7,612	3,987	−47
Tobacco products	1,695	1,233	−27

Source: U.S. Department of Commerce, Bureau of the Census, *Historical Statistics of the United States: Colonial Times to 1970, Part 1* (Washington, D.C.: U.S. Government Printing Office, 1976), 319.
[a] Prices in millions of dollars.

brands and one-third the price of standard brands. If Americans could afford fewer manufactured cigarettes in those dark days, they consoled themselves by rolling their own.[33] In 1934, the cigarette industry not only regained all lost ground but exceeded its previous sales record by six billion units. No other industry can make such a boast.[34]

In the 1940s, prosperity returned to the Pee Dee. World War II stimulated a tremendous increase in smoking. Indeed, Pete Daniel has written that smoking seemed to fit the mood of the war years. From FDR's cigarette to Churchill's cigar to Stalin's pipe, the Allies faced the enemy through a haze of tobacco smoke.[35] As in World War I, cigarettes assumed a quasi-patriotic quality. And as General Pershing had praised tobacco then, so did his successors plead for it now. Asked how to spend $10,000 raised for the war effort, General Douglas MacArthur told employees of Wright Aeronautical, "The entire amount should be used to buy American cigarettes which, of all personal comforts, are the most difficult to obtain here." Indeed, smokes were considered so important to morale that cigarettes were packaged in "C" and "K" rations issued to combat troops in the field. By 1944, one-quarter of all cigarette production was going to the military.[36]

More civilians were smoking too, and they were smoking more than ever. And thanks to federal crop controls, tobacco growers could expect to profit from increased demand as never before. In the past, rising leaf prices had stimulated excessive production, which, in turn, depressed the market. Under the revised AAA program, however, government controls managed the growers' response to rising demand and kept supply and price curves near optimal levels. Thus tobacco growers could enjoy the increasing popularity of their product without igniting a cycle of self-defeating overproduction.

The rewards of this rational approach to agriculture were considerable. The crop of 1941, the first under the new three-year contract, returned the highest prices since 1918. The extent of the recovery is revealed by comparing inflation-adjusted values for the crops of 1941 and 1931. In 1931, Pee Dee farmers sold 69.8 million pounds for $3.5 million (1900); in 1941, they received $9.8 million (1900) for the same amount of tobacco. Thus reckoned in constant dollars, one pound of the 1941 crop was worth almost three pounds of 1931 leaf. And prosperity was just beginning. Propelled by increasing demand for cigarette tobaccos, the USDA increased tobacco allotments 10 percent the following year.[37] See Table 13.

The tobacco crop of 1942 was a major economic event in the Pee Dee. Even before the market opened, growers were optimistic. The quality of the 1942 crop was excellent, and prices on bellwether Georgia markets were running nearly 50 percent above those for 1941. Merchants were optimistic as well. In market towns, shopkeepers were eager to hear the auctioneer's chant—and the ring of their cash registers. The *State* described the "festive atmosphere" of Pee Dee market towns as local businessmen pulled out all the stops to bring farm folks to town. For example, Lake City merchants sponsored a band concert, free movies, and a street dance to lure families into their shops.[38]

The optimism was justified. When sales began in August, enthusiastic reports poured in from around the region. Dillon reported "the best break in years" with prices twelve to fifteen cents above those in 1941. Pamplico had "the best opening in history," and Kingstree farmers were "jubilant" with prices there. At Timmonsville, tobacco prices were "sky high," the commercial district was "thronged with people," and "unprecedented business" was taking place.[39] As strong sales continued, the 1942 tobacco crop set several records in the Pee Dee. The yield of 1,075 pounds per acre,

TABLE 13
Bright Leaf Tobacco Production in South Carolina, 1939–1946

Year	Acreage (1,000s)	Poundage	Price (in cents per lb.)		Value ($1,000s)	
			current	(1900)[a]	current	(1900)
1939	142	133,480	14.6	(8.8)	19,488	(11,746)
1940	85	87,550	14.6	(8.7)	12,782	(7,617)
1941	81	69,660	24.8	(14.1)	17,276	(9,822)
1942	90	96,750	37.4	(19.2)	36,184	(18,576)
1943	92	86,480	38.9	(18.8)	33,641	(16,258)
1944	115	131,675	43.0	(20.5)	56,620	(26,993)
1945	128	139,520	43.9	(20.4)	61,249	(28,462)
1946	145	171,825	48.7	(20.9)	83,679	(35,911)

Source: South Carolina Agricultural Statistics Service, USDA National Agricultural Statistics Service (Columbia, 1992).

[a] Prices are reported in current and constant values with 1900 as the base year.

the average price of thirty-seven cents, and the crop's overall value of $36 million were all unprecedented. Even corrected for inflation, the crop of 1942 was worth almost double that of 1941.[40]

By 1944, demand for Bright Leaf had outstripped supply. Lucky Strike and Chesterfield could fill only 70 percent of their orders, and Camel smokers had to settle for about half the "humps" they wanted. The Big Four even suspended some minor brands so as to increase production of their sales leaders. "Voluntary" cigarette rationing began in some areas. Lines formed, carton sales ceased, and Camel smokers paid fifty cents a pack on the black market.[41] Clearly, a further production increase was justified, and tobacco allotments rose a substantial 25 percent.

Seeking to quell wartime inflation, the Office of Price Administration (OPA) set price ceilings on virtually all commodities and consumer goods. In 1943, the ceiling on flue-cured tobacco was forty-one cents. In 1944, growers and warehousemen lobbied the OPA to raise the ceiling to forty-three and a half cents per pound. In August, market openings were delayed a week to allow industry spokesmen time to plead their case in Washington. Although the OPA turned down their request, ceilings were raised to forty-five cents.[42] Indeed, tobacco buyers bid the limit for nearly everything. On opening day and for several days thereafter, farmers expressed surprise that tobacco companies were paying about the same for all grades of leaf. For example, only three cents separated "choice" from "fair" with one-cent increments for "fine" and "good."[43]

South Carolina tobacco growers received $56 million for their 1944 curings. The significance of such a sum is best appreciated in comparison with previous years. Measured in constant dollars, receipts for 1944 almost tripled 1941 and were three and a half times 1940 levels. Only wartime price ceilings kept leaf values from soaring even higher.[44] Records for production, price, and income were broken in 1945, and allotments were increased again for 1946. That year, proceeds topped $83 million—another record—and more than doubled what Pee Dee farmers had hailed as a great year in 1942.[45]

Production costs were also rising. By 1944, Pee Dee farmers were experiencing labor shortages. Despite record high prices, many warehousemen reported that tobacco was slow coming to market in part because of farm labor shortages. Not only were many Pee Dee farm hands leaving for military service, but good-paying defense jobs in Charleston, Wilmington, and other cities lured many more. Tobacco growers offered record wages to keep pace.[46]

They could well afford it. Although costs of producing tobacco inched upward during the war, expenses came nowhere near matching the growers' spectacular rise in income. In spite of inflation, tobacco farmers enjoyed prosperity unknown since 1918 and benefited more from the exigencies of war than producers of most other commodities. In 1943, the Office of Price Administration found that tobacco prices had risen nine times faster than costs, the second highest ratio of the thirty-four commodities studied. Leaf prices failed to reach parity only in 1941, and then by only six-tenths of a cent. By 1943, parity objectives had been exceeded by a healthy 19 percent.[47] Thus tobacco not only recovered its purchasing power during the war but reached value levels that have never been surpassed. Reckoned in constant dollars, the period 1944–48 returned the greatest real values for flue-cured tobacco in the twentieth century (see Appendix table "Bright Leaf Tobacco Production in South Carolina").[48]

A driving force behind rising leaf prices and expanding acreage was burgeoning demand for cigarettes. Higher wartime wages also played a part. Americans enjoyed greater incomes in the 1940s, and some of their earnings were literally going up in smoke. Vigorous advertising coupled with jittery wartime nerves also helped propel cigarette sales to record levels. Seizing the moment, the Big Four launched powerful advertising campaigns linking their brands to the war effort: "Our Fighting Men Rate the Best. Keep 'em Smoking—Chesterfield!" "On the Assembly Line, On the Front Line, Camel's the Favorite." Most memorable was "Lucky Strike Green Has Gone to War."[49] Some of the green was going into growers' pockets as well. Of the USDA's six "basic commodities," only tobacco increased in total acreage every year of the war, gaining a half-million acres between 1941 and 1945.[50]

Exports also played a role in increasing tobacco production and prosperity. Although dollar shortages and wartime priorities tended to inhibit tobacco purchases by foreign countries, the Lend-Lease program financed leaf sales to friendly nations irrespective of their ability to pay. Sales under Lend-Lease accounted for 46 percent of Bright Leaf exports during the war. While some observers questioned the wisdom of dedicating ever greater resources to producing a nonfood crop in wartime, the increases were fully justified by rising demand both at home and abroad. Despite substantial enlargement of tobacco production during the war, the nation's leaf inventories actually declined between 1940 and 1945.[51]

After the war, American farmers continued to benefit from government paternalism. Recalling the painful adjustment farmers suffered when crop prices plunged after World War I, Congress thoughtfully provided a safety net. The Steagall Amendment was characteristic of government largesse to agriculture in the postwar period. It protected farmers from a postwar depression by supporting commodity prices at 90 percent of parity for two years after the war was officially declared to be over. To aid farmers even further, President Harry Truman waited until 31 December 1946—sixteen months after V.J. Day—before starting the clock. Before this special protection expired in December 1948, Congress adjusted parity levels upward to reflect price increases during the war.[52]

In the late 1940s, Bright Leaf tobacco growers continued to embrace crop controls, and an obliging Congress continued to reward them. The Agricultural Act of 1949 set support levels for leaf tobacco that guaranteed minimum prices for growers who agreed to limit production. To administer the crop control/price support program, the Flue-Cured Tobacco Cooperative Stabilization Corporation was chartered as a government-sponsored grower cooperative. Bright Leaf growers joined by purchasing one share of stock for a nominal price of $5 and renewing their existing contract for three years. The stated purpose of the stabilization co-op was to provide growers with an orderly marketing program that eliminated drastic price fluctuations and "to protect the grower's interests, providing him with a guaranteed floor of 90 percent of parity in any part of the flue-cured belt."[53] The flue-cured tobacco regions were divided into ten geographical districts with the Pee Dee designated as District 3. Pee Dee tobacco growers elected Joe Blount of Loris to represent them on the co-op's Board of Directors.[54]

Under the stabilization co-op, growers continued to receive acreage allotments and market their leaf as usual. The tobacco was graded on the warehouse floor. Each grade was preassigned a support price based on current parity rates. Of course, better quality leaf was supported at higher levels than less desirable grades. If a pile of tobacco failed to bring the support price at auction, the leaf "went under loan," that is, the co-op bought the tobacco from the grower for the support price. Co-op purchases were funded by loans from the Commodity Credit Corporation. The co-op stored the leaf until it could be sold and the loan repaid.[55]

The tobacco program was expected to be self-supporting, and because leaf prices tended to rise, tobacco going under loan did not usually incur a loss. Some spoiled or otherwise unsalable leaf was charged off from time to time, however, and co-op financing was provided at below market rates by a government agency. Another indirect subsidy included free grading services provided by the Department of Agriculture. Therefore, the crop control/price support program for flue-cured tobacco entailed substantial expense to taxpayers for many years.[56]

Although price supports were linked to continued approval of USDA marketing quotas, the program did not want for grower support. Encouraging tobacco farmers to remain loyal to this highly profitable relationship was preaching to the choir; they were only too happy to comply. Growers renewed their commitment to crop controls in 1949, 1952, and 1955. Approval rates never fell below 90 percent. At last, solidarity among tobacco growers could be taken for granted.[57]

Government response to the farm crisis of the 1930s brought important changes to the South and the Pee Dee region. New Deal farm policies greatly enlarged government's role in American agriculture. Laissez-faire policies of the 1920s allowed irresponsible overproduction by growers to be exploited to an almost predatory extent by manufacturers. Growers' attempts to discipline themselves failed. Even the enthusiastic support of state and local government could not provide the necessary framework for reform. Only the overarching power of the federal government could restore equity. In essence, Congress imposed discipline on the tobacco industry from seedbed to cellophane. Only the national government could set and enforce production controls in every state. Washington could also compel the cooperation of stubborn manufacturers by threatening them with punitive licenses, audits, and fines.

Federal intervention in tobacco production and marketing in the 1930s helped to stabilize agriculture as a vital component of national recovery. Government's expanded role in agriculture in those years is consistent with Washington's broader involvement in the economic life of the nation as a whole. Though vulnerable to charges of paternalism, imposing discipline on a disorderly sector of the economy is not unlike, say, withholding Social Security contributions from current earnings, another legacy of the New Deal commonly accepted as necessary and proper.

By the late 1940s, Pee Dee tobacco growers were truly on the road to prosperity. Conceived in the crises of depression and war, the federal tobacco program was evolving into a long-term partnership of growers and government. The expansion of the crop control program to include price supports revealed the political clout tobacco growers were acquiring. Indeed "the program," as growers came to call it with near reverence, would become a familiar fixture of American politics in the 1950s and beyond.

*Driving the tobacco farmer out of business
isn't the answer.*
WENDELL BERRY, "OUR TOBACCO
PROGRAM," 1992

All we got to look to is tobacco.
MATTIE MACK, TOBACCO GROWER,
1998

8 Advance, Retreat, and Retrenchment, 1950–1990s

THE 1950S were the golden age of the golden leaf. Propelled by prosperity and powerful advertising, demand for cigarettes soared, and Pee Dee tobacco growers worked hard to supply the raw material. American agriculture was undergoing profound technological change as well. As industry returned to peacetime production in the late 1940s, farmers poured wartime profits into inexpensive, mass-produced farm machinery. Gasoline- and diesel-powered tractors were nearly universal by 1950, dramatically multiplying the horsepower available even to small farmers. Moreover, implements and attachments enabled tractors to serve in a greater range of roles.

Chemical technologies kept pace with mechanical ones. From field research stations came fertilizers custom-blended for specific soils. From laboratories came pesticides, fungicides, and herbicides to control plant pests and diseases. Genetically engineered seed enabled farmers to grow bigger, healthier plants. And crop science departments and extension services at Clemson and North Carolina State enabled farmers essentially to grow on order to meet buyers' requirements. All contributed to greater yields and profits for tobacco growers.[1]

The political underpinnings of the Bright Leaf culture were as vital as the new technologies. Government-sponsored crop controls and price supports virtually guaranteed tobacco growers a profit. Indeed, the land-bound tobacco allotment became a valuable franchise to landowners. And as the profitability of tobacco farming increased, so did the value of the tobacco allotment. In his excellent study of the federal tobacco program in North Carolina, Anthony Badger found that farms with tobacco allotments appreciated twice as fast as farms without them. Understandably, the tobacco allotment became an important factor in evaluating tobacco farms. Lenders were quick to recognize this new source of value, and they assessed tobacco allotments along with lands and buildings in appraising tobacco farms.[2]

Obviously, greater profitability and enhanced land values gave tobacco growers better access to credit. Before government regulation, the boom-or-bust nature of tobacco farming had made bankers nervous, and growers were forced back on the limited and sometimes usurious credit resources of supply merchants. But government-sponsored crop controls and price supports made farm credit good business for lenders. Tobacco growers' dependable cash flow and appreciating land values provided the credit resources to mechanize and consolidate Pee Dee agriculture in the 1950s and 1960s.

Crop controls had other benefits as well. Bright Leaf growers also saved on certain capital expenditures. With less tobacco to cure, farmers needed fewer curing barns. In fact, smaller farmers may have derived proportionally greater benefit from these savings than their more prosperous neighbors. Although such trends are difficult to confirm, there is anecdotal evidence that the number of active curing barns peaked in the late 1940s. Subsequent expenditures for curing facilities went mostly to upgrade or replace existing barns rather than to increase their numbers.[3] In any event, to whatever extent crop controls lowered expenses and rechanneled capital outlays, profits grew apace.

Tobacco farmers also benefited from federal commodity and conservation programs through more intelligent use of their soils. From 1936 onward, Soil Conservation Service and AAA marketing contracts required that lands withdrawn from tobacco production be dedicated to soil-building crops, food, and fodder.[4] These restrictions encouraged farmers to confine tobacco plantings to their best lands and devote idle acres to growing things they had formerly bought. Of course, the notion of "living at home" had been heeded by some, but constraints placed on acres "rented" by the government focused farmers' attention on expedient land use more sharply than ever.[5] Therefore, the revised AAA and its successors compelled many farmers who had not done so before to diversify. The 1949 Census of Agriculture confirms that greater livestock populations and more acreage were devoted to food crops in Pee Dee counties. This changed land use doubtless improved the diets of many in ways larger incomes alone did not.[6]

Fewer acres of tobacco also required less labor. Though difficult to measure, this side effect of crop controls must not be underestimated. Traditional tobacco farming was very labor-intensive. Before harvesting and curing were automated in the 1970s, the work routine was especially arduous. Throughout July and August, curing barns often required attention until late at night. The grower could thus be deprived of rest during the most physically demanding weeks of the year. Grower families welcomed any amelioration of this brutal regime as an improvement in their living standard.

The Bright Leaf crop control/price support program that evolved in the 1950s and 1960s had implications not clearly foreseen by New Deal policymakers in the 1930s. Crop controls and price supports basically assured even mediocre farmers a profit and more capable ones a real chance for prosperity. One reason for the high level of profitability was the way allotments were defined. Throughout the 1950s and early 1960s, marketing quotas were specified by the acre and price supports by the pound. Thus growers could profit from literally every leaf they could urge from their allotment. Obviously, the acreage allotment provided a powerful incentive to increase yields. From the record 1,075 pounds per acre set in

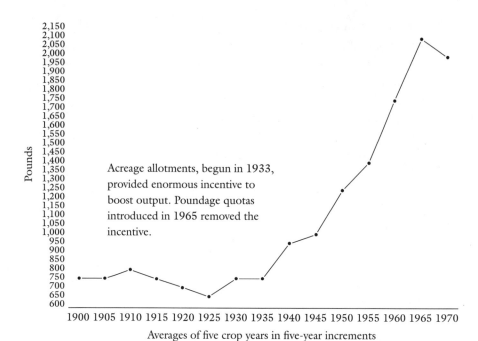

Pounds

Acreage allotments, begun in 1933, provided enormous incentive to boost output. Poundage quotas introduced in 1965 removed the incentive.

1900 1905 1910 1915 1920 1925 1930 1935 1940 1945 1950 1955 1960 1965 1970

Averages of five crop years in five-year increments

FIGURE 3
Five-Year Averages, Yields per Acre, Bright Leaf Tobacco in South Carolina,
1900–1970

1942, yields more than doubled, reaching 2,200 pounds per acre by 1964 (see Figure 3).

The spectacular rise in output per acre, at first welcomed by tobacco growers, ultimately threatened to upset the balance of supply and demand that ensured their prosperity. Pressures were mounting on both sides of the equation. On the supply side, the incentive to increase yields of open-ended acreage allotments not only encouraged overproduction but lowered quality as well. On the demand side, changes in cigarette manufacture reduced the amount of tobacco in a package of cigarettes. The popular filter-tipped brands introduced in the 1950s contained less tobacco than traditional unfiltered cigarettes.[7]

By the late 1950s, more and more tobacco was failing to bring the support price, and co-op leaf inventories were rising. To counter this trend, the secretary of agriculture ordered allotment reductions. But acreage cuts were at best a temporary solution. The urge to compensate for smaller allotments with greater yields proved irresistible to most farmers. They planted the broad-leaf Hicks variety that grew over six feet tall; they set plants closer together and applied a ton of fertilizer per acre; they side-dressed with concentrated nitrogen and potassium supplements. After a brief decline in the early 1960s, co-op stocks resumed their upward trend, passing one billion pounds in 1965. Storage and maintenance costs increased apace. Finally, in 1965 the USDA imposed poundage quotas in addition to acreage allotments. Poundage quotas controlled production more positively, and tobacco growers were no longer tempted to sacrifice quality for quantity.[8]

Tobacco farmers greeted poundage quotas with mixed feelings. Allotments specified in pounds had been imposed only once before—on the ill-fated crop of 1938—and were so unpopular they were withdrawn after one season. Moreover, shortsighted growers resented anything that capped their leaf output. As long as allotments were defined in acres only, growers viewed steadily increasing yields as a challenge to be met. But popular or not, poundage quotas saved the tobacco program and preserved the golden leaf's purchasing power remarkably well. Indeed, valued in constant dollars, tobacco prices varied little from the 1950s through the 1970s. As Figure 4 reveals, the line from 1949 to 1979 is virtually flat.

The 1960s brought other important changes to the tobacco program. When the original allotments were granted in 1933, tobacco production was frozen geographically. Therefore, growers wishing to expand could do so only by purchasing farms with tobacco allotments. This presented a host of problems. Some retiring growers were willing to sell their farms, but many resisted, preferring to hold on to lands that had sometimes been in their families for generations. But even when farms could be purchased, existing laws required that tobacco be grown on the farm where the allotment resided. This regulation posed a severe deterrent to consolidation since farms being worked by the same operator could be miles apart. Moving labor and equipment from farm to farm during the busy season was a logistical nightmare.[9] This regulation hobbled buyers and sellers alike. Logistical considerations tended to limit expansionists to their immediate neighborhoods while growers wishing to retire often had little choice but to sell in a very limited market.[10]

Another compelling reason to revise the crop control program was that allotment reductions had a damaging effect on small farmers. Acreage cuts in the 1950s had rendered many small tobacco farms uneconomical. Nevertheless, these small landowners wished to benefit from their allotments even though they were forced to seek part-time employment off the farm. At the same time, expansionists wanted to consolidate tobacco acreage into larger, more efficient units. Consolidation made good economic sense and had the further advantage of being politically expedient. The solution was the lease and transfer plan. Beginning in 1961, tobacco allotments could be leased and transferred between farms in the same county. Production could be consolidated into more economical units, and inactive farmers could profit from their tobacco allotments without planting a crop or selling their land. Lease income from tobacco allotments soon became an important boon to landowners in the Pee Dee.[11]

Consolidation proceeded slowly at first, but by the 1970s it was gaining momentum. Pee Dee tobacco farms became fewer and larger. Between 1974 and 1992, the number of tobacco farms in the Pee Dee declined by 70 percent.[12] Meanwhile, average tobacco acreage on surviving farms more than tripled, rising from eleven acres to thirty-five, and average output per farm rose from twenty-three thousand to seventy-nine thousand pounds. Before 1970, small tobacco farms were the rule; by 1990, they were the exception. Farms with fewer than nine acres of tobacco fell from 60 percent of the total to only 19 percent. At the same time, farms planting more than thirty-five acres rose from a mere 6 percent to 43 percent. There have been demographic consequences as well. Since black-owned tobacco farms were mostly in the small to mid-size range, the exit of African Americans from the culture has been disproportionately greater than that of whites.[13]

Consolidation helped to modernize tobacco farming in the Pee Dee by concentrating the marketing quota into units large enough to make new technologies practical. Before 1970, tobacco farming was only half mechanized. It had undergone a round of mechanization after World War II, but the technology of the 1940s modernized some tasks while leaving others unchanged. For example, tractors did the plowing and planting, but tobacco was still harvested by hand, one leaf at a time. The curing apparatus was upgraded from wood-fueled furnaces to kerosene burners, but such traditional tasks as handing and stringing were unchanged.

In the 1970s, however, a second wave of modernization swept the Bright Leaf culture. Reliable harvesting machines and oven-like bulk curing barns eliminated many labor-intensive tasks and improved curing efficiency. The new technologies saved farmers considerable fuel and labor costs and quickly paid for themselves on larger farms where economies of scale made them practical. For instance, mechanization reduced the labor required to harvest and cure Bright Leaf by more than half, from 6.4 hours per hundred pounds to less than 3 hours. As tobacco farming consolidated in the 1970s, cost-effective leaf harvesters and bulk curing barns became commonplace. By 1991, only 2 percent of Pee Dee tobacco was harvested manually.[14]

Just as consolidation made mechanization practical, so mechanization drove consolidation. Because profits from the new technology escalated with the scale of production, expansion-minded growers had an incentive to pursue marketing quota aggressively. As more growers attempted to lease quota, however, demand bid up the price. Government lending agencies and shortsighted bankers also fueled the inflation of quota lease rates in the 1970s. Unsound lending policies enabled some would-be expansionists to seek quotas, driving rates ever higher. Although this trend benefited allotment holders in the short term, it temporarily pushed quota lease rates beyond reasonable levels. This tended to penalize well-established farmers and favored less responsible operators who had nothing to lose. Predictably, many of the latter defaulted, and Pee Dee bankers emerged from the 1970s sadder and wiser.[15]

By the early 1980s it was clear to tobacco growers that the bloom was off the rose. After holding steady for thirty years, real values of leaf tobacco dropped sharply in the 1980s. For the first time in decades, current leaf prices failed to keep pace with inflation (see Figure 4). In 1990, the real value of a pound of Bright Leaf tobacco fell to 10.1 cents (1900), the lowest in fifty years. The inflation-adjusted value of the 1990 crop to South Carolina growers was only $11.1 million (1900), less than one-third that of 1955.[16] Declining real values cast in sharp relief the gap between large and small producers. Lower production costs enabled mechanized operators to enjoy considerable advantages in a soft market while declining purchasing power squeezed small growers ever tighter. In the 1980s, mounting pressures forced many small and middle-sized tobacco growers to sell or lease their farms and tobacco allotments.

While tobacco growers lost ground to inflation in the 1980s, manufacturers more than kept pace. Between 1980 and 1985, manufacturers' inflation-adjusted net profits after taxes rose from $207 million (1900) to $267 million (1900). And their rates of return increased as well. For the ten

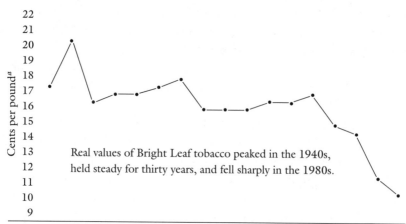

FIGURE 4

Bright Leaf Tobacco Prices in South Carolina, Three-Year Averages, 1943–1991

[a] Prices are reported in constant dollars with the year 1900 as a base.

years ending in 1985, tobacco companies' annual returns on shareholders' equity rose from 15 to 21 percent.[17] Even more spectacular was the manufacturers' expanding share of the consumer dollar. Cigarette price hikes coupled with flat leaf prices in the 1980s swelled manufacturers' already bloated margins. In 1980, manufacturers received 37 percent and farmers 7 percent of expenditures for tobacco products. By 1991, manufacturers were retaining fifty cents and growers only three cents of the retail dollar.[18]

Demographic changes compounded technological and economic ones. The rural exodus that began in the 1930s accelerated in the 1940s and 1950s. World War II played a major role in the diaspora. High-paying wartime jobs lured young men and women off the farm. Though some drifted back after the war, many did not, preferring to find a permanent place in the booming postwar economy. Understandably, the sons and daughters of the tenant class showed little interest in reentering agriculture at its lowest tier. In the prosperous decades after World War II, so many young people left Pee Dee agriculture that the ancient cycle of one generation following another into tenantry ended at last. Very few persons born after 1945 ever held tenant status as adults.[19]

The consolidation and mechanization of agriculture further hastened the decline of sharecropping and tenantry in the Pee Dee. As quota leasing merged traditional farms into modern ones, fewer hands were needed to make a crop. For example, bulk curing eliminated handing and stringing, two labor-intensive tasks traditionally done by women. Reduced labor requirements dovetailed with a dwindling labor pool and rising wages. Indeed, pay rates for many tasks doubled during the 1970s. With the decline of tenantry, there were simply fewer willing hands to do the work. Mexican migrant workers soon filled the need for seasonal labor in the tobacco fields and warehouses of the region.[20]

The civil rights revolution of the 1960s quickened the pace of black out-migration from the rural Pee Dee. After generations of toiling in the white man's fields as sharecroppers and tenants, thousands of African Americans shook the dust from their feet and moved to town. Of course, out-migration was not new to the Pee Dee—blacks had been moving north for decades—but the demise of Jim Crow enabled blacks to take greater advantage of improving opportunities closer to home. By the 1960s, most towns in the Pee Dee hosted one or more small industries eager to hire people accustomed to hard work. By the 1990s, Pee Dee towns and suburbs were populated with men and women of both races, reared on tobacco farms, who shared the memories and work ethic of the Bright Leaf culture.[21]

With the possible exception of alcohol during Prohibition, no consumer product in American history has experienced so spectacular an eclipse in public perception as cigarettes. For decades, cigarette smoking was viewed by most Americans as acceptable, even fashionable. By the early 1950s, however, evidence was accumulating that cigarette smoking caused cancer, heart disease, and a host of other health problems. During the last third of the twentieth century, increasing awareness of smoking-related illness gradually reversed the fashionable image of cigarettes. Far from the chic trend-setters of the 1940s and 1950s, cigarette smokers became increasingly isolated and stigmatized. Smoking regressed from a vogue to a vice.

Ironically, the retreat of the Pee Dee tobacco culture in the 1980s and 1990s is attributable to a reversal of the same trend that fastened it there a century earlier. Simply put, fewer people smoke. Per capita cigarette consumption in the United States peaked in the mid-1960s and has since declined sharply. In 1965, 42 percent of the nation's adult population smoked cigarettes; by 1990, only about 25 percent were smokers.[22] Objections to smoking are nothing new. From James I's "Counterblaste" of 1604 to the First Lady's banishment of tobacco from the White House in 1993, anti-smoking sentiment has flowed beneath the surface. It is fair to say, however, that public concerns about smoking and health have been increasing since the 1950s, and with good reason. Since the first definite links between cigarette smoking and lung cancer were published in 1953, the indictment against tobacco has grown very long.[23]

To say that government occupies an ambiguous position in the tobacco controversy risks understatement. Public Health Service research establishing a definite causal relationship between cigarette smoking and life-threatening illness was first published in Surgeon General Luther Terry's report *Smoking and Health* in January 1964. The report concluded that "cigarette smoking is a health hazard of sufficient importance in the United States to warrant appropriate remedial action."[24] Since then, the federal government has placed warnings on cigarette packages, banned cigarette advertising from radio and television, raised cigarette taxes, and severely restricted smoking on public conveyances and government property. Still, Congress has preserved most of the tobacco production control program.[25]

As the case against cigarette smoking mounted in the 1970s, the federal tobacco program came under increasing pressure. The wisdom, even morality, of maintaining costly programs that benefited tobacco growers were called into question. Seizing the high ground, critics charged that no policy operated at government expense and so hostile to public health should be continued. Congress responded with the No-Net-Cost Tobacco Program Act in 1982. Under the plan, tobacco growers and manufacturers reimburse government for expenses related to crop controls and price supports except administrative costs common to all crop programs.[26]

At first, growers bore the bulk of the no-net-cost program. Since 1985, however, the Consolidated Omnibus Budget Reconciliation Act has required manufacturers to share equally in program costs. In 1989, an additional sum, the tobacco marketing assessment, was levied to reduce the federal budget deficit. Beginning in 1994, leaf imports were assessed at a rate equal to the sum of fees paid by domestic producers and purchasers. Since 1982, growers' no-net-cost fees and assessments have ranged from twenty-five cents a pound to about two cents a pound.[27]

The no-net-cost program was an important change in the relationship of tobacco growers and government, and its impact was immediate and dramatic. For example, government expense for inspection and grading services fell from about $8 million per year to almost nil.[28] Besides paying for grading services, the no-net-cost program established a contingency fund to cover possible shortfalls in sales of leaf taken under loan. Before 1982, if sales of leaf held under loan did not equal borrowings, the deficit was written off as a cost of the program. Since 1982, shortages have been covered by the contingency fund. For example, in 1995 the contingency fund covered a deficit of $23 million. Program supporters have been quick to point out that before 1982 the tobacco price support program did entail expense to taxpayers, but losses on tobacco loans account for less than one-tenth of 1 percent of losses on all commodity support programs. The to-bacco program is by far the most economical major commodity program the government has undertaken.[29]

Shifting the burden of program costs to growers yielded unexpected re-sults. Since high support prices equaled high assessments, growers began to wean themselves from government largesse. Stung by very high assess-ments levied in 1985, growers requested that support levels be lowered. In 1986, support prices dropped, growers paid smaller assessments, and less tobacco went under loan. In fact, from 1987 through 1991, repayments of outstanding loans exceeded new loans by $1.6 billion. Ironically, lower sup-port prices made American tobacco more attractive to foreign customers and helped reverse the decline in Bright Leaf exports.[30]

In 1994, the Stabilization Cooperative's directors negotiated an extraor-dinary sale of its holdings to domestic manufacturers. Deliverable over sev-eral years, the buyout cleared a sizable backlog, reduced co-op leaf invento-ries, and placed the co-op on a firmer footing. Of course, storage costs for the smaller inventory dropped sharply as well. By the mid-1990s, the flue-cured tobacco program was operating very efficiently. Only 1.2 percent of the 1995 crop went under loan, the lowest in the co-op's fifty-year history.[31]

The no-net-cost plan protects taxpayers from losses on leaf taken under loan, but USDA administrative costs are not reimbursed. In the early 1990s, the federal government spent several million dollars per year administering the crop control/price support program and providing research, market-ing, and information services to tobacco growers. Subsidies of crop insur-ance premiums contributed to costs as well.[32] Although the residual ex-

pense of the tobacco program represents a tiny fraction (about one-fifth of
1 percent) of federal outlays for commodity price supports, assessments
could easily be adjusted to cover all costs associated with government tobacco programs. In 1995, no-net-cost fees of about 1 percent of the selling
price of flue-cured (and Burley) tobacco covered about two-thirds of all
tobacco-related costs. Since manufacturers match growers' contributions,
an additional cent or so per pound would fully fund all grower benefits.[33]

The no-net-cost plan has muted much criticism of the federal tobacco
program, yet philosophical opposition continues. Although emotion and
politics have tainted the rhetoric on both sides, some synthesis of the debate is possible. Opposition to the tobacco program can be distilled to a
single question: Given the harmful effects of cigarette smoking, is there any
legitimate reason for continued government sanction of tobacco production? To give this question the thought it deserves, one must consider what
outcomes opponents seek from ending the program and the probable consequences of doing so.

If the ultimate goal of program opponents is the cessation of cigarette
smoking by Americans, then scrapping the crop control/price support
program for tobacco would not accomplish that end. Indeed, it would not
prevent one cigarette from being manufactured or consumed. The American public is largely unaware of government agricultural policies, and altering them would have little influence on smoking behavior. The most
effective means of persuading smokers to quit is through antismoking education and higher cigarette taxes. Like most addictions, cigarette smoking
is relatively insensitive to price. Nevertheless, economists have determined
that for every 10 percent increase in cigarette prices, unit sales drop about
4.5 percent.[34]

Nor would ending federal crop controls reduce tobacco production.
Rather, abandoning the quota system would have the opposite effect; tobacco output would increase. The facts speak for themselves. The heart of
the tobacco program is production control. Currently, growers must own
or rent tobacco allotment in order to market tobacco. If quotas were abandoned, growers could plant as much as they wished, and production would
drift upward. Predictably, the selling price of leaf tobacco would decline.
Without price supports, leaf prices would drift downward toward world
market levels. Ironically, U.S. tobacco exports would likely increase. Price
supports have kept prices of American leaf above world market levels for
years, and lower prices would improve its competitive position.[35]

Who would benefit from abandoning crop controls? Obviously, manufacturers would reap the greatest rewards. Lower leaf prices have always equaled higher profits for tobacco companies. Although the cost of tobacco in a package of cigarettes contributes relatively little to its retail price, historically manufacturers have been quick to exploit both producers and consumers when the opportunity has arisen.[36] It may be worthwhile to recall the vigorous opposition manufacturers mounted to grower cooperatives in the 1920s and government crop controls in the 1930s to see where the companies perceive their interests to lie. Indeed, as recently as the 1980s, manufacturers capitalized on market conditions to augment their share of the consumers' tobacco dollar at the expense of growers.

Another beneficiary of abandoning crop controls would be growers who have historically leased all or most of the quota they plant. Expansionists pay considerable sums—as much as 25 percent of the selling price—to lease quotas, that is, for the right to grow tobacco. For some growers, quota leasing is their single greatest production cost. For them, lower leaf prices would be largely offset by not having to lease quota. Indeed, leaf prices could drop as much as 25 percent without affecting their bottom line.

A more competitive environment would also favor growers with the lowest production costs, that is, growers with the greatest commitment to automated harvesting and curing technologies. Without crop controls, large-scale, well-capitalized growers would likely grow tobacco on contract for manufacturers. Indeed, American manufacturers have been acquiring leaf on contract from growers in Brazil and Mexico for years.[37]

At the same time, however, lower prices would devastate small and mid-size farmers who have been planting their own allotments but lack the capital to expand. Since the 1930s, allotments have provided a more level playing field in the tobacco culture by helping small farmers stay profitable. If this leveling influence were lost, however, smaller growers unable to withstand price cuts sure to accompany unrestricted production would soon be forced out of business. Growers with the lowest costs of production would soon dominate the industry to the virtual exclusion of mid-size and smaller producers, and the consolidation of the Bright Leaf culture would likely accelerate.[38]

Another likely consequence of ending crop controls would be the disappearance of warehousemen, buyers, and auctioneers. Direct sales to manufacturers would surely bypass warehousemen to save sales commissions, auctioning fees, and handling costs. Although warehouse buildings could serve as temporary collection centers, contract sales would effectively end the traditional three-tiered tobacco marketing structure. Thousands of warehouse jobs in the tobacco states would be lost. Doubtless, the loss of sales facilities would deprive small growers of a convenient market for their leaf and hasten their exit from the culture.

Those who stand to lose most are retired growers, widows, and others who have heretofore received lease income from their tobacco allotments. Under the current program, the owner of a ten-acre allotment can expect lease income of about $8,000 per year. Moreover, the allotment can be sold for about $50,000. Thus the allotment owner would lose substantial income and capital value of his or her property. In summary, the crop control program for tobacco does not encourage cigarette smoking and ending it would not discourage smoking. Neither does it represent a significant cost to taxpayers. It only ensures that as long as tobacco is grown, it will be grown by those who have always grown it.[39]

Another threat to American tobacco growers is imported leaf. Worldwide production of Bright Leaf and Burley-type tobaccos increased substantially in the 1970s and 1980s. Indeed, since the 1960s American manufacturers have fostered tobacco production in the Third World, furnishing know-how and a ready market to novice growers in Asia, Africa, and South America. Abundant land and labor in these developing nations enable tobacco to be produced far cheaper than in the United States. For example, in 1996 Bright Leaf averaged $1.84 a pound in the United States, 93 cents in Brazil, and 77 cents in Zimbabwe.[40]

Predictably, more foreign leaf is going into American-made cigarettes. Leaf imports from Zimbabwe, for example, multiplied tenfold between 1987 and 1992.[41] For a brief period, U.S. tobacco growers were protected by the so-called domestic content law, a provision of the Omnibus Budget Reconciliation Act of 1993 that required that cigarette blends contain at least 75 percent American-grown leaf.[42] In 1995, however, this protection was revoked in compliance with the General Agreement on Tariffs and Trade. By 1997, foreign tobaccos accounted for 33 percent of U.S. cigarette production.[43]

The 1990s marked a century of Bright Leaf culture in South Carolina. The crop became a staple in the 1890s, peaked in the mid-

TABLE 14

Bright Leaf Tobacco Production in South
Carolina, by Decade, 1940s–1980s

Period	Absolute production (million pounds)	Relative production (1950s = 100)
1940–49	1,217.0	76.4
1950–59	1,592.7	100.0
1960–69	1,499.7	94.1
1970–79	1,459.1	91.6
1980–89	1,088.3	68.3

Source: South Carolina Agricultural Statistics Service;
USDA, National Agricultural Statistics Service
(Columbia, 1992).

twentieth century, and retreated in the 1980s (see Table 14). By 1993, tobacco production had fallen to the level of the late 1930s. The grower
population also dwindled. Facing allotment cuts, declining real values, and
pressures to "get big or get out," many growers chose the latter. As traditional Bright Leaf farms consolidated into large, capital-intensive enterprises, the economics and politics of tobacco also evolved. Fewer South
Carolinians depend on tobacco for their livelihood, and the prosperity of
market towns no longer hangs on the price of lugs and cutters. Still, if
tobacco growers are fewer, those who remain are more substantial.

Pee Dee tobacco growers in the 1990s face a complex challenge. While
pressures to diversify mount, tobacco farmers seeking an alternative cannot
simply plant something else. They are bound to tobacco in several ways.
Foremost is the crop's high value per acre. No other field crop comes close
to matching tobacco's income potential. For example, while tobacco occupied only 9 percent of cropland on producing farms in 1991, it yielded
70 percent of total income on those farms.[44]

Rising cotton prices in the early 1990s briefly revived interest in that
staple as an alternative to tobacco. (Admittedly, the prospect of King Cotton reclaiming his throne a century after tobacco usurped it has a certain
ironic appeal.) But while cotton gained ground, the white fiber still lagged
far behind the green leaf in value per acre. In 1993, South Carolina tobacco

growers produced 52,000 acres of Bright Leaf worth $184 million, or $3,538 per acre, while the state's cotton farmers harvested 198,000 acres of their staple worth $59 million, or $298 per acre. On the bottom line, an acre of tobacco is worth a dozen of cotton.[45]

Given the difference in value between the two crops, farmers simply cannot grow enough cotton to equal returns from tobacco. Nor should they try. Substantial increases in cotton production would surely force down prices of that commodity. After all, it was a cotton depression that drove Pee Dee farmers from that staple a century ago. The modest rise in cotton production in some Pee Dee counties in the 1990s may soften tobacco's decline, but it will not compensate for it.

Other alternatives to tobacco have limited appeal. Grains such as corn and soybeans can at best supplement a farmer's income or feed his animals. Few Pee Dee farmers have the acreage to compete with large-scale western and midwestern grain producers. Besides, income from corn and soybeans averaged only $250 per acre in the early 1990s. Raising chickens and turkeys on contract for meat processors, though profitable, is limited to relatively few individuals. Large-scale swine production has unpleasant environmental and social consequences and has encountered vigorous opposition in host communities.[46]

There are other obstacles to diversification, including growers' investments in tobacco-specific buildings and machinery. These assets have little value in used condition and cannot easily be exchanged for other equipment or adapted to other uses. Less tangible, perhaps, but still important is human capital. Tobacco farmers have accumulated valuable skills and experience that they are reluctant to abandon. Conversely, many tobacco growers, especially those middle-aged and older, often lack the education or other specialized skills needed to make a successful transition to another career.

Clearly, there is no magic bullet; no single crop will replace tobacco in the Pee Dee. Farmers will adapt their acres to a variety of uses. Some lands will leave agriculture altogether. Throughout the Pee Dee, hundreds of former tobacco fields have been reclaimed by forest. Moreover, as cities and suburbs expand, farmlands in the path of development will yield to new housing, shopping malls, manufacturing plants, and golf courses. Some farmers will lease their tobacco allotments to expansionists for cash and turn to other crops, including grains, vegetables, and livestock. Some will grow produce for grocery stores, restaurants, and farmers' markets. Others will combine crop and livestock production with seasonal or part-time jobs off the farm. Ironically, tobacco revenues have generated the capital that makes such diversification possible.[47]

In the 1990s, many tobacco growers have acquired a fundamentally different view of themselves, the tobacco industry, and the future. They are considering long-term solutions that are both pro-grower and pro-health. Best of all, some growers are distancing themselves from tobacco companies. Thoughtful growers recognize that there is a right side and a wrong side to the tobacco debate, and manufacturers are clearly on the wrong side. Just as clearly, the tobacco companies are not the growers' friends. They embrace growers only when they need to muster the greatest possible political clout to beat back federal sanctions. Manufacturers ask growers to defend their "common interests," yet growers get three cents of the consumers' dollar while manufacturers get fifty cents. Growers ask, How common is that? And even as the companies gather growers under their political tent, they foster tobacco production abroad that undermines American farmers. Thoughtful growers know the ultimate truth at the heart of the tobacco debate is that cigarettes hurt people. Will growers become martyrs to that truth? Or will they use their political leverage to make the best deal they can for themselves?

Various buyout plans have been considered, that is, cessation of the tobacco program with compensation for allotment holders. Some policy-makers have proposed sums as high as $8 per quota-pound to reimburse owners for lost lease income and depreciated capital value of land and equipment.[48] The situation is complex, however, and any solution must address human as well as capital issues. Some envision a kind of G.I. Bill for tobacco growers, a comprehensive plan to ease the transition from tobacco-centered economies to rewarding alternatives. The package could provide special tax incentives to refit former tobacco farms for other uses. Growers could be offered scholarships for higher education or vocational training. For those who continue to plant tobacco, cash payments could help growers adjust to the new economic landscape. Others—retirees, for example—could choose to receive payment in interest-bearing government bonds with staggered maturities. This option would provide financial stability to former growers while spreading the cost over several years. The plan could be funded through higher cigarette taxes and assessments on manufacturers.

Meanwhile, Pee Dee farmers continue to plant tobacco for its unrivaled value per acre, for despite the ironclad case against cigarettes, many people continue to smoke. And as long as people smoke, tobacco will be grown in the Pee Dee. The region's climate and soils place the Pee Dee among the world's best leaf-producing areas. Further, many Pee Dee tobacco growers have invested in expensive harvesting and curing equipment that has no other use. Last, Pee Dee farmers are highly skilled in growing tobacco and are unlikely to abandon the crop while it remains profitable unless they are offered an attractive alternative.

Changes in the federal tobacco program in the 1980s partially weaned growers from the high levels of price support they once enjoyed. If crop controls end, well-capitalized growers, no longer compelled to lease quota, will likely grow on contract for manufacturers. Chemical and mechanical technologies will continue to evolve, and growers will continue refining the production process. Economies of scale will be applied; unit costs will decline. Bright Leaf will not dominate the region's agriculture as it once did, but neither will it disappear.

The retreat of South Carolina's tobacco culture at the end of the twentieth century offers sharp contrast to earlier instances of decline. When tobacco disappeared in the 1690s and again about 1800, it was displaced by new crops showing greater possibilities. In the first instance, tobacco was displaced by rice; in the second, it yielded to cotton. Rising demand for these staples coupled with the comparative advantages of the culture areas fastened rice to the lowcountry and cotton to the backcountry. Obedient to the same economic laws, Bright Leaf entered the Pee Dee in the 1880s. The region's staples were in decline, and rising demand for cigarette tobaccos offered new possibilities for Pee Dee farmers. Compatible soils, a congenial climate, and a hardworking population raised the possibility to a certainty.

Such is not the case with the decline of Bright Leaf in the late twentieth century. Tobacco is not being supplanted by a crop showing greater possibilities; it is being undermined by the erosion of demand caused by health concerns. And no new crop is waiting in the wings. At this writing, the search for alternatives continues. The problem is finding a crop with comparable value per acre to enable tobacco growers to subsist on their modest holdings. Another contrast with previous declines is the persistence of the culture. When tobacco retreated in the 1690s and 1800s, it virtually disappeared. Now, however, significant amounts continue to be grown in South Carolina.

Since the 1960s, health concerns have added a new page to the ancient ledger of market forces. Certainly, not since Prohibition has a consumer product suffered such a reversal of fortunes. These concerns have forced a third and probably final retreat of the long green leaf. But in a larger sense, tobacco has been a very mixed blessing for the Pee Dee. As a staple crop, it was certainly better than what it replaced. Even so, few tobacco farmers ever got rich. And if Bright Leaf culture raised the living standard of the Pee Dee for nearly a century, cigarette smoking also shortened the lives of many of these same people.

In this respect, tobacco presents a moral quandary for Pee Dee farmers in the 1990s. For decades, cigarette smoking was acceptable, even fashionable. The tobacco industry was well respected, and tobacco farming carried no moral burden. Since the 1960s, however, increasing awareness of smoking-related illness has brought the entire industry—growers, warehousemen, and manufacturers—under a cloud. Producers have seen their product and profession retrospectively maligned. Generations of tobacco growers met a demand considered entirely respectable even as their product funneled a quarter-trillion current dollars into state and federal coffers.[49] Yet the same society, even some of the same individuals, who happily smoked for years and who made the cigarette a cultural icon, later accused the tobacco industry of being little better than drug pushers. Nevertheless, there seems to be broad public sympathy for tobacco farmers who have worked hard, played by the rules, and harmed no one.

While the justice of the charge and apportionment of blame can be debated, one thing is sure: Bright Leaf tobacco has lost its preeminence in the Pee Dee economy. Most of the region's farmers and their counterparts in other leaf belts must and will diversify. But though tobacco is down, it is not out. Although reduced, demand for tobacco will continue. And Pee Dee farmers will help meet that demand. A cadre of highly specialized and well-capitalized Pee Dee tobacco growers could survive the loss of crop controls and price supports.

In the 1990s, the Pee Dee observed a century of tobacco culture. Although the Bright Leaf ledger reveals debits as well as credits, perhaps the most valuable and lasting legacy of the Pee Dee's tobacco century is its people. The generations who toiled in fields, barns, and warehouses learned the virtue of work and the satisfaction of a task well and faithfully performed. The collective memory of the Bright Leaf culture runs deep in the Pee Dee, and respect for the region's agrarian past endures.

Appendix

Labor Contract of Chicora Wood Plantation, 18 January 1870

State of South Carolina
Georgetown County
Chicora Wood Plantation

Articles of Agreement between C. Petigru Allston, Agent for Mrs Adele Petigru Allston, and the Freedmen & women subscribed; witnesseth

Art-I The Freedmen & women subscribed, agree to hire themselves as Laborers on the aforesaid plantation for the year ending 31$^{\underline{st}}$ December 1870—to conduct themselves honestly & civilly, and to exact the same from their families; to perform any and all labor pertaining to said plantation that may be required of them by the said Allston or his Agent; to obey all orders, rules, and regulations for the government and for the peaceful and successful working of the plantation that are now or may hereafter be established by said Allston, his Agent or anyone appointed Agent in his place by Mrs Adele P. Allston until the 1$^{\underline{st}}$ day of January 1871.

Art-II They agree to perform the usual tasks on Rice Plantations as full or fractional Hands as they shall rate themselves under the direction of Foremen to be appointed by said Allston.

Art-III They agree to forfeit for each day's work lost to the plantation, one peck of Rough Rice for full hands, proportionally for fractionals—and if they absent themselves without permission or without being sick; for each day of such absence, one Bushel of Rough Rice; if absent more than once in this manner, or if disobedient, insubordinate or thieving, such offender shall be dismissed [from] the plantation with loss of all interest in the crop at the discretion of said Allston.

Art-IV They agree to care for all tools, implements, flats, boats, carts, & animals & and all things belonging to plantation that may be intrusted to their care, to return the same at the expiration of this contract, or if lost, destroyed or injured, the one so losing or injuring to pay the cost value of same.

Art-V They agree that a plantation Record of all work shall be kept by said Allston or his Agent which shall be evidence in court.

Art-VI They agree that if any extra work beyond their force is required by the crop, it shall be done, the payment to be advanced by said Allston & $\frac{2}{3}$ to be returned to him from that portion of the Crop coming to the Freedmen & women.

Art-VII They agree that the Rice resulting from the deductions for absence & sickness shall be Equally divided, one half to go to said Allston, one half to go to the Freedmen & women who have labored best.

Art-VIII In consideration of the above services faithfully performed C. P. Allston or any Agent of Mrs Allston agrees to divide the crop raised in the following proportions. To wit. 1ˢᵗ deduct *one fourth* for plantation Expenses. 2ⁿᵈ Deduct seed used in planting. 3ʳᵈ Divide remainder with the Freedmen *one half* for *them*, one half to Mrs Allston—their half to be divided according to the Plantation Book.

Art-IX They agree to do what ditching is required and to bear the expense of extra labor if such should be necessary. They agree to furnish one Watchman from their portion of the crop.

Art-X The said Allston also agrees that if they plant ten acres of rice land to the hand he will give them four months provisions of corn.

Jan 18ᵗʰ 1870

C Petigru Allston Agt Mrs A P Allston

Nelson Thompson

his Charles ✕ Gallant 1 mark	his Bowen ✕ Banon 1 mark
his Moses ✕ Lancet 1 mark	his January ✕ Banon 1 mark
his Sam ✕ Cash 1 mark	his Friday ✕ Rothmoller 1 mark
his Tobey ✕ Gallant 1 mark	his Moses ✕ Lancet Sr ¾ mark
his Job ✕ Mention 1 mark	her Hagar ✕ Grate ¾ mark
his Ancum ✕ Small 1 mark	her Patty ✕ Small ¾ mark
his Coleman ✕ McCants ¾ mark	his Johnny ✕ Cohen ¾ mark
her Henrietta ✕ Cohen ¾ mark	her Eve ✕ Grate ¾ mark
his Charles ✕ Cooper 1 mark	his Ephraim ✕ Green ½ mark

                    her
Elizabeth ✕ Lee ½ by Jan Banon
                  mark
                    her
     Diana ✕ Robertson ½ by Charles Cooper
                  mark
                    her
    Yaniky ✕ Gallant ¾
                  mark
                    her
      Rena ✕ Green ½
                  mark
                    his
Charles ✕ Robinson 1
                  mark
                    his
Solomon ✕ Casey 1
                  mark
                    his
      Micky ✕ Small ¾ by Scipio Small
                  mark
                    his
       Ben ✕ Keith
                  mark

                    her
Mazerium ✕ Walker ¾
                  mark
                    her
     Celia ✕ Alston 1
                  mark
                    her
  Rebecca ✕ Mention ¾
                  mark
                    his
     David ✕ Robertson 1
                  mark
                    his
    Harris ✕ Washington 1
                  mark
                    his
     Scipio ✕ Small 1
                  mark
                    her
Penelope ✕ Gallant ¾
                  mark

Bright Leaf Tobacco Production in South Carolina, 1900–1992

Year	Acreage (1,000s)	Poundage (1,000s)	Price (in cents per lb.)		Value of production ($1,000s)	
			current	(1900)[a]	current	(1900)
1900	28	21,280	7.0	(7.0)	1,490	(1,490)
1901	29	20,590	7.0	(6.9)	1,441	(1,421)
1902	34	28,050	7.0	(6.8)	1,964	(1,907)
1903	40	28,600	5.1	(4.8)	1,459	(1,373)
1904	13	10,920	8.2	(7.7)	895	(841)
1905	15	11,175	8.7	(8.2)	972	(916)
1906	13	8,840	10.5	(9.7)	928	(857)
1907	20	8,400	10.7	(9.5)	899	(798)
1908	24	19,680	10.0	(9.1)	1,968	(1,791)
1909	30	25,500	7.3	(6.7)	1,862	(1,709)
1910	25	19,750	8.6	(7.5)	1,698	(1,481)
1911	21	15,750	12.6	(11.1)	1,984	(1,748)
1912	35	27,650	10.9	(9.3)	3,014	(2,571)
1913	45	36,900	13.8	(11.6)	5,092	(4,280)
1914	47	35,250	9.7	(8.1)	3,419	(2,855)
1915	63	46,620	7.0	(5.8)	3,263	(2,704)
1916	42	27,300	14.0	(10.8)	3,822	(2,948)
1917	72	56,160	23.1	(15.1)	12,972	(8,480)
1918	88	64,240	31.0	(17.2)	19,914	(11,050)
1919	114	78,860	20.1	(9.7)	15,811	(7,650)
1920	98	66,150	23.8	(9.9)	15,744	(6,549)
1921	66	43,230	11.2	(5.2)	4,842	(2,248)
1922	66	43,560	20.5	(9.6)	8,930	(4,182)
1923	102	77,214	20.9	(10.3)	16,138	(7,953)
1924	94	47,530	16.2	(7.9)	7,700	(3,755)
1925	97	72,750	16.5	(7.9)	12,004	(5,747)
1926	81	57,915	23.6	(11.2)	13,668	(6,486)
1927	101	79,083	20.2	(9.7)	16,275	(7,671)
1928	148	84,360	12.7	(6.2)	10,714	(5,230)
1929	118	87,320	15.5	(7.6)	13,535	(6,636)
1930	116	98,600	12.0	(6.0)	11,832	(5,916)
1931	102	69,870	9.2	(5.1)	6,428	(3,563)
1932	68	39,440	11.3	(6.9)	4,457	(2,721)
1933	103	88,580	12.6	(8.1)	11,161	(7,175)
1934	72	56,880	21.6	(13.5)	12,286	(7,678)
1935	96	89,760	18.8	(11.5)	16,875	(10,322)

Year	Acreage (1,000s)	Poundage (1,000s)	Price (in cents per lb.)		Value of production ($1,000s)	
			current	(1900)[a]	current	(1900)
1936	90	73,350	19.9	(12.0)	14,597	(8,802)
1937	112	108,080	20.8	(12.1)	22,481	(13,078)
1938	104	98,800	22.2	(13.1)	21,934	(12,943)
1939	142	133,480	14.6	(8.8)	19,488	(11,746)
1940	85	87,550	14.6	(8.7)	12,782	(7,617)
1941	81	69,660	24.8	(14.1)	17,276	(9,822)
1942	90	96,750	37.4	(19.2)	36,184	(18,576)
1943	92	86,480	38.9	(18.8)	33,641	(16,258)
1944	115	131,675	43.0	(20.5)	56,620	(26,993)
1945	128	139,520	43.9	(20.4)	61,249	(28,462)
1946	145	171,825	48.7	(20.9)	83,679	(35,911)
1947	137	155,495	41.8	(15.7)	64,997	(24,413)
1948	104	131,560	50.3	(17.5)	66,175	(23,023)
1949	111	147,075	49.0	(17.2)	72,067	(25,297)
1950	114	150,480	54.3	(18.9)	81,711	(28,440)
1951	132	175,560	50.6	(16.3)	88,833	(28,616)
1952	132	172,920	51.9	(16.4)	89,745	(28,359)
1953	122	172,630	56.4	(17.6)	97,363	(30,383)
1954	126	148,050	49.0	(15.3)	72,544	(22,652)
1955	116	197,200	54.5	(17.0)	107,474	(33,524)
1956	102	173,400	52.4	(16.1)	90,862	(27,917)
1957	78	128,700	59.7	(17.8)	76,834	(22,909)
1958	76	131,100	59.9	(17.3)	78,569	(22,680)
1959	81	142,965	63.0	(18.1)	90,068	(25,867)
1960	80	147,600	61.5	(17.4)	90,774	(25,682)
1961	80	151,600	65.7	(18.4)	99,601	(27,894)
1962	84	190,260	61.1	(16.9)	116,249	(32,154)
1963	80	162,400	60.0	(16.4)	97,440	(26,663)
1964	72	156,240	60.0	(16.2)	93,744	(25,311)
1965	66	134,808	53.3	(14.1)	88,030	(19,008)
1966	69	127,305	69.1	(17.8)	87,968	(22,660)
1967	76	165,722	64.5	(16.1)	106,891	(26,681)
1968	63	122,383	66.4	(16.0)	81,262	(19,581)
1969	69	136,658	72.8	(16.6)	99,487	(22,685)
1970	68	141,075	71.9	(15.5)	101,433	(21,867)
1971	63	133,245	75.8	(15.7)	101,000	(20,919)
1972	62	131,130	85.3	(17.0)	111,854	(22,292)

(*continued*)

Year	Acreage (1,000s)	Poundage (1,000s)	Price (in cents per lb.) current	Price (in cents per lb.) (1900)[a]	Value of production ($1,000s) current	Value of production ($1,000s) (1900)
1973	67	132,660	86.9	(16.4)	115,282	(21,756)
1974	80	172,000	103.9	(17.6)	178,708	(30,272)
1975	90	189,000	99.5	(15.5)	188,055	(29,295)
1976	75	153,375	112.0	(16.5)	171,780	(25,307)
1977	68	138,720	123.3	(17.0)	171,042	(23,582)
1978	71	150,520	137.6	(17.6)	207,116	(26,492)
1979	57	117,705	141.5	(16.3)	166,553	(19,186)
1980	65	125,450	139.5	(14.1)	175,003	(20,448)
1981	68	148,580	165.5	(15.2)	245,900	(22,584)
1982	59	124,195	176.5	(15.3)	219,204	(19,002)
1983	54	112,860	180.9	(15.2)	204,164	(17,155)
1984	47	105,515	181.3	(14.6)	191,299	(15,405)
1985	43	98,900	172.7	(13.4)	170,800	(13,253)
1986	37	75,480	144.2	(11.0)	198,842	(8,303)
1987	42	94,080	160.7	(11.8)	151,187	(11,101)
1988	45	100,125	161.4	(11.4)	161,602	(11,414)
1989	48	103,680	166.3	(11.2)	172,420	(11,612)
1990	51	109,905	158.6	(10.1)	174,309	(11,100)
1991	51	111,180	171.5	(10.5)	190,674	(11,698)
1992	52	112,320	169.9	(10.1)	190,832	(11,393)

Source: South Carolina Agricultural Statistics Service, USDA National Agricultural Statistics Service (Columbia, 1992). Production data may vary slightly from South Carolina Department of Agriculture, Commerce, and Industries annual reports.

[a] Prices are reported in current and constant values with 1900 as the base year.

Costs of Producing One Acre of Tobacco, 1923

Cost items (labor at one dollar per day)	Cost per acre	Percentage of total cost
Preparing plant bed	$ 2.00	2.0
Fertilizer and seed for plant beds	.90	.9
Canvas for plant beds	.90	.9
Picking or weeding plant bed	.70	.7
Plowing tobacco land	3.00	3.0
Disking and harrowing land	1.00	1.0
Bedding or listing land	1.50	1.5
Fertilizer	16.70	16.7
Distributing fertilizer	.80	.8
Transplanting or setting plants	3.20	3.2
Resetting and hoeing	2.00	2.0
Cultivating	4.00	4.0
Topping and suckering	4.30	4.3
Poison and applying poison for hornworms	1.60	1.6
Harvesting and barning	12.90	12.9
Curing	8.00	8.0
Grading, tying, and preparing for market	15.50	15.5
Hauling to market	3.00	3.0
Use of land and depreciation of barns	14.00	14.0
Miscellaneous costs	4.00	4.0
TOTAL COST	$100.00	100.0

Average cost to produce one acre $ $\frac{100.00}{785}$ = 12.7 cents per pound
Average yield, pounds per acre

Source: South Carolina Department of Agriculture, Commerce, and Industries, *Annual Report,* 1923.

Tobacco Markets and Warehouses in South Carolina, 1927–1932

Market	1927	1928	1929	1930	1931	1932
Andrews	2	2	1	1	–	–
Conway	3	3	3	3	2	3
Darlington	4	4	4	3	3	3
Dillon	2	3	3	3	2	2
Florence	2	2	1	–	–	–
Hartsville	2	2	2	2	–	–
Johnsonville	2	2	2	2	2	–
Kingstree	3	3	3	2	3	3
Lake City	4	4	4	4	4	3
Lake View	2	3	–	–	–	–
Lamar	3	3	3	2	2	–
Loris	3	3	2	2	2	3
Manning	2	2	2	1	1	–
Marion	2	2	2	1	1	–
Mullins	7	7	6	6	6	6
Nichols	2	2	2	–	–	–
Olanta	3	2	–	–	–	–
Orangeburg	–	1	–	–	–	–
Pamplico	3	3	3	2	2	2
Sumter	2	2	2	–	–	–
Timmonsville	5	4	3	3	3	4
Total warehouses	58	59	48	37	33	29
Total markets	20	21	18	15	13	9

Source: South Carolina Department of Agriculture, Commerce, and Industries, *Annual Reports, 1927, 1928, 1929, 1930, 1931, 1932.* Comparisons for August 1 in stated years.

Notes

INTRODUCTION

1. The "colonial economy" thesis was set forth by C. Vann Woodward in *Origins of the New South, 1877–1913* (Baton Rouge: Louisiana State University Press, 1951). A more recent treatment is Gavin Wright, *Old South, New South: Revolutions in the Southern Economy Since the Civil War* (New York: Basic Books, 1986). The debate is reviewed in C. Vann Woodward, *Thinking Back: The Perils of Writing History* (Baton Rouge: Louisiana State University Press, 1986), 66–81.

2. See Stanley M. Elkins, *Slavery: A Problem in American Institutional and Intellectual Life,* 3d ed. (Chicago: University of Chicago Press, 1976), 81–139. Elkins reviews the "Sambo" myth in the historiography of American slavery.

CHAPTER ONE: Tobacco Doth Here Grow Very Well, 1670–1810

1. On the operation of market forces in the economy of colonial South Carolina, see Peter A. Coclanis, *The Shadow of a Dream: Economic Life and Death in the South Carolina Lowcountry, 1670–1920* (New York: Oxford University Press, 1989), 53–58.

2. See Robert M. Weir, *Colonial South Carolina: A History* (Millwood, N.Y.: KTO Press, 1983), 141–42; Joyce E. Chaplin, *An Anxious Pursuit: Agricultural Innovation and Modernity in the Lower South, 1730–1815* (Chapel Hill: University of North Carolina Press, 1993); on citrus, wine, and olives, see ibid., 150–51; on silk, see ibid., 162–64.

It was believed the Carolina climate was too cold for cotton. See Governor West to Lord Ashley, 21 March 1671, and Joseph Dalton to Lord Ashley, 20 January 1672, in Langdon Cheves, ed., "The Shaftesbury Papers and Other Records Relating to Carolina and the First Settlement on the Ashley River Prior to the Year 1676," in *Collections of the South Carolina Historical Society,* vol. 5 (Richmond: William E. Jones, 1897), 297, 376. Hereafter cited as "Shaftesbury Papers."

3. Proprietors to Governor and Council at Charles Town in W. Noel Sainsbury et al., transcribers, *Records in the British Public Records Office Relating to South Carolina, 1663–1684,* 5 vols. (Columbia: Crowson-Stone, 1928–46), 1:55. These transcripts were made in London in the 1890s by Sainsbury and his staff. Microfilm copies of the entire series are available at the South Carolina Department of Archives and History. Volumes 1–5 were published in facsimile editions by the Historical Commission between 1928 and 1946 and are available from the University of South Carolina Library System.

4. On tobacco as a temporary staple in Barbados, see Richard S. Dunn, *Sugar and Slaves: The Rise of the Planter Class in the English West Indies, 1624–1713* (New York: Norton, 1972), 49–54, 59–61. Apparently Barbadian leaf was of poor quality.

John Winthrop described his son's tobacco crop as "fowle, full of stalkes, and evill colored." An English merchant wrote the epitaph for Barbadian weed in 1637: "Your tobacco of Barbados of all the tobacco that cometh to England is accompted the worst."

5. Lewis C. Gray, *The History of Agriculture in the Southern United States to 1860*, 2 vols., consecutively paginated (1932; rpt. Gloucester: Peter Smith, 1958), 264–65.

6. Maurice Williams to Lord Ashley, 30 August 1671, "Shaftesbury Papers," 334. See also Gray, *History of Agriculture*, 53–54. Cf. Linda Marie Pett, "Changing Spatial Patterns of Tobacco Production in South Carolina" (M.A. thesis, University of South Carolina, 1976), 14–17.

7. See Ashley, Craven, Carterette, and Colleton to Captain Mathias Halstead, 1 May 1671, "Shaftesbury Papers," 321. See also Mary Parramore, "Preservation Plan for Historic Tobacco Related Resources," State Historic Preservation Office, South Carolina Department of Archives and History, Columbia, 1990.

8. "Shaftesbury Papers," 349, from a summary of correspondence to the Lords Proprietors abstracted by John Locke, executive assistant and secretary to Lord Anthony Ashley Cooper, Earl of Shaftesbury. See also Parramore, "Preservation Plan"; cf. Andrew Browning, ed., *English Historical Documents, 1660–1714*, vol. 8 (New York: Oxford University Press, 1953), 537–38. Farmers in several English counties were growing tobacco. English leaf was said to be of fair quality but did not cure well. See David Ogg, *England in the Reign of Charles II*, 2d ed. (Oxford: Clarendon Press, 1956), 74–75.

9. On tobacco prices in the mid-1670s, see Gray, *History of Agriculture*, 1:265; "Shaftesbury Papers," 309. See "An Account of the Province of Carolina by Samuel Wilson, 1682," in Alexander S. Salley, comp. and ed., *Narratives of Early Carolina, 1650–1708* (New York: Charles Scribner's Sons, 1911), 175.

10. Governor West to Lord Ashley, 21 March 1671, "Shaftesbury Papers," 300; see also "Council Journal" for 2 November 1675, ibid., 473; see also ibid., 212, 352.

11. Stephen Bull to Proprietors, "Shaftesbury Papers," "Council Journal" entry for 2 November 1675, in ibid., 473.

12. See Salley, *Narratives*, 147; see also remarks of Samuel Wilson, ibid., 175; cf. John Locke abstracts in "Shaftesbury Papers," 352.

13. Imperial Tobacco Company, *A History of the Tobacco Trade: Information Brochure No. 2* (Nottingham: Forman and Sons, n.d.), 7. The quote comes from David Harley, "The Beginnings of the Tobacco Controversy: Puritanism, James I, and the Royal Physicians," *Bulletin of the History of Medicine* 67 (Spring 1993): 34.

14. Imperial Tobacco Company, *History of the Tobacco Trade*, 12. The source gives the larger sum as "3s.6d.," or three shillings six pence. Since this obsolete monetary form is not familiar to some readers, the equivalent sum of forty-two pence is given to aid comparison. See Gray, *History of Agriculture*, 1:265–66. Charles II reigned from 1660 to 1685.

15. Lord Shaftesbury to Charles II, in Sainsbury et al., trans., *Records*, 1:80. The city's name was Charles Town until officially changed to Charleston in 1783.

16. Lord Craven to Gov. Joseph West, ibid., 2:204; Weir, *Colonial South Carolina*, 88.

17. Lord Colleton et al. to Gov. Joseph West, 6 July 1685, Sainsbury et al., trans., *Records*, 2:77. See also James II to Lord Craven, 26 June 1685, ibid., 71–72. James II reigned from 1685 to 1688.

18. See correspondence of Thomas Ashe in Salley, *Narratives*, 147.

19. There is a substantial literature on colonial rice culture. A good summary, citing much of the older literature, is Sam B. Hilliard, "Antebellum Tidewater Rice Culture in South Carolina and Georgia," in *European Settlement and Development in North America: Essays on Geographical Change in Honor and Memory of Andrew Hill Clark*, James R. Gibson, ed. (Toronto: University of Toronto Press, 1978), 91–115. Other sources are Weir, *Colonial South Carolina*, 145, and Charles W. Joyner, *Down by the Riverside: A South Carolina Slave Community* (Urbana: University of Illinois Press, 1984), 13–14. A classic source is Alexander S. Salley Jr., *The Introduction of Rice Culture into South Carolina* (Columbia: Historical Commission of South Carolina, 1919).

20. Coclanis, *Shadow of a Dream*, 133–34.

21. Wolfgang Schivelsbusch, *Tastes of Paradise: A Social History of Spices, Stimulants, and Intoxicants* (New York: Pantheon Books, 1992), 96–146.

22. On naval stores, see Gray, *History of Agriculture*, 1:151–60. A good local treatment is Charles W. Joyner, "The Far Side of the Forest," *Independent Republic Quarterly* 18 (Fall 1984): 13–17.

23. Gray, *History of Agriculture*, 1:153–54; Weir, *Colonial South Carolina*, 143.

24. Converse D. Clowse, *Economic Beginnings in Colonial South Carolina, 1670–1730* (Columbia: University of South Carolina Press, 1971), 60. See also Weir, *South Carolina*, 145–46; also "Letter of Edmund Randolph to the Board of Trade, 1699" in Salley, *Narratives*, 203–9.

25. Clowse, *Economic Beginnings*, 256–58.

26. For a detailed analysis of Johnson's plan, see Robert L. Meriwether, *The Expansion of South Carolina, 1729–1765* (Kingsport, Tenn.: Southern Publishers, 1940), 17–30; on the relative growth rates of black and white populations in colonial South Carolina, see Coclanis, *Shadow of a Dream*, 65.

27. Meriwether, *Expansion of South Carolina*, 20–21, 29–30. Eventually, an astonishing £60,000 sterling was appropriated for this purpose from slave duties.

28. Weir, *Colonial South Carolina*, 147–49, 175, 209–10. See Julian J. Petty, *The Growth and Distribution of Population in South Carolina* (1943; rpt., Spartanburg: Reprint Co., 1975), 40.

29. Petty, *Growth and Distribution of Population*, 174–75, 209–10.

30. Gray, *History of Agriculture*, 1:155–57.

31. See "An Account of the Several Species and Quantities of Commodities, of the Produce of South Carolina which were exported from thence at the port of Charles Town, in One Year, from 1st November 1747 to 1st November 1748; together with the Rate and Amount of the Value of each, in sterling money and in South

Carolina Currency," in James Glen, *A Description of South Carolina* . . . (1761; rpt. Columbia: University of South Carolina Press, 1951), 58–63. An abstract of this lengthy table appears in Coclanis, *Shadow of a Dream,* 80–81.

32. Glen, *Description of South Carolina,* 95.

33. Lacy K. Ford Jr., *Origins of Southern Radicalism: The South Carolina Up-country, 1800–1860* (New York: Oxford University Press, 1988), 1; on self-sufficiency see ibid., 54.

34. U.S. Department of Commerce, Bureau of the Census, *Historical Statistics of the United States: Colonial Times to 1970, Part II* (Washington, D.C.: U.S. Government Printing Office, 1976), 1197. Percentage calculated on increase from 17.71 shillings to 32.50 shillings. On tobacco prices in the 1760s, see also Jacob Price, *Capital and Credit in British Overseas Trade: The View from the Chesapeake, 1700–1776* (Cambridge, Mass.: Harvard University Press, 1980), 12, 128, 130.

35. On the introduction of tobacco in the backcountry, see Chaplin, *Anxious Pursuit,* 279–80. See also Parramore, "Preservation Plan"; Charles F. Kovacik and John J. Winberry, *South Carolina: A Geography* (Boulder: Westview Press, 1987), 75; South Carolina Department of Agriculture, Commerce, and Industries, *Tobacco Report, 1938* (Columbia: Gonzales and Bryan, 1939), 14. Although none of these sources mention Marylanders as carriers of tobacco culture, that colony had considerable experience with leaf production, so it is likely they played a part.

36. Charles J. Gayle, "The Nature and Volume of Exports from Charleston, 1724–1774," *Proceedings of the South Carolina Historical Society* 33 (1937). Early figures often give tobacco exports in hogsheads. Although the weight of individual hogsheads varied, one thousand pounds was about average. On tobacco in upcountry agriculture, see D. Huger Bacot, "The South Carolina Up Country at the End of the Eighteenth Century," *American Historical Review* 28 (July 1923): 682–98, esp. 684, 685, 691, 693.

37. *South Carolina Gazette* (Charleston), 5 December 1771; see also Rachel N. Klein, *Unification of a Slave State: The Rise of the Planter Class in the South Carolina Backcountry, 1760–1808* (Chapel Hill: University of North Carolina Press, 1990), 19.

38. John Drayton, *A View of South Carolina as Respects Her Natural and Civil Concerns* (Charleston: W. P. Young, 1802), 168. These figures reflect exports from Charleston only. Some leaf was also shipped down the Pee Dee River from Cheraw to Georgetown, and South Carolina farmers along the Savannah River shipped tobacco through the port of Savannah, Georgia. Although impossible to determine precisely, the state's leaf production was doubtless higher than Drayton's figures for Charleston alone.

39. H. Roy Merrens, ed., *The Colonial South Carolina Scene: Contemporary Views, 1697–1774* (Columbia: University of South Carolina Press, 1977), 265; also Klein, *Unification of a Slave State,* 16–17.

40. Kovacik and Winberry, *South Carolina,* 76.

41. William Willis Boddie, *History of Williamsburg County* (1924; rpt. Spartan-

burg: Reprint Company, 1980), 249–50; also Alexander Gregg, *History of the Old Cheraws* (1867; rpt. Spartanburg: Reprint Company, 1965), 112n.

42. Klein, *Unification of a Slave State*, 244.

43. On problems of tobacco inspection, see *De Bow's Commercial Review* 2 (July 1846): 42–53. The article discusses problems common to the tobacco trade in several markets.

44. Parramore, "Preservation Plan"; Thomas Cooper and David J. McCord, eds., *Statutes at Large of South Carolina*, 10 vols. (Columbia: A. L. Johnston, 1836–55), 4:237.

45. *De Bow's Commercial Review* 1 (July 1846): 42–45; see also Marjorie S. Mendenhall, "A History of Agriculture in South Carolina, 1790–1860: An Economic and Social Study (Ph.D. dissertation, University of North Carolina, 1940), 56. See Act No. 1574, "An Act to Regulate the Inspection and Transportation of Tobacco," 13 March 1789, Articles X and XXXI, in Cooper and McCord, *Statutes*, vol. 4. Such draconian penalties, while commonly provided for, were seldom enforced. "Benefit of Clergy" would usually be invoked for a first offense.

46. Cooper and McCord, eds., *Statutes*, 4:604, 681.

47. *Papers of the General Assembly*, Petitions, 1789 (0010 003 1789 00103 00), South Carolina Department of Archives and History, Columbia. See also Parramore, "Preservation Plan."

48. Cooper and McCord, eds., *Statutes*, 5:113–14, 133. Export figures from Drayton, *View of South Carolina*, 168, 173. These figures reflect exports from Charleston only.

49. South Carolina Department of Agriculture, *Tobacco Report 1938*, 14–16.

50. Michael E. Stevens, ed., *Journal of the House of Representatives, 1789–1790* (Columbia: University of South Carolina Press, 1984), 330.

51. *Papers of the General Assembly*, Petitions, 1796 (0010 003 1796 00143). See also Parramore, "Preservation Plan." The petition had 270 signatures.

52. See Singleton's obituary in *Charleston City Gazette and Daily Advertiser*, 23 October 1798; also article of Huger Bacot in *Charleston News and Courier*, 31 July 1938. Thomas Singleton was the grandfather of William Gilmore Simms through his daughter Harriet Ann Singleton.

53. See J. B. D. De Bow, *A Statistical View of the United States . . . Being a Compendium of the Seventh Census* (Washington, D.C.: Beverly Tucker, 1854), 174.

54. Paul J. Mantoux, *The Industrial Revolution in the Eighteenth Century* (London: J. Cape, 1961), 191: "The rapid transformation of the cotton industry, wrought by a succession of technical inventions, made it the earliest and also the classic example of modern large-scale industry."

55. C. F. McCay, "An American Professor Sketches the Principal English Inventions Affecting Textiles," in *Cotton and the Growth of the American Economy, 1790–1860*, comp. and ed. Stuart Bruchey (New York: Brace and World, 1967), 48–50. McCay was a professor at the University of Georgia and a frequent contributor on

the subject of cotton to *De Bow's Commercial Review*. The article was first published in 1868.

56. McCay, "American Professor," 18, 45. There were twelve pence in a shilling; five shillings were worth about $1.25 in 1800. On early cotton production in colonial South Carolina, see Chaplin, *Anxious Pursuit*, 220–26.

57. McCay, "American Professor," 45.

58. Edward C. Bates, "The Story of the Cotton Gin," *New England Magazine*, May 1890, 288–92.

59. Eli Whitney Jr. to Eli Whitney, 11 September 1793, in Matthew B. Hammond, "Correspondence of Eli Whitney Relative to the Invention of the Cotton Gin," *American Historical Review* 3 (October 1897): 99–101. The cotton gin was subsequently improved to the extent that by 1810 Whitney could assert that the gin multiplied the labor of one man a thousandfold. See Tench Coxe, *A Statement of the Arts and Manufactures of the United States of America for the Year 1810* (Philadelphia: A. Corman Jr., 1814), ix.

60. Ford, *Origins of Southern Radicalism*, 7–8.

61. Gray, *History of Agriculture*, 2:681; Ford, *Origins of Southern Radicalism*, 8.

62. David Ramsay, *Ramsay's History of South Carolina from Its First Settlement in 1670 to the Year 1809* (1809; rpt. Newberry: W. J. Duffie, 1858), 120. See also Lacy K. Ford Jr., "Self-Sufficiency, Cotton, and Economic Development in the South Carolina Upcountry, 1800–1860," *Journal of Economic History* 45 (June 1985): 262–65.

63. On the transition from tobacco to cotton in the up-country, see Gray, *History of Agriculture*, 2:609, 684–85; Chaplin, *Anxious Pursuit*, 297–303.

64. *Papers of the General Assembly*, Petitions (0010 003 ND00 01536 00). (Although undated, the petition is from the early 1800s.) See also Parramore, "Preservation Plan"; Cooper and McCord, eds., *Statutes*, 5:433–34. On adaptation of tobacco equipment to cotton, see Chaplin, *Anxious Pursuit*, 302–3.

65. Arthur H. Cole, *Wholesale Commodity Prices in the United States, 1700–1861* (1938; rpt. New York: Johnson Reprint Co., 1969), appendix C, 210.

66. De Bow, *Statistical View*, 178.

67. Coclanis, *Shadow of a Dream*, 142.

CHAPTER TWO: Years of the Locust, 1865–1885

1. The literature on antebellum South Carolina is vast. For a review of antebellum historiography, see David Moltke-Hansen, "Protecting Interests, Maintaining Rights, Emulating Ancestors: U.S. Constitution Bicentennial Reflections on 'The Problem of South Carolina,' 1787–1860," *South Carolina Historical Magazine* 89 (July 1988): 160–82. An excellent source on the growing ideological alienation of South Carolina in the 1840s and 1850s is Michael O'Brien and David Moltke-

Hansen, eds., *Intellectual Life in Antebellum Charleston* (Knoxville: University of Tennessee Press, 1986).

2. J. W. Ogilvie, "Reminiscences," *Horry Herald,* 9 September 1909. A reprint appears in *Independent Republic Quarterly* 3 (January 1969): 19–27.

3. George C. Rogers Jr., *The History of Georgetown County, South Carolina* (Columbia: University of South Carolina Press, 1970), 445.

4. See, for example, county summaries in *Charleston News and Courier,* 4 February 1884.

5. On the lack of industrial development in the region, see David L. Carlton, "The Piedmont and Waccamaw Regions: A Comparison," *South Carolina Historical Magazine* 88 (April 1987): 83–100. A graphic representation of the lack of industry in the region is David L. Carlton, *Mill and Town in South Carolina* (Baton Rouge: Louisiana State University Press, 1982), 47. On the economic history of South Carolina, including some Pee Dee counties, see Peter A. Coclanis and Lacy K. Ford Jr., "The South Carolina Economy Reconstructed and Reconsidered: Structure, Output, and Performance, 1670–1985," in *Developing Dixie: Modernization in a Traditional Society,* ed. Winfred B. Moore (New York: Greenwood Press, 1990), 93–110.

6. *Marion Star,* 8 September 1886.

7. U.S. Department of Commerce, Bureau of the Census, *Historical Statistics of the United States: Colonial Times to 1970, Part I* (Washington, D.C.: U.S. Government Printing Office, 1976), 1:462. See also Eugene Lerner, "Southern Output and Agricultural Income, 1860–1880," *Agricultural History* 33 (1959): 117. On the Pee Dee region, see Twelfth Census (1880), *History of Agriculture,* South Carolina, County Tables.

8. On the uncertainties of South Carolina agriculture after the Civil War, see Joel Williamson, *After Slavery: The Negro in South Carolina During Reconstruction* (Chapel Hill: University of North Carolina Press, 1965), esp. chap. 2. See also Coclanis and Ford, "South Carolina Economy," 101.

9. On restrictions, the pass system, and slave movements in the Pee Dee, see interviews of former slaves in George Rawick, ed., *The American Slave: A Composite Autobiography,* 41 vols. (Westport, Conn.: Greenwood Press, 1972–79), 2: pt. 1, pp. 21, 101, 246. The interviews were conducted by Annie Ruth Davis in Marion County, South Carolina, 1937–38. On postwar movements of former slaves in South Carolina, see Williamson, *After Slavery,* 33, 39, 44. Patience Johnson is quoted in William W. Ball, *The State That Forgot: South Carolina's Surrender to Democracy* (Indianapolis: Bobbs-Merrill, 1932), 128.

10. See interviews with former slaves Washington Dozier and Hester Hunter conducted by Annie Ruth Davis in Marion County, South Carolina, 1937, in Rawick, ed., *American Slave,* 2: pt. 1, pp. 334–35, and pt. 2, p. 340.

11. Leon F. Litwack, *Been in the Storm So Long: The Aftermath of Slavery* (New York: Knopf, 1979), 162, citing Grace Elmore Diary, entry for 4 March 1865.

12. Williamson, *After Slavery*, 44.

13. *Darlington New Era*, 25 July 1865. The *New Era* was a "carpetbag" paper dedicated to "Reconstruction, Reform and Reunion of the States." It circulated widely among occupying forces in the Pee Dee region.

14. *New York Times*, 7 October 1866. Benjamin F. Perry, a staunch Unionist, was appointed provisional governor of South Carolina in 1865 by President Andrew Johnson. He was succeeded by James L. Orr in 1866.

15. On conditions in the Pee Dee and attitudes of planters there, see C. B. Berry, ed., "Diary of Col. Daniel Jordan," *Independent Republic Quarterly* 15 (April 1981): 25–26.

16. See Charles Ravenel, "Southern Deficits," *Business and Economic Review*, July 1984, 22–23. On the status of slaves as capital in the antebellum South, see Stanley Engerman, "The Effects of Slavery on the Southern Economy: The Recent Debate," *Explorations in Entrepreneurial History* 4 (Winter 1967).

17. Banknote values and exchange rates were published regularly in the commercial sections of newspapers. For example, see the *Marion Crescent*, 30 October 1867; *Darlington Southerner*, 11 August 1865.

18. *Charleston Daily Courier*, 4 April 1867.

19. Rogers, *History of Georgetown County*, 435.

20. Ibid., 454–55, 528. Snow Island is on the Great Pee Dee near Johnsonville. The area became part of Florence County in the 1880s.

21. Some Republicans advocated confiscating the lands of prominent planters to help defray the costs of the war. Rumors of confiscation, pro and con, abound in the postwar southern press. See "Land Confiscations" in *Darlington New Era*, 25 July 1865, and *Darlington Southerner*, 11 August 1865.

22. The persistence of these rumors can be seen in the *Marion Crescent* (quoting the *Wilmington Dispatch*), 20 March 1867, warning against extending credit because of "the certainty of the passage of confiscation laws during the present session of the Fortieth Congress."

23. On the effects of rumors of land confiscation on postwar commerce, see the *Charleston Mercury*, 3 January 1867.

24. Newspapers routinely published warnings of such schemes. See *Marion Crescent*, October–December 1867, passim.

25. On the land question in South Carolina, see Carol R. Bleser, *The Promised Land: The History of the South Carolina Land Commission, 1869–1890* (Columbia: University of South Carolina Press, 1969), xii–xv, 6–14.

26. See interview with former slave Ezra Adams conducted by Henry Grant (n.d.) in Rawick, ed., *American Slave*, 1: pt. 1, p. 5.

27. Interview with Tinney Shaw, in Rawick, ed., *American Slave*, 15: pt. 2, p. 268. Shaw was interviewed by Mary Hicks (n.d.).

28. *Marion Star*, 6 June 1866.

29. On cotton prices see U.S. Department of Commerce, Bureau of the Census, *Statistical Abstract of the United States, 1900* (Washington, D.C.: U.S. Government

Printing Office, 1901), 426. Cotton sold for an average of 11 cents in 1860 and 43 cents in 1866. Wartime inflation seriously eroded the dollar, however, and the 1860 dollar has been indexed at $1.91 in 1866 money. Therefore, 43-cent cotton in 1866 was worth 22.5 cents by 1860 standards, still an impressive advance. See John J. McCusker, *How Much Is That in Real Money?: A Historical Price Index for Use as a Deflator of Money Values in the Economy of the United States* (Worcester, Mass.: American Antiquarian Society, 1992), 316–31.

30. *Charleston Daily Courier,* 31 May 1865.

31. On the development and expectations of the contract system in South Carolina, see Martin Abbott, *The Freedmen's Bureau in South Carolina, 1865–1872* (Chapel Hill: University of North Carolina Press, 1967), 66–81.

32. On the role of Freedmen's Bureau agents, see Abbott, *Freedmen's Bureau in South Carolina,* 67; on conditions in the Pee Dee, see *Darlington New Era,* 25 July 1865, and reports in *Charleston Mercury,* 15, 30 January 1867. On the role of B. H. Smith, see Rogers, *History of Georgetown County,* 431–44.

33. See contracts in Peter B. Bacot Papers, Southern Historical Collection, University of North Carolina, Chapel Hill. On terms of labor contracts, see Abbott, *Freedmen's Bureau in South Carolina,* 68; see also Rogers, *History of Georgetown County,* 434.

34. On crop share compensation in Marion District, see interview with Washington Dozier in Rawick, ed., *American Slave,* 2: pt. 1, pp. 334–35; interview of John Glover at Timmonsville, August 1937, by H. Grady Davis, ibid., 141. See also contracts in Horry Deas Papers and Joseph Glover Papers, South Caroliniana Library, University of South Carolina, Columbia. On Georgetown County, see Rogers, *History of Georgetown County,* 434. The contracts specified an equal division after one-fifth was deducted for expenses, hence a two-fifths share for labor. On Darlington, see contracts in Bacot Papers; see also contract forms in *Darlington New Era,* 25 July 1865. A good general source on labor contracts in postbellum South Carolina is Ralph Shlomowitz, "The Origins of Southern Sharecropping," *Agricultural History,* July 1979, 557–75.

35. See labor contracts, Woodward Manning Papers, 28-652/655, South Carolina Historical Society, Charleston. Manning was a planter, merchant, and innkeeper in Marion County.

36. See published contracts and commentary in the *Darlington New Era,* 25 July 1865.

37. On the free labor ideology, see Daniel T. Rodgers, *The Work Ethic in Industrial America, 1850–1920* (Chicago: University of Chicago Press, 1978); Eric Foner, *Free Soil, Free Labor, Free Men: The Ideology of the Republican Party Before the Civil War* (New York: Oxford University Press, 1970). Ironically, traditional views of the role of labor were becoming an anachronism in the North by the mid-nineteenth century as serious labor unrest in the 1870s would soon reveal.

38. On southern inexperience with and misunderstanding of free labor principles, see Eric Foner, "Reconstruction and the Crisis of Free Labor," in *Politics*

and Ideology in the Age of the Civil War (New York: Oxford University Press, 1980), 97–127, esp. 102–7. A good summary is Foner's *Reconstruction: America's Unfinished Revolution, 1863–1877* (New York: Harper & Row, 1988), 28–31.

39. Attempts by northerners to establish cotton plantations in postwar South Carolina ended in failure, which northern capitalists typically blamed on the free black laborers. One observed of freedmen that they "looked better at a distance." See Francis B. Simkins and Robert H. Woody, *South Carolina During Reconstruction* (Chapel Hill: University of North Carolina Press, 1932), 243.

40. Peter Bacot's labor contract lists twenty names, and Adele Petigru Allston's involved thirty-three freedmen. See Bacot Papers and Allston Family Papers, South Caroliniana Library, University of South Carolina, Columbia.

41. See Bacot Papers. See also Williamson, *After Slavery*, 132.

42. See Shlomowitz, "Origins of Southern Sharecropping."

43. "F. A. W. S." to *Charleston Courier*, 3 October 1865.

44. Contract of Adele Petigru Allston, 18 January 1870, Allston Family Papers, reprinted in the Appendix. Rice accumulating from fines and forfeitures was divided among those "who have labored best."

45. Contract of Adele Petigru Allston, 18 January 1870, Allston Family Papers.

46. See printed and MS contracts in Bacot Papers; also sample contract in *Darlington New Era*, 25 July 1865.

47. Abbott, *Freedmen's Bureau in South Carolina*, 70–74.

48. See MS and printed contract forms in Bacot Papers.

49. *Nation* 1 (November 1865): 651. See also Williamson, *After Slavery*, 89. On the confusion surrounding the land question, see Bleser, *Promised Land*, 1–14.

50. Maj. Gen. O. O. Howard to Brig. Gen. Wager Swayne, 3 November 1865, in *Selected Series of Records Issued by the Commissioner of the Bureau of Refugees, Freedmen, and Abandoned Lands, 1865–1872* (Washington, D.C.: National Archives Microfilm Publications), roll 1, p. 421; also Howard to Asst Commissioners, 11 November 1865, roll 1, p. 424.

51. Some freedmen were still hoping for land grants as late as Christmas 1868. See Abbott, *Freedmen's Bureau in South Carolina*, 71–78.

52. Charles W. Joyner, *Down by the Riverside: A South Carolina Slave Community* (Urbana: University of Illinois Press, 1984), 83–85. See also Litwack, *Been in the Storm So Long*, 158.

53. Rogers, *History of Georgetown County*, 431–33; Williamson, *After Slavery*, 90. The site of the gathering was about nine miles south of Kingstree, probably near Greeleyville.

54. Quoted in Litwack, *Been in the Storm So Long*, 417. On the bureau's continuing support of the contract system, see remarks by Gen. O. O. Howard in *Charleston Mercury*, 9 January 1867.

55. Rogers, *History of Georgetown County*, 433–34.

56. Ibid.

57. Litwack, *Been in the Storm So Long*, 418.

58. Rogers, *History of Georgetown County*, 453. On the regionwide decline of productivity after the Civil War, see Roger Ransom and Richard Sutch, *One Kind of Freedom: The Economic Consequences of Emancipation* (Cambridge, Eng.: Cambridge University Press, 1977), 10.

59. On planters' hostility to the Freedmen's Bureau and confusion of the labor situation, see *Marion Star*, 6 June, 29 August 1866.

60. Darlington Agricultural Society, Minute Book, vol. 1 (1846–80), entry for 29 August 1865, Darlington County Historical Commission, Darlington, S.C. A facsimile edition of the minute book was published by the society in observance of its sesquicentennial in 1996.

61. *Darlington New Era*, 26 September, 3 October 1865. Benjamin F. Whittemore, late chaplain in the Union army, was elected to Congress during Reconstruction. He was later expelled for selling appointments to West Point.

62. Benjamin F. Williamson (1814–87). See European Immigration File, Benjamin F. Williamson Papers, Darlington Historical Commission, Darlington, S.C. See also G. Wayne King, *Rise Up So Early: A History of Florence County, South Carolina* (Spartanburg: Reprint Company, 1981), 73; Williamson, *After Slavery*, 142.

63. *Marion Star*, 20 June, 29 August 1866.

64. Rogers, *History of Georgetown County*, 433–34. On recruitment of Chinese labor in the postwar South, see James W. Loewen, *The Mississippi Chinese: Between Black and White* (Cambridge, Mass.: Harvard University Press, 1971).

65. Cruthers and Brown contract, 18 December 1821, manuscript court records, Darlington County Historical Commission, Darlington, S.C. Share tenancy was common in other areas of the antebellum South. See, for example, Steven Hahn, *The Roots of Southern Populism: Yeoman Farmers and the Transformation of the Georgia Upcountry, 1850–1890* (New York: Oxford University Press, 1983), 64.

66. On wage preferences, see editorial "Labor at the South," *Charleston Daily Courier*, 31 May 1865.

67. See advertisements for labor in *Marion Star*, December 1866, passim. The going rate for "prime females" was about $9 per month.

68. See labor cost estimates in *Marion Crescent*, 25 December 1867, and *Charleston Daily Courier*, 30 March 1866. Estimates are based on 31-cent cotton. (The average price for a pound of middling cotton in 1867 was 31.5 cents.) On cotton prices, see U.S. Department of Commerce, Bureau of the Census, *Statistical Abstract, 1900*, 426. Labor costs for one prime hand were as follows:

cash wages	$100.00
120 lbs. bacon @.20	24.00
13 bushels corn @ 1.50	19.50
miscellaneous	10.00
total labor expense	$153.50

Planters estimated the average production per worker at three four-hundred-pound bales. At thirty-one cents per pound, twelve hundred pounds of cotton was worth

$372. Thus cash wages of about $153 yielded $372 of produce. Under sharecropping, equal division of the proceeds increased the laborer's wages to half of $372, or $186—a very meaningful increase of $33. Advances made to croppers were repaid from the croppers' share and thus did not affect the result. Note that no cash value is accorded to housing, which was furnished to laborers under both plans.

69. *Charleston Mercury*, 3 January 1867.

70. On attitudes of planters toward free black labor, see *Charleston Mercury*, 3 January 1867, and *Marion Crescent*, 20 November 1867.

71. *Charleston Mercury*, 3 January 1867; *Marion Crescent*, 20 November 1867.

72. *South Carolina Leader* (Charleston), 9 December 1865.

73. On labor shortages in the Pee Dee, see *Charleston Daily Courier*, 26, 30 March, 4 May 1866.

74. Walter Gregg to Mrs. Gregg, 26 December 1867, cited in Amelia Wallace Vernon, *African Americans at Mars Bluff, South Carolina* (Baton Rouge: Louisiana State University Press, 1993), 145.

75. *Charleston Daily Courier*, 30 March, 4 May 1866.

76. *Darlington Southerner*, 17 August 1866.

77. On labor shortages in the Pee Dee, see *Charleston Daily Courier*, 30 March, 4 May 1866. The quote is from *Marion Crescent*, 20 November 1867.

78. *Sumter Watchman*, 5 September 1866; "A Negro Public Meeting in Sumter District," *New York Times*, 30 November 1866, 2.

79. Darlington Agricultural Society, Minute Book, vol. 1, entries for 29 August 1865 and 14 August 1866.

80. *Southern Cultivator* 27 (January 1869): 54; see also Ransom and Sutch, *One Kind of Freedom*, 67.

81. See report of Mr. Edgecombe in *Charleston Mercury*, 5 January 1867. Fifteen dollars per month was well above the prevailing rate of about $12. Wage rates in Georgia also peaked at $15 per month. See Hahn, *Roots of Southern Populism*, 155.

82. On provisions of sharecropping agreements in the Pee Dee see Bacot Papers; cf. James M. Carson Papers, South Caroliniana Library, University of South Carolina, Columbia. On the structure and evolution of sharecropping in the South, see the last chapter of Gavin Wright, *The Political Economy of the Cotton South: Households, Markets, and Wealth in the Nineteenth Century* (New York: Norton, 1978). On traditional hunting and fishing rights in other parts of the South, see Hahn, *Roots of Southern Populism*, 242–43.

83. Contemporaries estimated that the labor expense of sharecropping fell below wage labor when cotton sold at fifteen cents a pound. See *Marion Crescent*, 25 December 1867.

84. The scale of tidewater rice production was not as conducive to family-unit arrangements as was cotton. Gang labor and communal housing persisted longer in rice areas. See Williamson, *After Slavery*, 130; Rogers, *History of Georgetown County*, 445.

85. On conditions in the Pee Dee, see for example, contracts in Carson Papers. A fine treatment of sharecropping told in the first person is Theodore Rosengarten, *All God's Dangers: The Life of Nate Shaw* (New York: Knopf, 1974). On mobility, see ibid., 117–18, 126–28; on transferring croppers' debts between landlords, see ibid., 144–46. On problems with sharecropping throughout the region, see Gilbert C. Fite, *Cotton Fields No More: Southern Agriculture, 1865–1980* (Lexington: University Press of Kentucky, 1984), 10–29.

86. For a defense of sharecropping, see Joseph D. Reid Jr., "Sharecropping as an Understandable Market Response: The Post-Bellum South," *Journal of Economic History* 33 (March 1973): 106–30; Stephen DeCanio, *Agriculture in the Postbellum South: The Economics of Production and Supply* (Cambridge, Mass.: MIT Press, 1974); and Robert Higgs, *Competition and Coercion: Blacks in the American Economy, 1865–1914* (Cambridge, Eng.: Cambridge University Press, 1977). On the other side of the debate, see Ransom and Sutch, *One Kind of Freedom;* Pete Daniel, *The Shadow of Slavery: Peonage in the South, 1901–1969* (Urbana: University of Illinois Press, 1972), and Daniel, "The Metamorphosis of Slavery, 1865–1900," *Journal of American History* 65 (June 1979): 88–99.

87. See, for example, John W. Cell, *The Highest State of White Supremacy: The Origins of Segregation in South Africa and the American South* (Cambridge, Eng.: Cambridge University Press, 1982), 108–16.

88. Contract labor did not disappear from the Pee Dee for several years. Sharecropping did not lend itself well to rice culture. In rice areas—mostly Georgetown County—an arrangement evolved by which workers were paid in rice according to a sliding production scale. See labor contracts in Allston Family Papers and the contract reprinted in the Appendix.

89. For example, see rental contracts in Carson Papers. See also Williamson, *After Slavery,* 126–31.

90. There were many tenancy arrangements in the rural South. See Jack Temple Kirby, *Rural Worlds Lost: The American South, 1920–1960* (Baton Rouge: Louisiana State University Press, 1987), 140–45; Hahn, *Roots of Southern Populism,* 159–60.

91. Percentages extracted from the Twelfth Census (1900), *Agriculture,* 118–21. Horry County had a very high incidence of land ownership among blacks. Percentages for 1890 are not available. Tenure classifications were not separated by race in the census of 1890. See "Classification of Farms by Acreage and Tenure," Eleventh Census (1890), *Agriculture,* 178–79. Unfortunately, the manuscript records of the Eleventh Census were destroyed.

92. The Wilmington and Manchester Railroad ran east and west through the Pee Dee region. See advertisements for factors in *Darlington Southerner, Marion Star,* and *Marion Crescent,* 1866–67, passim; Walker and James, *Southern Business Directory* (Charleston: Walker and James, 1854).

93. On the factorage system and problems after the Civil War, see Harold D. Woodman, "The Decline of Cotton Factorage After the Civil War," *American His-*

torical Review 71 (July 1966): 1219–36. A rich source on antebellum factorage in Charleston is the records of C. T. Mitchell & Co., 1850–64, South Carolina Historical Society, Charleston.

94. On the National Banking and Currency Act of 1863 (amended 1864), see Robert P. Sharkey, *Money, Class, and Party: An Economic Study of the Civil War and Reconstruction* (Baltimore: Johns Hopkins University Press, 1959), 221–37. After 1900, national banks could be chartered with a minimum of $25,000 capital in towns with populations under three thousand. See Chester Krause and Robert Lemke, *Standard Catalogue of U.S. Paper Money*, 8th ed. (Iola, Wisc.: Krause Publications, 1989), 58–60. By 1878, only four South Carolina banks were issuing national currency and then only in $1 and $2 denominations. The Pee Dee's first national bank, Darlington National, was chartered in 1881. See Robert Friedberg, *Paper Money of the United States*, 14th ed. (Clifton, N.J.: Coin and Currency Institute, 1995), 74–77, 294.

95. Sharkey, *Money, Class, and Party*, 221–37.

96. There is substantial literature on rural merchants. An excellent general treatment is Thomas D. Clark, *Pills, Petticoats and Plows: The Southern Country Store* (Norman: University of Oklahoma Press, 1944).

97. On the rural credit system after the Civil War, see Harold D. Woodman, *King Cotton and His Retainers: Financing and Marketing the Cotton Crop of the South, 1800–1925* (Lexington: University Press of Kentucky, 1968); Ransom and Sutch, *One Kind of Freedom*, 120–23; Williamson, *After Slavery*, 175; Hahn, *Roots of Southern Populism*, 173–76.

Clarence Poe, editor of the *Progressive Farmer*, was an outspoken critic of time prices. See Poe, *How Farmers Co-operate and Double Profits: First Hand Reports on All the Leading Forms of Rural Co-operation in the United States and Europe— Stories That Show How Farmers Can Co-operate by Showing How They Have Done It and Are Doing It* (New York: Orange Judd Co., 1915), 44–45; Poe, *My First 80 Years* (Chapel Hill: University of North Carolina Press, 1963), 65. A defense of rural credit is Claudia D. Goldin, "'N' Kinds of Freedom," *Explorations in Economic History* 16 (January 1979): 18–29.

98. South Carolina's lien law was enacted 20 September 1866. For local coverage, see *Marion Star*, 10 October 1866. See also contracts of Henry Spain (28 January 1880) and Jack Drayton (21 January 1881) with James M. Carson, Carson Papers.

99. See contracts of Abraham Robinson (26 January 1881) and Isaac White (5 February 1880) in Carson Papers. On lien law in the postwar South, see Harold D. Woodman, "Post–Civil War Agriculture and Agricultural Law," *Agricultural History* 53 (1979): 311. See also Fite, *Cotton Fields No More*, 2–16; Ransom and Sutch, *One Kind of Freedom*, 176; Hahn, *Roots of Southern Populism*, 174. Contrasting opinions are presented in articles by Claudia D. Goldin, Joseph D. Reid Jr., and Peter Timin in *Explorations in Economic History* 16 (January 1979).

100. On naval stores as a basis of credit, see reminiscences of J. W. Ogilvie, *Independent Republic Quarterly* 3 (January 1969); also James S. Rogers III, "The

History of Horry County, South Carolina" (M.A. thesis, University of South Carolina, 1972).

101. The territoriality of the supply merchant was common throughout the South. See Ransom and Sutch, *One Kind of Freedom,* 126–48, and Hahn, *Roots of Southern Populism,* 176–86.

102. See sales ledgers of the Holliday Company, March–July 1886, Holliday Company Papers, South Caroliniana Library, University of South Carolina, Columbia; also liens in Francis Marion Dwight Papers, ibid. See also advertisements of Burroughs and Cooper, *Horry Weekly News,* 3 September 1869, reprinted in *Independent Republic Quarterly* 3 (January 1969): 9–10. Barter was common across the rural South. See Hahn, *Roots of Southern Populism,* 190–92.

103. George Simpson, *The Cokers of Carolina* (Chapel Hill: University of North Carolina Press, 1956), 86.

104. Joseph W. Holliday, "Horry and the Tobacco Industry," *Independent Republic Quarterly* 2 (April 1968): 7–8.

105. See Charles W. Joyner, "The Far Side of the Forest," *Independent Republic Quarterly* 18 (Fall 1984): 13–17.

106. Extracted from Janet H. Woodard, ed., *1850 Census of Horry County South Carolina* (Greenville: A Press, 1980). On Georgetown, see Joyner, *Down by the Riverside,* 36.

107. Julian J. Petty, *The Growth and Distribution of Population in South Carolina* (1943; rpt. Spartanburg: Reprint Company, 1975), 75–77, 227–28.

108. Twelfth Census (1900), *Agriculture,* 118–21. Average farm size in Horry County was 143.3 acres, Darlington 69.9 acres, and Clarendon 70.1 acres.

109. Rogers, *History of Georgetown County,* 456; Lucille Godfrey to Samuel G. Dargan, reprinted in *Independent Republic Quarterly* 15 (Winter 1981): 9.

110. Daniel R. Headrick, *The Tools of Empire: Technology and European Imperialism in the Nineteenth Century* (New York: Oxford University Press, 1981), esp. 142–150.

111. H. P. Dew, *Report to the Commission on Port Development and the Utilities Commission* (Columbia: State Printers, 1929). See also Edward L. Ayers, *The Promise of the New South: Life After Reconstruction* (New York: Oxford University Press, 1992), 125. On the decline of naval stores in Horry in the 1890s, see "Horry," *Charleston News and Courier,* 3 January 1896.

112. The literature on cotton is vast. See Woodman, *King Cotton and His Retainers;* on overdependence, see Fite, *Cotton Fields No More;* on declining demand, see Wright, *Old South, New South,* 56.

113. Britain began developing alternative sources of cotton during the Civil War. See Gavin Wright, "Cotton Competition and the Post-Bellum Recovery of the American South," *Journal of Economic History* 34 (September 1974): 610–35.

114. Data on growth of cotton demand are from Wright, *Political Economy,* 94; data on cotton production from U.S. Department of Commerce, Bureau of the Census, *Historical Statistics of the United States: Colonial Times to 1970, Part I*

(Washington, D.C.: U.S. Government Printing Office, 1976), 1:518. The figure of 5.3 percent annual growth was calculated from base acreage of 7,666,000 increasing to 19,839,000 over 30 years.

115. See Richard Easterlin, "Regional Income Trends, 1840–1950," in *American Economic History,* ed. Seymour Harris (New York: McGraw-Hill, 1961), 528.

116. Elizabeth Etheridge, *The Butterfly Caste: A Social History of Pellagra in the South* (Westport, Conn.: Greenwood Press, 1972), 2–16; Fred A. Shannon, *The Farmers' Last Frontier: Agriculture, 1860–1897* (New York: Holt, Rinehart, and Winston, 1966), 94; Kirby, *Rural Worlds Lost,* 188.

117. See Lewis P. Jones, "History of Public Education in South Carolina," in *Public Education in South Carolina: Historical, Political and Legal Perspectives,* ed. Thomas R. McDaniel (Spartanburg: Converse College, 1984), 20–21; South Carolina Division of Research and Statistical Services, *South Carolina Statistical Abstract* (Columbia: State Printers, 1977); see also *Annual Report of the Superintendent of Education for the Year 1897* (Columbia: State Printing, 1898).

118. Lewis P. Jones, *South Carolina: A Synoptic History for Laymen,* 4th ed. (Orangeburg, S.C.: Sandlapper Press, 1971), 200–201. See also Louis R. Harlan, *Separate and Unequal: Public School Campaigns and Racism in the Southern Seaboard States, 1900–1915* (New York: Atheneum, 1968), 240–65.

119. W. H. Spivey to "My Dear Brother," 5 October 1885, in author's possession.

CHAPTER THREE: Pearl of the Pee Dee, 1885–1918

1. An excellent summary of the history of cigarette smoking in the United States is Robert Sobel, *They Satisfy: The Cigarette in American Life* (New York: Anchor Press/Doubleday, 1978).

2. Nannie May Tilley, *The Bright Tobacco Industry, 1860–1929* (Chapel Hill: University of North Carolina Press, 1948), 507–8. In the 1860s, Charleston tobacconists routinely advertised "seegars," pipe tobaccos, and other smoking products without mentioning cigarettes. For example, see *Charleston Daily Courier,* 30 March 1866.

3. Tilley, *Bright Tobacco,* 507.

4. The nausea experienced by novice smokers and the body's initial rejection of tobacco were graphically represented in antitobacco tracts as early as the 1630s. See Wolfgang Schivelbusch, *Tastes of Paradise: A Social History of Spices, Stimulants, and Intoxicants* (New York: Pantheon Books, 1992), 99–101.

5. Tilley, *Bright Tobacco,* 24–25.

6. The North Carolina border–Virginia tobacco area known as the Old Belt includes the North Carolina counties of Alamance, Caswell, Durham, Forsyth, Granville, Guilford, Orange, Person, Rockingham, Stokes, and Vance. The Virginia counties of the Old Belt include Franklin, Halifax, Henry, Mecklenberg, Patrick, and Pittsylvania. See ibid., 12.

7. See advertisements in *Southern Planter,* June 1868.

8. Tilley, *Bright Tobacco,* 24–88, 507–9. There were several competing flue-

curing technologies. See W. H. Snow, *Snow's Modern Barn System of Raising and Curing Tobacco*, 4th ed. (Baltimore: Friedenwald, 1895).

9. All data on tobacco manufacture and consumption are from U.S. Department of Commerce, Bureau of the Census, *Historical Statistics of the United States: Colonial Times to 1970, Part I* (Washington, D.C.: U.S. Government Printing Office, 1976), 690–91. Of course, many smokers "rolled their own" using granulated tobacco.

10. Sobel, *They Satisfy*, 31.

11. Tilley, *Bright Tobacco*, 569.

12. Robert F. Durden, *The Dukes of Durham, 1865–1929* (Durham: Duke University Press, 1975), 26; see also Tilley, *Bright Tobacco*, 570–74.

13. Sobel, *They Satisfy*, 33.

14. See "Dates of Internal Revenue Acts and Rates of Tax Imposed on Tobacco Products" in U.S. Department of Agriculture, *Statistical Bulletin No. 58: First Annual Report on Tobacco Statistics* (Washington, D.C.: U.S. Government Printing Office, 1937), 135. Revenue collections on cigarettes fell from $929,000 in 1882 to $454,000 in 1883.

15. W. K. Boyd, *The Story of Durham, City of the New South* (Durham: Duke University Press, 1925), 87–93; American Tobacco Company, *"Sold American!": The First Fifty Years* (New York: American Tobacco Company, 1954), 19.

16. U.S. Department of Commerce, Bureau of the Census, *Historical Statistics*, 609–10.

17. J. R. Dodge, "Report on Agriculture," *Tenth Census*, 1883, 3:57; Tilley, *Bright Tobacco*, 327.

18. *Charleston News and Courier*, 4 December 1886.

19. U.S. Department of Commerce, Bureau of the Census, *Statistics of Agriculture in the United States* (Washington, D.C.: U.S. Government Printing Office, 1895), 449.

20. As a young man, Rogers (1857–1945) signed his name "junior." By the 1930s, however, he was referred to as "senior." The Rogers farm was located between Mars Bluff and Black Creek along SC 327 near the present Country Club of South Carolina. This area was transferred to Florence County in 1888. Biographical information is from F. M. Rogers File, Frank M. Rogers Papers, Darlington Historical Commission, Darlington, S.C. See also *Cyclopedia of Eminent and Representative Men of the Carolinas of the Nineteenth Century*, vol. 1 (Madison, Wisc: Brant and Fuller, 1892), 606–7; G. Wayne King, *Rise Up So Early: A History of Florence County, South Carolina* (Spartanburg: Reprint Company, 1981), 91–101.

21. *Charleston News and Courier*, 28 January 1889. The Rogers family attended nearby Christ Episcopal Church.

22. See article by Frank Mandeville Rogers for the "Golden Anniversary Jubilee" in *Florence Morning News*, 8 October 1935. See also South Carolina Department of Agriculture, Commerce, and Industries, *South Carolina Tobacco Report, 1938* (Columbia: Gonzales and Bryan, 1939), 14–16. The report includes an article by the

Works Progress Administration Federal Writers' Project on the origins of Bright Leaf in South Carolina. An interview with Frank Mandeville Rogers is cited.

23. There is some confusion about the year of Rogers's first tobacco experiment, but the best evidence dates it to 1884. Rogers stated in 1935 that he planted his first experimental crop in that year, but accounts published in 1889 imply that the first crop was planted in 1883. See *Charleston News and Courier,* 28 January 1889; *Florence Morning News,* 8 October 1935.

24. *Charleston News and Courier,* 28 January 1889, 3 August 1958. See also South Carolina Department of Agriculture, Commerce, and Industries, *Tobacco Report, 1938,* 2. Granville County, North Carolina, produced extraordinarily fine tobacco.

25. On Richard E. Rives, see Rogers's article in *Florence Morning News,* 8 October 1935; South Carolina Department of Agriculture, Commerce, and Industries, *Bulletin, 1938,* 15; also South Carolina Department of Agriculture, *Tobacco Report, 1947* (Columbia: State Printers, 1948), 2–6. (Some sources render the name "Rivers.") Robert Eugene "Dad" Currin (1868–1948) married Claude Ashby of Mars Bluff in 1891. See article on R. E. Currin in *Florence Morning News,* 4 September 1947. Currin is buried in Mount Hope Cemetery, Florence.

26. *Darlington News,* 17 November 1887; *Charleston News and Courier,* 12 June 1889, 2 October 1891. On leaf tobacco prices in the mid-1880s, see commodity price reports in *Charleston News and Courier,* 11 December 1886.

27. On costs of producing cotton in South Carolina, see Paul F. Hammond in *Annual Report of the Commissioner of Agriculture, 1885* (Columbia: State Printers, 1886). In 1886, the commissioner of agriculture reckoned the average net profit from an acre of cotton to be $12.43.

28. On early tobacco growers at Mars Bluff, see King, *Rise Up So Early,* 121. See also *Charleston News and Courier,* 28 January 1889.

29. Until 1888, Mars Bluff was in Darlington County.

30. *Darlington News,* 17 November 1887, 27 September 1888, 12 December 1889. Rogers later sold his 1888 crop for $8,634. See *Charleston News and Courier,* 12 June 1889.

31. On Francis Warrington Dawson (1840–89), see E. Culpepper Clark, *Francis Warrington Dawson and the Politics of Restoration: South Carolina, 1874–1889* (University: University of Alabama Press, 1980).

32. See, for example, *Charleston News and Courier,* 26 October, 11 November 1885, 11 December 1886. The seed, a Cuban cigar leaf variety, did not thrive in South Carolina. The seed and pamphlets were obtained from R. L. Ragland, a Virginia tobacco expert.

33. See *Charleston News and Courier,* 12 January, 30 December 1886, 10 February 1887, 12 June 1889, 2 October 1891, 26 January 1895. Dawson also donated a quantity of seed to the South Carolina Agricultural and Mechanical Society for distribution to members.

34. An outstanding example of the *Charleston News and Courier*'s tobacco boosterism is the issue of 26 January 1895. The entire front page of this Saturday

edition was dedicated to Bright Leaf success stories from Darlington and Florence County tobacco growers.

35. *Columbia State,* 1, 9 February 1892; Mary Parramore, "Preservation Plan for Historic Tobacco Related Resources," State Historic Preservation Office, South Carolina Department of Archives and History, Columbia, 1990.

36. *Columbia State,* 27 January 1892. On Gonzales, see Lewis P. Jones, *Stormy Petrel: N. G. Gonzales and His State* (Columbia: University of South Carolina Press, 1970).

37. *Columbia State,* 5 September 1892.

38. *Baptist Courier* (Greenville), 13 March 1889.

39. Ibid., 6 November 1890.

40. *Charleston News and Courier,* 18 December 1885.

41. Pete Daniel, *Breaking the Land: The Transformation of Cotton, Rice, and Tobacco Cultures Since 1880* (Urbana: University of Illinois Press, 1985), 37. Farms producing both cotton and tobacco became commonplace in many Pee Dee counties. For example, of Darlington's 4,650 farms, 4,259 planted cotton and 1,779 planted tobacco in 1925. Obviously, considerable overlap took place. See U.S. Department of Commerce, Bureau of the Census, *Census of Agriculture, 1925,* 389; *Thirteenth Census* (1910) Statistics for South Carolina, 628–31; *Fourteenth Census* (1920) South Carolina Compendium, 54, 68–72.

42. *Charleston News and Courier,* 18 December 1885.

43. Ibid., 20 January 1886.

44. Ibid. South Carolina then had thirty-four counties. Two samples were received from Colleton, Greenville, and Sumter Counties. There was no sample reported from Barnwell County.

45. Ibid., 1 March 1887.

46. Ibid.

47. *Florence Morning News,* 8 October 1935.

48. *Marion Star,* 20 July, 10 August 1892. Wrapper, so called because it was used to wrap plugs of chewing tobacco, was highly prized and very valuable. See E. D. Lewis, "History of the Mullins Tobacco Market," in *The City of Opportunity: Centennial Commemorative Book About Mullins, 1872–1972,* ed. Frank G. Mason (N.p.: Mullins Centennial Commission, 1972).

49. On William Henry Daniel (1841–1915), see Herbert Ravenel Sass, *The Story of the South Carolina Lowcountry,* 3 vols. (West Columbia, S.C.: J. F. Hyer, 1956), 3:624–27; also *Mullins Enterprise,* Fortieth Anniversary Edition, 26 August 1937.

50. *Marion Star,* 5 September 1894. Daniel's first crop was planted by a mill pond near Mullins. See *Mullins Enterprise,* Fortieth Anniversary Edition, 26 August 1937.

51. *Marion Star,* 6 February 1895; see also *Mullins Enterprise,* Fortieth Anniversary Edition, 26 August 1937.

52. The first record of flue-cured tobacco in Horry County is a report to the *Charleston News and Courier* of 1 January 1889 that "three gentlemen in the Powell-

ville section" had employed a North Carolinian to "superintend a tobacco crop" for them in 1889. Though unnamed in the report, the *Horry Herald* and *Charleston World* later identified James C. Bryant as the grower. It is probable that John P. Derham was one of the others. The *Charleston News and Courier* report was submitted by "R. B. S."—Robert Bethea Scarborough.

53. *Charleston News and Courier,* 1 March 1887.

54. *Horry Herald,* 22 August 1889. See reprint from *Charleston World* in *Horry Herald,* 29 August 1889.

55. Joseph William Holliday (1827–1904). See *Horry Herald,* 22 March, 21 June, 5 July, 16 August 1894; Joseph W. Holliday, "Horry Tobacco Planting," *Independent Republic Quarterly* 2 (April 1968): 6–8; "The Ferry," *Independent Republic Quarterly* 1 (October 1967): 10.

56. See Janet H. Woodard, ed., *1850 Census of Horry County, South Carolina* (Greenville: A Press, 1980), 56; Charles W. Joyner, *Down by the Riverside: A South Carolina Slave Community* (Urbana: University of Illinois Press, 1984), 29–30.

57. Henry Lee Buck II (1844–1902). A *Charleston News and Courier* article of 23 February 1941 reprinted in the *Independent Republic Quarterly* (April 1969) is filled with inaccuracies.

58. Peter A. Coclanis, *Shadow of a Dream: Economic Life and Death in the South Carolina Low Country, 1670–1820* (New York: Oxford University Press, 1989), 155.

59. *Georgetown Times,* 8 October 1892. On Josiah Doar, see J. C. Garlington, *Men of the Time: Sketches of Living Notables* (Spartanburg: Author, 1902), 115.

60. *Georgetown Times,* 10 April, 10 August 1895, 6 September 1902. Georgetown County's first warehouse opened in Andrews in 1915, though many Georgetown farmers were closer to markets in Lake City, Hemingway, and Johnsonville. On preference for markets, see *Georgetown Times,* 28 July 1915.

61. Joseph W. Holliday, "Early Tobacco Planting," *Independent Republic Quarterly,* Tricentennial Edition, 1970, 20.

62. King, *Rise Up So Early,* 169.

63. In 1890, Florence County produced more than half of South Carolina's tobacco crop. See U.S. Department of Commerce, Bureau of the Census, *Eleventh Census* (1890), Agriculture Schedules, 449. On the expansion of Bright Leaf culture in Florence County, see King, *Rise Up So Early,* 167–78.

64. *Florence Morning News,* 23 July 1969; South Carolina Department of Agriculture, *Tobacco Report, 1938,* 2; King, *Rise Up So Early,* 169.

65. *Charleston News and Courier,* 2 October 1891, 1 February 1896; King, *Rise Up So Early,* 65, 75.

66. *Charleston News and Courier,* 2 October 1891; King, *Rise Up So Early,* 65, 75, 171–72, 177, 184, 238, 282, 284, 374, 380.

67. *Charleston News and Courier,* 2 October 1891.

68. *Columbia State,* 2 October 1891.

69. The Sanborn Map of 1893 shows the "Florence Tobacco W. Ho. Co." facing north on Darlington Street just east of Dargan. The building was fifty feet

wide by two hundred feet long with the narrow side fronting the street. The Florence Tobacco Co. "Tobacco Factory," with areas for "prizing, rolling, grading and storage," stood south and slightly west of the warehouse. See "Sanborn Map of Florence, S.C." (1893), South Caroliniana Library, University of South Carolina, Columbia.

70. *Charleston News and Courier,* 2 October 1891; *Columbia State,* 2 October 1891.

71. *Charleston News and Courier,* 2 October 1891; *Columbia State,* 2 October 1891. The bid of $2.05 per pound was inflated. It was customary for a visiting dignitary to "buy" the first pile of the season at an inflated price. Harmon estimated the actual value of the tobacco at from "75 cents to $1 per pound."

72. On the Darlington Tobacco Company, see *Columbia State,* 14 September 1892; on the farming operations of Dargan, McCullough, Ward, and Wipple, see *Charleston News and Courier,* 25 January 1895; on McCullough's cotton interests, see *Charleston News and Courier,* 26 August 1893; on Darlington Warehouse, see *Darlington News,* 11 August, 8 September, 27 September 1892; *Charleston News and Courier,* 18, 28 September 1892. C. S. McCullough later served as mayor of Darlington.

73. The hurricane of 27 August 1893 was extensively covered in all South Carolina newspapers. See especially the *Charleston News and Courier,* 29 August–15 September 1893. The cotton crop of South Carolina was estimated to be short one hundred thousand bales. See *Horry Herald,* 12 October 1893.

74. *Charleston News and Courier,* 14 September 1893.

75. Ibid., 8, 14 September 1893.

76. Ibid., 30 September, 4, 5 October 1893.

77. See "Clarendon," ibid., 2 January 1895.

78. See "Williamsburg," ibid., 2 January 1895.

79. *Marion Star,* 2 September 1891.

80. See "Clarendon," *Charleston News and Courier,* 2 January 1895.

81. Ibid.

82. See "Williamsburg" and "Clarendon," *Charleston News and Courier,* 2 January 1895.

83. "Williamsburg," ibid., 2 January 1895; "Darlington," ibid. The quote is from *Charleston News and Courier,* 26 January 1895.

84. Tilley, *Bright Tobacco,* 145. The *Southern Tobacco Journal* was published in Winston, North Carolina. The Atlantic Coast Line Railroad consolidated several smaller lines in the 1890s.

85. King, *Rise Up So Early,* 176.

86. *Columbia State,* 30 August 1895.

87. This is not Captain John McSween, the pioneer tobacco grower near Mars Bluff but another bearing the same name. This John McSween moved to Timmonsville about 1870, established a business, and was later cashier in the Bank of Timmonsville.

88. *Columbia State,* 30 August 1895; *Charleston News and Courier,* 31 August

1895; see drawing of the Timmonsville Warehouse in *Charleston News and Courier,* 1 February 1896. See especially Charles A. Smith's letter to the *Charleston News and Courier,* 2 September 1895.

89. *Columbia State,* 30 August 1895; *Charleston News and Courier,* 31 August, 20 December 1895; *South Carolina Tobacconist* (Sumter), 3 March 1896. The depot formerly served the Charleston, Sumter and Northern Railroad.

90. On the Florence Warehouse, see *Columbia State,* 30 August 1895.

91. *Florence Weekly Times,* 25 April, 11 July 1895; *Charleston News and Courier,* 26 January, 26 August 1895; *Columbia State,* 23, 30 August 1895; *Darlington News,* 22 August 1895. The factory was operated by the Burch brothers of Durham.

92. See community columns in *Marion Star* 1893 and 1894, passim; for example, 26 July 1893, 1 August 1894.

93. *Marion Star,* 1 May, 24 July, 21 August, 4 September 1895. Hutchings received $200 per month plus expenses.

94. Ibid., 4 September 1895.

95. Ibid.; *Mullins Enterprise,* Fortieth Anniversary Edition, 26 August 1937; J. E. Norment, *The Pee Dee Tobacco Belt of South Carolina: A Condensed Review of the Tobacco Industry, with Special Reference to the Home Markets at Mullins, Timmonsville, Florence, and Darlington* (Columbia: State Publishing, 1903), 6–10.

96. *Charleston News and Courier,* 10 September 1895; *Marion Star,* 4 September 1895; see also reminiscences of M. M. Byrd, *Mullins Enterprise,* Fortieth Anniversary Edition, 26 August 1937.

97. *Horry Herald,* 8, 29 June, 6, 27 July 1899. John Edmond Coles remained in Conway and helped found St. Paul's Episcopal Church about 1913.

98. *Horry Herald,* 8, 29 June, 6, 27 July 1899.

99. *Horry Herald,* 3 August 1899.

100. Ibid., 27 July, 24 August 1899.

101. U.S. Department of Commerce, Bureau of the Census, *Report on the Statistics of Agriculture in the United States at the Eleventh Census: 1890* (Washington, D.C.: U.S. Government Printing Office, 1895), 449.

102. *Columbia State,* 30 August 1895. In the 1890s, Marion County included what in 1910 became Dillon County. Statistics for Marion County from *Eleventh Census* (1890), *Report on the Statistics of Agriculture,* 43; *Twelfth Census* (1900), *Agriculture,* pt. 2, Crops and Irrigation, 53.

103. "Darlington," *Charleston News and Courier,* 3 January 1896.

104. See Eli Gregg & Son, ledgers and account books, 1890–91, bound volumes, South Caroliniana Library, University of South Carolina, Columbia.

105. On free tobacco seeds, see advertisements of Center Brick Warehouse in *Darlington News and Press,* 28 December 1911, 13 February 1913.

106. *Marion Star,* 11 December 1889.

107. See tenancy agreement of Dr. Horace Williamson and Julia D. Coburn, 8 June 1895, Judgement Roll No. 4230, Darlington County Historical Commission, Darlington, S.C.

108. In 1925, Horry County had only half the cotton acreage of Marion County, one-third that of Florence, one-fifth that of Williamsburg, and one-seventh that of Marlboro. See *Census of Agriculture, 1925,* South Carolina, County Tables, 378–82. Between 1889 and 1929, tenancy in Horry County grew from 16.4 percent of the farm population to 45.6 percent. See Tilley, *Bright Tobacco,* 94–95.

109. Tilley, *Bright Tobacco,* 94–95.

110. See Thomas Benton Young for Clemson College, *Tobacco Culture in South Carolina: Popular Bulletin No. 86* (Columbia: R. L. Bryan, 1904).

111. See South Carolina Experiment Station of Clemson Agricultural College, *Fortieth Anniversary Report, 1947* (N.p.: Clemson College, n.d.); also South Carolina Department of Agriculture, Commerce, and Industries, *Tobacco Report, 1947.*

112. *Florence Times,* 7 August 1913.

113. U.S. Department of Commerce, Bureau of the Census, *Thirteenth Census, 1910,* vol. 3, Population, 649–50. See also Tobacco Institute, *South Carolina and Tobacco: A Chapter in America's Industrial Growth* (Washington, D.C.: Tobacco Institute, 1977), 16.

114. *Columbia State,* 30 September 1895.

115. *Florence Times,* 7 August 1913.

116. John G. Sproat and Larry Schweikart, *Making Change: South Carolina Banking in the Twentieth Century* (Columbia: South Carolina Bankers Association, 1990), 193–97.

117. *Columbia State,* 19 April 1906.

118. *South Carolina Handbook, 1907* (Columbia: State Printers, 1908), 329–31.

119. *Columbia State,* 19 April 1906.

120. Norment, *Pee Dee Tobacco Belt,* 6–13. See also *Columbia State,* 23 October 1892.

121. *Columbia State,* 1 February 1896.

122. Durwood T. Stokes, *History of Dillon County, South Carolina* (Columbia: University of South Carolina Press, 1978), 202; King, *Rise Up So Early,* 317.

123. Sproat and Schweikart, *Making Change,* figure 7, 208, and figure 9, 210.

124. South Carolina Department of Agriculture, Commerce, and Industries, *Seventh Annual Report, 1910* (Columbia: State Printers, 1911). On the boom of the early twentieth century, see Sproat and Schweikart, *Making Change,* 35–37.

125. Daniel, *Breaking the Land,* 35. On the Tobacco Trust, see Reaves Cox, *Competition in the American Tobacco Industry, 1911–1932: A Study of the Effects of the Partition of the American Tobacco Company by the Supreme Court* (New York: Columbia University Press, 1942).

126. For local reaction to the effect of war on Pee Dee tobacco growers, see *Georgetown Times,* 8 August 1914 and 18 September 1915. See also Sproat and Schweikart, *Making Change,* 42.

127. U.S. Department of Commerce, Bureau of the Census, *Historical Statistics,* 208.

128. Sobel, *They Satisfy,* 84–86.

129. Tilley, *Bright Tobacco*, 613; Robert C. Joseph, *Tobacco in America* (New York: Knopf, 1952), 234.

130. Compiled from *Thirteenth Census* (1910), vol. 7, *Agriculture*, 516–19, and *Fourteenth Census* (1920), vol. 6, pt. 2, pp. 286–90. See also Compendium for South Carolina (1920).

131. South Carolina Department of Agriculture, Commerce, and Industries, *Tobacco Report: Statistics for the Production and Marketing of Tobacco in South Carolina in 1920, Bulletin No. 76* (Columbia: Gonzales and Bryan, 1920), 25.

Georgetown offers a good example of the wartime tobacco boom. By 1920, two warehouses and a stemmery were operating there. The Georgetown Warehouse was located on the northeast side of Highmarket Street between Frazier and Hazard Streets. A stemmery was located next door. New Planters' Warehouse opened in July 1920. See *Georgetown Times,* 1 October 1918, 26 February 1919, *Georgetown Times-Index,* 9 April, 9 July 1920.

132. Two good general treatments of the agrarian revolt are Theodore Saloutos, *Farmer Movements in the South, 1865–1933* (Berkeley and Los Angeles: University of California Press, 1960), and Robert C. McMath Jr., *Populist Vanguard: A History of the Southern Farmers' Alliance* (Chapel Hill: University of North Carolina Press, 1975).

CHAPTER FOUR: Reform and Reaction, 1918–1926

1. U.S. Department of Agriculture, *Yearbook 1922* (Washington, D.C.: U.S. Government Printing Office, 1923), 434–36; also T. J. Woofter Jr., *The Plight of Cigarette Tobacco* (Chapel Hill: University of North Carolina Press, 1931), 43–44.

2. South Carolina Department of Agriculture, Commerce, and Industries, *Tobacco Report: Statistics for the Production and Marketing of Tobacco in South Carolina in 1920, Bulletin No. 76* (Columbia: Gonzales and Bryan, 1920), 25.

3. Interview with C. P. Brewer by Eldred E. Prince Jr. and Robert Simpson, Loris, S.C., 18 May 1992. Brewer was born in 1902.

4. South Carolina Department of Agriculture, Commerce, and Industries, *Eleventh Annual Report, 1914* (Columbia: Gonzales and Bryan, 1915), 51–52.

5. South Carolina Department of Agriculture, Commerce, and Industries, *Tobacco Report, 1920,* 11.

6. On pinhookers, see Nannie May Tilley, *The Bright Tobacco Industry, 1860–1929* (Chapel Hill: University of North Carolina Press, 1948), 298–303; South Carolina Department of Agriculture, Commerce, and Industries, *Seventeenth Annual Report, 1920,* 57.

7. Aaron Sapiro, "Rolling Their Own," *Survey,* 1 April 1923, quoted in Woofter, *Plight of Cigarette Tobacco,* 43–44.

8. Interview with Edward Walden by author, Tabor City, North Carolina, 21 July 1991.

9. Tilley, *Bright Tobacco,* 398–400; interview with Walden, 21 July 1991. London

factors traditionally charged 2.5 percent in the seventeenth century. It was also the customary rate among cotton factors. See Harold D. Woodman, *King Cotton and His Retainers: Financing and Marketing the Cotton Crop of the South, 1800–1925* (Lexington: University Press of Kentucky, 1968), 49–51.

10. Tilley, *Bright Tobacco,* 401–5. On the Farmers' Alliance, see Robert C. McMath, *Populist Vanguard: A History of the Southern Farmers' Alliance* (Chapel Hill: University of North Carolina Press, 1975).

11. See minutes published in *South Carolina Tobacconist,* 17 March 1896; also *Florence Daily Times,* 9 March 1896, 11 April 1895; G. Wayne King, *Rise Up So Early: A History of Florence County, South Carolina* (Spartanburg: Reprint Company, 1981), 380.

12. *Acts of South Carolina, 1899* (Columbia: State Printing, 1900), 91–92. The law exempted three Pee Dee counties from compliance, ostensibly because those markets were small and required higher charges to survive on the smaller amounts of leaf they handled.

13. South Carolina Department of Agriculture, Commerce, and Industries, *Eleventh Annual Report, 1914; Columbia State,* 13 December 1914; also *Journal of the House of Representatives,* General Assembly, Regular Session, 1915, 79, 438, 548–49.

14. William H. Nicholls, *Price Policies in the Cigarette Industry* (Nashville: Vanderbilt University Press, 1951), 62.

15. Tilley, *Bright Tobacco,* 279–80.

16. Anthony J. Badger, *Prosperity Road: The New Deal, Tobacco, and North Carolina* (Chapel Hill: University of North Carolina Press, 1980), 18–20.

17. U.S. Department of Agriculture, *Yearbook 1922* (Washington, D.C.: U.S. Government Printing Office, 1921), 444; also Woofter, *Plight of Cigarette Tobacco,* 11, 72.

18. Woofter, *Plight of Cigarette Tobacco,* 11, 40–41.

19. U.S. Department of Agriculture, *Yearbook 1922,* 439; see also Woofter, *Plight of Cigarette Tobacco,* 10–12, 23–24.

20. Woofter, *Plight of Cigarette Tobacco,* 11–15.

21. Department of Agriculture, Commerce, and Industries, *Fourteenth Annual Report, 1917* (Columbia: Gonzales and Bryan, 1918), 33–34.

22. On David R. Coker, see James Rogers with Larry E. Nelson, *Mr. D. R.: A Biography of David R. Coker* (Hartsville, S.C.: Coker College Press, 1994), quotes from 108 and 116.

23. *Columbia State,* 26 October 1919.

24. South Carolina Department of Agriculture, Commerce, and Industries, *Tobacco Report, 1920,* 3.

25. South Carolina Department of Agriculture, Commerce, and Industries, *Sixteenth Annual Report, 1919* (Columbia: Gonzales and Bryan, 1920), 40–41.

26. *Columbia State,* 26 July 1919; *Progressive Farmer,* 7 August 1920.

27. South Carolina Department of Agriculture, Commerce, and Industries, *Tobacco Report, 1920,* 15–16. See also Bright Williamson Tobacco File, Bright Wil-

liamson Papers, Darlington Historical Commission, Darlington, S.C. On Bright Williamson, see J. C. Garlington, *Men of the Time: Sketches of Living Notables* (Spartanburg: Author, 1902), 455.

28. *Marion Star,* 5 January 1921. On James Yadkin Joyner's remarkable career, see George-Anne Willard in William S. Powell, ed., *Dictionary of North Carolina Biography,* vol. 3 (Chapel Hill: University of North Carolina Press, 1979), 336–38. On Joyner's leadership of the Tobacco Growers Association, see *Columbia State,* 15 July 1925.

29. On the career of Aaron Sapiro, see Grace Larsen and Henry Erdman, "Aaron Sapiro: Genius of Farm Cooperative Marketing," *Mississippi Valley Historical Review* 49 (September 1962): 242–68; see also Theodore Salutous and John D. Hicks, *Agricultural Discontent in the Middle West, 1900–1939* (Madison: University of Wisconsin Press, 1951), 255–85.

30. *Progressive Farmer,* 4 June 1921.

31. The co-op recognized five belts: the Old Belt, Eastern North Carolina, South Carolina, Dark Fired, and Sun Cured. See *Horry Herald,* 31 March 1921; also *Marion Star,* 5 January 1921; *Kingstree County Record,* 9 January 1922.

32. On Clarence Hamilton Poe (1881–1964), see Joseph A. Cote, "Poe, Clarence Hamilton," in Charles R. Wilson and William Ferris, eds., *Encyclopedia of Southern Culture* (Chapel Hill: University of North Carolina Press, 1989), 43–44.

33. Clarence H. Poe, *How Farmers Co-operate and Double Profits: First Hand Reports on All the Leading Forms of Rural Co-operation in the United States and Europe—Stories That Show How Farmers Can Co-operate by Showing How They Have Done It and Are Doing It* (New York: Orange Judd Co., 1915).

34. Clarence H. Poe, *My First 80 Years* (Chapel Hill: University of North Carolina Press, 1963). See, for example, *Progressive Farmer,* 26 February, 4 June, 23 July, 2 September 1921. An annual circulation of 10,400,000 was claimed by the *Progressive Farmer.* See issue of 23 February 1923.

35. Poe, *How Farmers Co-operate and Double Profits.*

36. A good summary of the cooperative marketing movement is David E. Hamilton, *From New Day to New Deal: American Farm Policy from Hoover to Roosevelt, 1928–1933* (Chapel Hill: University of North Carolina Press, 1991), 13–19; see also Larsen and Erdman, "Aaron Sapiro." In the Pee Dee press see *Marion Star,* 2 March 1922, 25 January 1923; see also letter of James C. Stone, *Kingstree County Record,* 8 February 1922. On the prune growers co-op, see *Progressive Farmer,* 4 June 1921.

37. Larsen and Erdman, "Aaron Sapiro," 254–55.

38. See sample co-op contract in box 256.5, cooperative marketing folder, Clarence Hamilton Poe Papers, North Carolina Division of Archives and History, Raleigh; U.S. Department of Agriculture, *Yearbook 1922,* 441–42; *Columbia State,* 8 August 1922; *Progressive Farmer,* 16 July 1921.

39. U.S. Department of Agriculture, *Yearbook 1922,* 440; South Carolina Department of Agriculture, Commerce, and Industries, *Tobacco Report, 1920,* 5–8, 15.

40. State of South Carolina, *Acts and Resolutions of the South Carolina Assembly, 1921* (Columbia: State Printers, 1922), 339–50; quote from Article 24.

41. Thomas B. Young to Bright Williamson, 18 July 1921, Bright Williamson Tobacco File, Bright Williamson Papers.

42. On enrollment efforts in the spring of 1921 see *Horry Herald,* 31 March 1921. On the co-op's decision not to market the 1921 crop, see Tilley, *Bright Tobacco,* 454.

43. *Kingstree County Record,* 21 July 1921; *Columbia State,* 20 July 1921.

44. *Marion Star,* 27 July 1921.

45. Ibid. See also *Columbia State,* 18 August 1921.

46. *Marion Star,* 20 July 1921; *Progressive Farmer,* 26 November 1921.

47. *Columbia State,* 4 July 1922; *Horry Herald,* 20 April 1922. The Kentuckians were mostly Burley producers and the Virginians mostly dark-fired growers.

48. *Horry Herald,* 15 June 1922.

49. *Marion Star,* 9 November 1921.

50. See *Kingstree County Record,* 6 April 1922; *Horry Herald,* 20 April, 15 June, 3 August 1922; *Columbia State,* 11 July 1922.

51. U.S. Department of Agriculture, *Yearbook 1922,* 445.

52. *Marion Star,* 9 November 1921.

53. *Kingstree County Record,* 11 May 1922; *Horry Herald,* 11 May, 15 June 1922; *Columbia State,* 8 August 1922. On former warehousemen employed by the co-op, see Tilley, *Bright Tobacco,* 479. The locations and numbers of co-op warehouses were Andrews (2), Aynor (2), Bamberg (1), Conway (1), Darlington (3), Dillon (2), Georgetown (1), Hartsville (3), Hemingway (3), Johnsonville and Kingstree (5), Lake City (1), Lake View (3), Lamar (1), Latta (1), Loris (2), Mullins (1), Nichols (1), Olanta (1), Pamplico (1), Summerville (1), and Timmonsville (2).

54. *Columbia State,* 8 August 1922.

55. Ibid.; *Kingstree County Record,* 10 August 1922; *Columbia State,* 24 August 1922; *Marion Star,* 23 March 1923.

56. *Columbia State,* 22 August 1922.

57. Ibid., 16 August 1922.

58. *Marion Star,* 14 September, 9 November 1922.

59. *Horry Herald,* 31 August 1922.

60. *Marion Star,* 1 August 1923.

61. Nathaniel C. Browder, *The Tri-State Tobacco Growers Association, 1922–1925: The Co-op That Failed* (1940; rpt. N.p.: N.p., 1983), 12; *Progressive Farmer,* 2 September 1922.

62. *Horry Herald,* 24 August 1922; see numerous complaint and summons forms of Tobacco Growers Cooperative Association, agriculture section, tobacco files, Darlington County Historical Commission, Darlington, S.C.

63. Browder, *Tri-State Tobacco Growers Association,* 19; *Kingstree County Record,* 26 April 1923.

64. Browder, *Tri-State Tobacco Growers Association,* 19.

65. *Horry Herald,* 16 August 1923. F. L. Willcox of the Florence firm of Willcox and Willcox represented the co-op. See summons and complaints of Tobacco Growers Cooperative Association in agricultural section, tobacco files, Darlington County Historical Commission. Some defendants in Darlington County were M. Knotts, S. E. Truett, W. B. Blackmon, Elliott Wilds, W. A. Windham, E. P. Sexton, J. B. Stokes, E. C. Jeffords, and W. T. Suggs.

66. *Horry Herald,* 16 August 1923; *Progressive Farmer,* 21 October 1922.

67. *Marion Star,* 26 March 1924; *Kingstree County Record,* 10 April 1924.

68. *Kingstree County Record,* 15 March 1923.

69. *Progressive Farmer,* 16 July 1921.

70. *Kingstree County Record,* 19 July 1923; *Columbia State,* 19 July 1923. Unfortunately, the papers of Senator Ellison D. Smith no longer exist. See Kathryn Jacob and Elizabeth Hornyak, eds., *Guide to Research Collections of Former United States Senators, 1789–1982* (Washington, D.C.: U.S. Senate Historical Office, 1983), 238.

71. *Kingstree County Record,* 9 August 1923.

72. *Horry Herald,* 22 March 1923; *Marion Star,* 21 March 1923; *Kingstree County Record,* 15 March 1923.

73. *Marion Star,* 21 March 1923.

74. Ibid., 1 August 1923.

75. Ibid., 29 August 1923.

76. Interview with C. P. Brewer, 18 May 1992.

77. South Carolina Department of Agriculture, Commerce, and Industries, *Twentieth Annual Report, 1923* (Columbia: State Printers, 1924), 41.

78. *Kingstree County Record,* 19 July 1923.

79. Ibid., 12 September 1923; *Progressive Farmer,* 22 January 1927.

80. Clarence H. Poe to John W. Gold, 22 October 1926, box 256.10, tobacco folder, Poe Papers. See also *Progressive Farmer,* 22 January 1927.

81. *Columbia State,* 15 July 1925. Joyner received $6,000 per year in 1922, 1923, and 1924. In 1925, Joyner collected $1,249 for expenses. Bright Williamson, who represented Pee Dee growers on the co-op's board of directors for four years, received $5 for his services. See *Progressive Farmer,* 22 January 1927.

82. Tilley, *Bright Tobacco,* 471, 474.

83. Larsen and Erdman, "Aaron Sapiro," 267; also Browder, *Tri-State Tobacco Growers Association,* 11; *Southern Tobacco Journal,* 8 May 1923; Tilley, *Bright Tobacco,* 474–77.

84. *Columbia State,* 5 August 1925; Browder, *Tri-State Tobacco Growers Association,* 12–13; see *Acts and Joint Resolutions of the South Carolina General Assembly, 1924* (Columbia: State Printers, 1925), 993–96.

85. On pledging partial crops, see *Progressive Farmer,* 22 January 1927.

86. *Horry Herald,* 4 January 1923. The actual figure reported for South Carolina was 15,356,949 pounds. For 1923 see South Carolina Department of Agriculture, Commerce, and Industries, *Annual Report, 1923,* 43. On 1924 see South Carolina

Department of Agriculture, Commerce, and Industries, *Twenty-first Annual Report, 1924* (Columbia: State Printers, 1925), 61. In 1924, the co-op reported sales of 11,075,474 pounds of South Carolina leaf of a total crop of 45,521,604 pounds, or 24.3 percent. For 1925, see South Carolina Department of Agriculture, Commerce, and Industries, *Twenty-second Annual Report, 1925* (Columbia: State Printers, 1926), 110.

87. "Annual Report of the Tri-State Tobacco Growers' Cooperative for 1924," box 256.10, tobacco folder, Poe Papers.

88. Tilley, *Bright Tobacco,* 462; *Columbia State,* 19 July 1923; Woofter, *Plight of Cigarette Tobacco,* 38; *Kingstree County Record,* 2 March 1922. R. J. Reynolds and Liggett & Myers also purchased substantial amounts of leaf from the Burley Growers Co-op in Kentucky.

89. See "Special Report on European Trip" in Bright Williamson Tobacco File, Bright Williamson Papers. See also Browder, *Tri-State Tobacco Growers Association,* 21; Tilley, *Bright Tobacco,* 462, 481; *Marion Star,* 23 July 1924.

90. Browder, *Tri-State Tobacco Growers Association,* 14–15.

91. Ibid., 15; also *Columbia State,* 15 July 1923.

92. *Kingstree County Record,* 19 July 1923; *Columbia State,* 19 July 1923.

93. *Columbia State,* 15 July 1925.

94. Browder, *Tri-State Tobacco Growers Association,* 6.

95. *Kingstree County Record,* 19 July 1923; *Marion Star,* 31 December 1924. See also *Horry Herald,* 14 September 1922.

96. *Columbia State,* 5 August 1925.

97. *Marion Star,* 26 March 1924; *Kingstree County Record,* 27 March 1924; Browder, *Tri-State Tobacco Growers Association,* 8; Tilley, *Bright Tobacco,* 460, 468.

98. See Tilley, *Bright Tobacco,* 460, 468; Browder, *Tri-State Tobacco Growers Association,* 17.

99. See "Annual Report of the Tri-State Tobacco Growers' Cooperative for 1924," box 256.10, tobacco folder, Poe Papers.

100. Ibid.; see also co-op advertisement in *Columbia State,* 1 August 1925.

101. *Horry Herald,* 24 December 1925; *Marion Star,* 27 May 1926.

102. The executives were R. R. Patterson, sales manager, and T. C. Watkins, warehouse manager. See Aaron Sapiro to George Norwood, 12 March 1926, carbon copy in box 256.5, co-op marketing folder, Poe Papers; see also *Progressive Farmer,* 22 January 1927; Tilley, *Bright Tobacco,* 482–83; Browder, *Tri-State Tobacco Growers Association,* 22–23. For local coverage, see *Horry Herald,* 28 January 1926.

103. *Columbia State,* 1 July 1926; Browder, *Tri-State Tobacco Growers Association,* 31, 33; *Progressive Farmer,* 22 January 1927, 4.

104. See Woofter, *Plight of Cigarette Tobacco,* 82–83, 93–95.

105. Poe, *How Farmers Co-operate and Double Profits,* 8.

106. *Horry Herald,* 7 August 1924; Tilley, *Bright Tobacco,* 450.

107. Some observers recognized at the time that some farmers had unrealistic

hopes for cooperative marketing as a panacea for all their troubles. See *Columbia State,* 22 July 1924.

108. Extract from 1920 census geographically depicted in the *Horry Herald,* 23 February 1922. The five counties were Cherokee, Chesterfield, Dillon, Horry, and Marlboro.

109. Browder, *Tri-State Tobacco Growers Association,* 7; Tilley, *Bright Tobacco,* 465; interview with C. P. Brewer, 18 May 1992.

110. Clarence Poe had warned against farmers who expected to profit from co-op activity but refused to join. See *Progressive Farmer,* 23 July 1921.

CHAPTER FIVE: The Abyss, 1926–1932

1. Lewis Cecil Gray, *History of Agriculture in the Southern United States to 1860,* 2 vols. (1932; rpt. Gloucester, Mass.: Peter Smith, 1958), 1:260.

2. Ibid., 260–66. The tobacco depression of the 1680s convinced struggling South Carolina leaf growers to abandon the crop in favor of rice. It proved a wise choice.

3. See John G. Miller, *The Black Patch War* (Chapel Hill: University of North Carolina Press, 1936). A good summary is Fred Shannon, *American Farmers' Movements* (Princeton: D. Van Nostrand, 1957), 75–77, 161–66. See also Theodore Salutous, *Farmer Movements in the South, 1865–1933* (Berkeley and Los Angeles: University of California Press, 1960), 167–83.

4. Shannon, *American Farmers' Movements,* 75–77, 161–66; Salutous, *Farmer Movements in the South,* 167–83.

5. T. J. Woofter Jr., *The Plight of Cigarette Tobacco* (Chapel Hill: University of North Carolina Press, 1931), 67.

6. Percentages are based on production of 1.289 billion pounds in 1926 rising to 1.648 billion pounds in 1930. Cigarette consumption in the United States increased from 92.5 billion in 1926 to 124.2 billion in 1930; see United States Department of Commerce, Bureau of the Census, *Historical Statistics of the United States: Colonial Times to 1970, Part J* (Washington, D.C.: U.S. Government Printing Office, 1976), 1:690, 517. Although a substantial amount of Bright Leaf was exported, this tobacco was manufactured into cigarettes in Great Britain. Woofter concluded that cigarette sales were a valid index of demand for leaf tobacco.

7. Woofter, *Plight of Cigarette Tobacco,* 72–74.

8. Anthony J. Badger, *Prosperity Road: The New Deal, Tobacco, and North Carolina* (Chapel Hill: University of North Carolina Press, 1980), 32.

9. For Bailey's remarks, see *Congressional Record,* 73d Cong., 2d sess., 5420–21. See William S. Powell, ed., *Dictionary of North Carolina Biography* (Chapel Hill: University of North Carolina Press, 1979), s.v. "Josiah William Bailey."

10. *Columbia State,* 11 August 1926; *Kingstree County Record,* 12 August 1926; see also South Carolina Department of Agriculture, Commerce, and Industries, *Yearbook, 1926* (Columbia: General Assembly, 1927), 18–21.

11. South Carolina produced 250.7 million pounds from 1927 to 1929. The previous record for a three-year period was 1918–20, when 209 million pounds were harvested in South Carolina.

12. *Horry Herald*, 5 January 1928.

13. Ibid., 9, 23 August 1928; South Carolina Department of Agriculture, Commerce, and Industries, *Yearbook, 1928* (Columbia: General Assembly, 1929), 38–40. The tobacco crops of 1928 and 1929 were compared in the *Columbia State*, 31 July 1929; see also John G. Sproat and Larry Schweikart, *Making Change: South Carolina Banking in the Twentieth Century* (Columbia: South Carolina Bankers Association, 1990), 60.

14. *Columbia State*, 7 August 1928.

15. Ibid., 8 August 1928.

16. Determining the laid-in cost of a labor-intensive product depends on how labor is valued. When much of the labor is supplied by the producer himself, it must be accounted for at the prevailing hire rate for that kind of labor. The laid-in cost of producing Bright Leaf tobacco was determined in the 1920s by the South Carolina Department of Agriculture, Commerce, and Industries by consolidating forty-seven field studies. The department calculated the prevailing labor rate at one dollar per day. See its *Twentieth Annual Report, 1923* (Columbia: State Printers, 1924); also Woofter, *Plight of Cigarette Tobacco*, 20.

17. Interview with C. P. Brewer by Eldred E. Prince Jr. and Robert Simpson, Loris, S.C., 18 May 1992.

18. David R. Coker to George Seay, 22 September 1928, and Coker to Daniel C. Roper, 21 September 1928, Coker Papers, South Caroliniana Library, University of South Carolina, Columbia. See also Sproat and Schweikart, *Making Change*, 60.

19. *Horry Herald*, 18 October, 27 December 1928.

20. Sproat and Schweikart, *Making Change*, 50; see James A. Rogers with Larry E. Nelson, *Mr. D. R.: A Biography of David R. Coker* (Hartsville, S.C.: Coker College Press, 1994), 174–75, 188. David Coker forestalled runs on the Bank of Hartsville and the Peoples Bank by guaranteeing their deposits with his personal fortune.

21. Rogers and Nelson, *Mr. D. R.*, 188.

22. *Horry Herald*, 21 February 1929.

23. Ibid., 28 February 1929; interview with Edward Walden by author, 21 July 1991.

24. *Horry Herald*, 23 August 1928.

25. *Columbia State*, 5 September 1928, 11.

26. *Marion Star*, 8 January 1930; also South Carolina Department of Agriculture, Commerce, and Industries, *Yearbook, 1929* (Columbia: General Assembly, 1930), 81.

27. *Horry Herald*, 6, 13 September 1928.

28. South Carolina's tobacco acreage declined from 148,000 to 118,000; overall tobacco production in all belts rose from 1,864,000 acres in 1928 to 1,980,000 in

1929. See U.S. Department of Commerce, Bureau of the Census, *Historical Statistics*, 1:517.

29. Encouraging tobacco culture in new areas to keep prices low was a common strategy of tobacco manufacturers. Besides the example referred to in the text, the American Tobacco Company helped organize Burley production in Ohio after being forced to pay higher prices to Kentucky growers. Company representatives even distributed Kentucky seed free to Ohio farmers. See Salutous, *Farmer Movements in the South*, 180.

30. *Columbia State*, 28, 31 July 1929. The Georgia tobacco crop matures earlier than the Carolinas'. Consequently, Georgia–Florida Belt markets traditionally open a week to ten days before the North Carolina–South Carolina Border Belt. Carolina tobacco interests generally regard Georgia prices as a bellwether for the season.

31. *Columbia State*, 4, 5 September 1929.

32. Ibid., 16 August 1929.

33. Ibid., 4, 5 September 1929.

34. On the evolution of Hoover's agricultural policy, see David E. Hamilton, *From New Day to New Deal: American Farm Policy from Hoover to Roosevelt, 1928–1933* (Chapel Hill: University of North Carolina Press, 1991), 26–49.

35. Ibid., 39.

36. On the Federal Farm Board, see William H. Peterson, *The Great Farm Problem* (Chicago: Henry Regnery, 1959), 93–96; Luther G. Tweeten, *Foundations of Farm Policy* (Lincoln: University of Nebraska Press, 1970), 300–301; Don Paarlberg, *American Farm Policy* (New York: Wiley, 1964), 151–52.

37. Peterson, *Great Farm Problem*, 95.

38. *Progressive Farmer*, 21 September 1929.

39. Ibid., 21 September 1927.

40. *Columbia State*, 11 August 1929.

41. *Marion Star*, 26 March, 9, 23 April 1930.

42. See sample contract in *Marion Star*, 22 January 1930.

43. *Horry Herald*, 11 September 1930.

44. See Badger, *Prosperity Road*, 30; also *Marion Star*, 8, 15, 22 January 1930, and especially 23 April 1930.

45. *Progressive Farmer*, 21 September 1929; *Marion Star*, 8 January 1930, 15 July 1931.

46. *Marion Star*, 9 April 1930.

47. See letter of H. K. Cooke, ibid., 9 October 1929.

48. *Horry Herald*, 21 August 1930.

49. *Marion Star*, 8 January, 26 March 1930.

50. *Horry Herald*, 24 July 1930.

51. Ibid., 7 August 1930; *Columbia State*, 3 August 1930.

52. *Columbia State*, 1 August 1930.

53. *Macon News*, 1 August 1930.

54. *Columbia State,* 2 August 1930. Stone was an organizer and manager of the Kentucky Burley Tobacco Growers Association.

55. *Marion Star,* 9 October 1930.

56. *Progressive Farmer,* 11 September 1930.

57. *Marion Star,* 1 October 1930; *Columbia State,* 2 August 1930; Interview with Harvey Graham by author, Loris, S.C., 23 June 1992.

58. *Columbia State,* 5 August 1930.

59. Interview with Brewer; *Columbia State,* 2, 3 August 1930.

60. *Columbia State,* 5 August 1930.

61. Ibid., 6 August 1930.

62. Ibid.; *Marion Star,* 13 August 1930.

63. *Columbia State,* 8 August 1930; *Horry Herald,* 9 August 1930; *Marion Star,* 13 August 1930; *Mullins Enterprise,* 27 August 1930.

64. *Columbia State,* 9 August 1930; on per acre operating losses, see *Marion Star,* 6 August 1930; see also ibid., 13 August 1930; *Horry Herald,* 11 September 1930. Some sources spell the name Paullett.

65. *Horry Herald,* 11 September 1930.

66. On earnings of tobacco companies, see Nannie M. Tilley, *The R. J. Reynolds Tobacco Company* (Chapel Hill: University of North Carolina Press, 1985), 575. On reaction in the Pee Dee to manufacturers' profits, see *Horry Herald,* 14 August 1930. On women smoking, see Robert Sobel, *They Satisfy: The Cigarette in American Life* (New York: Anchor Press/Doubleday, 1978), 95.

67. *New York Journal of Commerce,* 29 August 1929. Portions of the interview were quoted in the *Progressive Farmer,* 21 September 1929.

68. Badger, *Prosperity Road,* 23; William Nicholls, *Price Policies in the Cigarette Industry* (Nashville: Vanderbilt University Press, 1951), 73. The wholesale price rose from $6.40 per thousand to $6.85 per thousand. One thousand cigarettes equals fifty packages of twenty smokes. Although tobacco companies stubbornly denied charges of collusion and price fixing, all four announced identical price increases on the same day.

69. Nicholls, *Price Policies,* 72.

70. On per capita income, see Richard Easterlin et al., *Population Redistribution and Economic Growth, United States, 1870–1950,* vol. 1 (Philadelphia: American Philosophical Society, 1957), 753.

71. American Tobacco Company, *"Sold American!": The First Fifty Years* (New York: American Tobacco Company, 1954), 82. Hill's arrogance and personal eccentricities also rankled. An urbane New Yorker, Hill began affecting an enormous, white cowboy hat and traveled by limousine with a pair of dachshunds named "Lucky" and "Strike." See Sobel, *They Satisfy,* 94.

72. American Tobacco Company, *"Sold American!,"* 73–82.

73. Jane Carmichael for the Graylyn Conference Center, *The Story of Graylyn* (Winston-Salem: Wake Forest University, 1984), passim. The mule's name was Ida.

74. See South Carolina Department of Agriculture, Commerce, and Industries, *Yearbook, 1930* (Columbia: State Printers, 1931), 25; also *Horry Herald,* 11 September 1930.

75. *Columbia State,* 17 September 1930.

76. On Farm Board policy, see Peterson, *Great Farm Problem,* 93–96; Tweeten, *Foundations of Farm Policy,* 300–301; Paarlberg, *American Farm Policy,* 151–52.

77. Salutous, *Farmer Movements in the South,* 273–74.

78. *Horry Herald,* 5 February 1931.

79. Jefferson Boone Aiken to W. W. Long, 7 April 1931, carbon copy in box 256.10, tobacco folder, Poe Papers.

80. J. T. Lazar to W. W. Long, 7 April 1931, carbon copy, ibid.

81. J. C. Hudson, USDA Bureau of Statistics, quoted in *Columbia State,* 5 August 1930.

82. *Horry Herald,* 2 April 1931.

83. Gardner's program was widely quoted in both Carolinas. See *Raleigh News and Observer* article reprinted in *Horry Herald,* 9 April 1931.

84. On Gardner's plan, see Badger, *Prosperity Road,* 26–27. On rural life in South Carolina in the 1920s and 1930s, see Ben Robertson, *Red Hills and Cotton: An Upcountry Memory* (1960; rpt. University of South Carolina Press, 1991).

85. On efforts to establish co-ops in North Carolina and Virginia, see Badger, *Prosperity Road,* 23, 28–30, and Salutous, *Farmer Movements in the South,* 276; also *Horry Herald,* 9 April 1931. On lack of grower participation in these states, see J. R. Hutcheson to Clarence Poe, 1 April 1931, James C. Stone to J. R. Page (carbon copy), and "Report by William Collins of a survey made in the Eastern North Carolina Tobacco Territory," all in box 256.10, tobacco folder, Poe Papers.

86. See *Horry Herald,* 3 April 1931; *Marion Star,* 2 April 1931.

87. U.S. Department of Commerce, Bureau of the Census, *Historical Statistics,* 517–18.

88. *Columbia State,* 30 July, 4 August 1931.

89. Ibid., 5 August 1931.

90. Interview with Brewer, 18 May 1992.

91. *Marion Star,* 12 August 1931.

92. Ibid., 19, 26 August 1931.

93. Ibid., 2 September 1931.

94. Ibid., 9 September 1931; *Darlington News and Press,* 10 September 1931; *Horry Herald,* 10 September 1931.

95. Open letter to members reprinted in *Marion Star,* 2 September 1931.

96. See South Carolina Department of Agriculture, Commerce, and Industries, *Yearbook, 1931* (Columbia: State Printers, 1932), 22, 26–27.

97. Interview with Edward Walden by author, 21 July 1991.

98. Sproat and Schweikart, *Making Change,* 50.

99. *Marion Star,* 16 December 1931. The First National Bank and the Bank of

Mullins posted notices on Saturday, 12 December 1931. Weekends are a good time to go broke.

100. South Carolina Department of Agriculture, Commerce, and Industries, *Yearbook, 1931,* 23.

CHAPTER SIX: The Lord, Mr. Roosevelt, and Bright Leaf Redemption, 1933–1935

1. In 1927 and 1928, Congress passed two versions of the so-called McNary-Haugen Plan to raise commodity prices in the United States by dumping surpluses on the export market. Critics suggested that commodities be dumped into the sea instead. At least the sea would not retaliate. Both bills were vetoed by Calvin Coolidge. On the Farm Bloc and its activities in the 1920s, see Don Paarlberg, *American Farm Policy* (New York: Wiley, 1964).

2. Interview with Edward Walden by author, 21 July 1991.

3. Harold B. Rowe, *Tobacco Under the AAA* (Washington, D.C.: Brookings Institution, 1935), 55.

4. *Horry Herald,* 9 September 1933. Pete Daniel refers to this letter in *Breaking the Land: The Transformation of Cotton, Rice, and Tobacco Culture Since 1880* (Urbana: University of Illinois Press, 1985), 115.

5. Agricultural Adjustment Act of 12 May 1933, *Statutes at Large,* vol. 48, chap. 25, pp. 31–41; quotes from sec. 1, Introduction, p. 31 and sec. 2, paragraph 1, p. 32. The Agricultural Adjustment Act will be cited hereafter as AAA, section (paragraph), and page number. A good contemporary summary of parity and disparity is William S. White for Associated Press in *Columbia State,* 7 January 1936.

6. AAA, sec. 2(3), p. 32.

7. AAA, sec. 11, p. 38.

8. Anthony J. Badger, *Prosperity Road: The New Deal, Tobacco, and North Carolina* (Chapel Hill: University of North Carolina Press, 1980), 40, 45.

9. Rowe, *Tobacco Under the AAA,* 78. The tax rate was $3 per thousand cigarettes or six cents per pack of twenty cigarettes. See U.S. Department of Agriculture, *Statistical Bulletin No. 58: First Annual Report of Tobacco Statistics* (Washington, D.C.: U.S. Government Printing Office, 1937), 135–36.

10. AAA, sec. 10(a), p. 37; also R. Charles Brooks and J. C. Williamson Jr., *Flue-Cured Tobacco Programs, 1933–1958,* Agricultural Economics Information Series No. 66 (Raleigh: North Carolina State College, 1958), 15–16; Badger, *Prosperity Road,* 40, 45; Daniel, *Breaking the Land,* 112.

11. AAA, sec. 9(c), p.36. On determining parity levels, see Paul R. Johnson, *The Economics of the Tobacco Industry* (New York: Praeger, 1984), 26.

12. AAA, sec. 2(1), p. 32. Parity price for flue-cured tobacco from Rowe, *Tobacco Under the AAA,* 88.

13. AAA, sec. 2(1), p. 32.

14. Rowe, *Tobacco Under the AAA,* 94–95. North Carolina senator Josiah Bailey opposed the AAA, voting against his party, his president, and the interests of thousands of his constituents. The bill was also opposed by cigarette manufacturers.

15. AAA, sec. 8 (1), p. 34; AAA, sec. 12(a), p. 38.

16. Rowe, *Tobacco Under the AAA,* 87.

17. For a more thorough discussion of this problem, see Badger, *Prosperity Road,* 39.

18. AAA, sec. 8 (3), p. 35.

19. AAA, sec. 9(b), p. 36.

20. See Johnson, *Economics of the Tobacco Industry,* 55; also Daniel, *Breaking the Land,* 126.

21. *Columbia State,* 1, 2 August 1933.

22. *Charleston News and Courier,* 5 August 1933; *Columbia State,* 3, 4 August 1933; Talmadge quote from Badger, *Prosperity Road,* 48.

23. *Columbia State,* 2 September 1933.

24. *Charleston News and Courier,* 5 August 1933; *Columbia State,* 3, 4 August 1933.

25. *Columbia State,* 3, 4 August 1933.

26. *Charleston News and Courier,* 11 August 1933; *Columbia State,* 11, 12, 13 August 1933.

27. *Charleston News and Courier,* 18 August 1933, and especially 30 August 1933; *Columbia State,* 22, 30 August 1933; Badger, *Prosperity Road,* 49. Lugs are the bottom leaves of the tobacco plant and generally the least valuable.

28. *Charleston News and Courier,* 30 August 1933.

29. Ibid., 26 August 1933; *Columbia State,* 26 August 1933.

30. *Columbia State,* 31 August 1933. On Governor I. C. Blackwood, see biographical entry in David D. Wallace, *The History of South Carolina,* vol. 4 (New York: American Historical Society, 1934), 1.

31. *Charleston News and Courier,* 1 September 1933; *Columbia State,* 1 September 1933. In fairness to Blackwood, it should be mentioned that he was ill with laryngitis at the time.

32. *Columbia State,* 1 September 1933; Badger, *Prosperity Road,* 50–52.

33. Studs Terkel, *Hard Times* (New York: Pantheon Books, 1970), 252–53.

34. *Charleston News and Courier,* 1 September 1933.

35. *Columbia State,* 1 September 1933; *Charleston News and Courier,* 1 September 1933; Badger, *Prosperity Road,* 52–53. Georgia's marketing season was about over, and Virginia's had not opened.

36. *Charleston News and Courier,* 29 August, 2 September 1933; *Columbia State,* 31 August 1933; Badger, *Prosperity Road,* 52–53; Interview with C. P. Brewer by Eldred E. Prince Jr. and Robert Simpson, Loris, S.C., 18 May 1992.

37. *Marion Star,* 30 August 1933; *Columbia State,* 31 August 1933; *Charleston News and Courier,* 30 August, 2 September 1933. One of the Pee Dee growers who

went to Washington was R. Eugene Currin, who helped introduce Bright Leaf to the Pee Dee in 1887.

38. See Gilbert C. Fite, *Cotton Fields No More: Southern Agriculture, 1865–1980* (Lexington: University Press of Kentucky, 1984). On the plow-up in South Carolina, see *Charleston News and Courier,* 19 July 1933.

39. Rowe, *Tobacco Under the AAA,* 102–3; Badger, *Prosperity Road,* 49–50.

40. Rowe, *Tobacco Under the AAA,* 103.

41. Badger, *Prosperity Road,* 49; Rowe, *Tobacco Under the AAA,* 104.

42. *Charleston News and Courier,* 31 August 1933; *Columbia State,* 31 August 1933; Badger, *Prosperity Road,* 49–50. Williams's proposal called for pro-rata contributions based on purchases of Internal Revenue stamps affixed to each package of cigarettes. Since identical stamps were used on all brands regardless of the selling price, Williams's plan would discriminate against low-priced brands.

43. *Columbia State,* 2 September 1933.

44. On USDA meetings with growers, see ibid., 5, 6 September 1933; see also sample contract in Rowe, *Tobacco Under the AAA,* 294–95. Wallace and Hutson did not forget about Georgia. Farmers there participated on practically the same basis as the Carolinians.

45. *Horry Herald,* 7 September 1933; on Clemson's role in the campaign, see *Columbia State,* 8, 11 September 1933.

46. *Kingstree County Record,* 7 September 1933; *Columbia State,* 7, 13 September 1933.

47. *Marion Star,* 13 September 1933; *Columbia State,* 10, 13 September 1933.

48. *Horry Herald,* 14 September 1933; *Dillon Herald,* 14 September 1933; *Georgetown Times,* 14 September 1933.

49. *Columbia State,* 23 September 1933; Rowe, *Tobacco Under the AAA,* 103–10; Badger, *Prosperity Road,* 58.

50. *Columbia State,* 17 September 1933.

51. Ibid., 18 September 1933.

52. Ibid., 18, 19, 20 September 1933.

53. William H. Nicholls, *Price Policies in the Cigarette Industry* (Nashville: Vanderbilt Univesity Press, 1951), 62.

54. Rowe, *Tobacco Under the AAA,* 80; Nicholls, *Price Policies,* 181.

55. Robert Sobel, *They Satisfy: The Cigarette in American Life* (New York: Anchor Press/Doubleday, 1978), 114–16.

56. Nicholls, *Price Policies,* 95, 105. The new "standard" retail price became two packs for a quarter. Thus increased volume compensated somewhat for lower margins.

57. Badger, *Prosperity Road,* 59.

58. *Columbia State,* 23 September 1933; Rowe, *Tobacco Under the AAA,* 110–13; Badger, *Prosperity Road,* 58–59.

59. *Marion Star,* 27 September 1933; *Columbia State,* 27 September 1933.

60. Interview with Edward Walden, 21 July 1991.

61. *Columbia State,* 1 October 1933.

62. The text of Ehringhaus's telegram was released to the press. See *Columbia State,* 1 October 1933.

63. Government access to records of leaf purchases and consumption was included in section 2(b). The text of the marketing agreement appears in Rowe, *Tobacco Under the AAA,* 263–72. The quote appears on page 272.

64. *Horry Herald,* 19 October 1933; *Columbia State,* 14 October 1933; *Marion Star,* 22 November 1933; Rowe, *Tobacco Under the AAA,* 295.

65. *Marion Star,* 4 October 1933.

66. South Carolina Department of Agriculture, Commerce, and Industries, *Yearbook, 1933–1934* (Columbia: State Printers, 1935), 13; Badger, *Prosperity Road,* 65; quote from *Columbia State,* 28 August 1934.

67. Rowe, *Tobacco Under the AAA,* 283.

68. *Columbia State,* 28 August 1934.

69. Rowe, *Tobacco Under the AAA,* 148, 294. The processing tax was 4.2 cents per pound and the inventory tax amounted to 6.2 cents per thousand cigarettes; see Brooks and Williamson, *Flue-Cured Tobacco Programs,* 18–19, 25.

70. See Jack Temple Kirby, *Rural Worlds Lost: The American South, 1920–1960* (Baton Rouge: Louisiana State University Press, 1987), 64–68.

71. Badger, *Prosperity Road,* 73–74, 200.

72. Rowe, *Tobacco Under the AAA,* 172.

73. Tobacco Control Act of 28 June 1934, *Statutes at Large,* 48:1275–81.

74. Badger, *Prosperity Road,* 87–88. Senator Smith's papers have been destroyed.

75. Badger, *Prosperity Road,* 122; U.S. Department of Agriculture, *Tobaccos,* table 97.

CHAPTER SEVEN: War and Peace, 1936–1950

1. On the events leading to the Court's decision on *The Franklin Process Company* v. *Hoosac Mills,* see Theodore Saloutos, *The American Farmer and the New Deal* (Ames: Iowa State University Press, 1982), 125–34. Justice Owen J. Roberts is quoted in *Columbia State,* 7 January 1936. For coverage in the South Carolina press, see ibid., 7 January 1936, and *Charleston News and Courier,* 7 January 1936. The complete text of majority and minority opinions was reprinted in the *News and Courier.*

2. *Charleston News and Courier,* 11 January 1936.

3. *Columbia State,* 8, 18 January 1936; *Charleston News and Courier,* 10 January 1936. In Iowa, angry corn producers hanged the six concurring justices in effigy. See Saloutos, *American Farmer and the New Deal,* 136; Anthony J. Badger, *Prosperity Road: The New Deal, Tobacco, and North Carolina* (Chapel Hill: University of North Carolina Press, 1980), 122–23.

4. *Charleston News and Courier,* 10 January 1936; *Columbia State,* 11, 12 January 1936.

5. *Columbia State,* 11 January 1936.

6. On the Soil Conservation and Domestic Allotment Act of 29 February 1936, see Saloutos, *American Farmer and the New Deal,* 237–39.

7. On tobacco provisions, see Paul R. Johnson, *The Economics of the Tobacco Industry* (New York: Praeger, 1984), 33; see also R. Charles Brooks and J. C. Williamson, *Flue-Cured Tobacco Programs, 1933–1958,* Agricultural Economics Information Series No. 66 (Raleigh: North Carolina State College, 1958), 26–27.

8. Badger, *Prosperity Road,* 124.

9. *Darlington News and Press,* 26 March 1936.

10. *Charleston News and Courier,* 14 August 1936; *Darlington News and Press,* 20 August 1936; U.S. Department of Commerce, Bureau of the Census, *Historical Statistics of the United States: Colonial Times to 1970, Part I* (Washington, D.C.: U.S. Government Printing Office, 1976), 517; U.S. Department of Agriculture, Bureau of Agricultural Economics, *Tobaccos of the United States: Acreage, Production, Price and Value by States, 1866–1945, and by Types and Classes, 1919–1945* (Washington, D.C.: U.S. Government Printing Office, 1948), 74. South Carolina's production fell from 89.7 million pounds to 73.3 million pounds.

11. Johnson, *Economics of the Tobacco Industry,* 33. On drought conditions in the Pee Dee, see *Charleston News and Courier,* 11 August 1936.

12. On tobacco production, prices, and income in South Carolina, see Table 11. On cigarette consumption and demand for leaf tobacco, see U.S. Department of Commerce, Bureau of the Census, *Historical Statistics,* 690–91. See also Johnson, *Economics of the Tobacco Industry,* 33.

13. The complete title was Agricultural Adjustment Act of 1938 (P.L. 75–430). See Brooks and Williamson, *Flue-Cured Tobacco Programs,* 32.

14. Johnson, *Economics of the Tobacco Industry,* 33–34; Brooks and Williamson, *Flue-Cured Tobacco Programs,* 32.

15. Badger, *Prosperity Road,* 162–63; Saloutos, *American Farmer and the New Deal,* 245; Johnson, *Economics of the Tobacco Industry,* 33–34. On dissatisfaction with poundage quotas, see Pete Daniel, *Breaking the Land: The Transformation of Cotton, Rice, and Tobacco Culture Since 1880* (Urbana: University of Illinois Press, 1985), 129.

16. Badger, *Prosperity Road,* 162–63; Saloutos, *American Farmer and the New Deal,* 245; Johnson, *Economics of the Tobacco Industry,* 33–34.

17. See text of Poe's radio address in box 256.14, crop control folder, Clarence Poe Papers, North Carolina Division of Archives and History, Raleigh.

18. Brooks and Williamson, *Flue-Cured Tobacco Programs,* 34.

19. On returns by states and counties, see *Horry Herald,* 15 December 1939.

20. U.S. Department of Agriculture, *Tobaccos of the United States,* 74.

21. *Columbia State,* 8–9 September 1939; *Charleston News and Courier,* 8–9 September 1939; Johnson, *Economics of the Tobacco Industry,* 34.

22. Badger, *Prosperity Road,* 180.

23. *Marion Star,* 13 September 1939; *Horry Herald,* 14 September 1939.

24. *Marion Star,* 13 September 1939; *Horry Herald,* 14 September 1939.

25. See *Marion Star,* 20 September 1939.

26. Ibid.

27. Badger, *Prosperity Road,* 177.

28. *Marion Star,* 27 September 1939.

29. Ibid., 4 October 1939.

30. *Horry Herald,* 12 October 1939. On black voting, see Robert E. Martin, "Negro-White Participation in the AAA Cotton and Tobacco Referenda in North and South Carolina: A Study in Differential Voting and Attitudes in Selected Areas" (Ph.D. dissertation, University of Chicago, 1947).

31. Johnson, *Economics of the Tobacco Industry,* 34–35; Badger, *Prosperity Road,* 182–83; Brooks and Williamson, *Flue-Cured Tobacco Programs,* 34. This tobacco was eventually sold to Britain under the Lend-Lease Act.

32. Brooks and Williamson, *Flue-Cured Tobacco Programs,* 36; Badger, *Prosperity Road,* 193. South Carolina leaf prices averaged about eighteen cents in the 1920s and twenty-one cents in 1934–38. Alben W. Barkley served as Senate majority leader from 1937 to 1947.

33. William H. Nicholls, *Price Policies in the Cigarette Industry* (Nashville: Vanderbilt University Press, 1951), 100, 111.

34. U.S. Department of Commerce, Bureau of the Census, *Historical Statistics,* 319.

35. Daniel, *Breaking the Land,* 256.

36. Robert Sobel, *They Satisfy: The Cigarette in American Life* (Anchor Press/ Doubleday, 1978), 131–36.

37. On acreage increases during World War II, see Bella Gold, *Wartime Economic Planning in Agriculture: A Study in the Allocation of Resources* (New York: Columbia University Press, 1949), 114–15, 121, 126. See also Brooks and Williamson, *Flue-Cured Tobacco Programs,* 38.

38. *Columbia State,* 6 August 1942.

39. Ibid., 7 August 1942.

40. The crop of 1942 was worth $18,576,000 (1900) compared with 1941's value of $9,822,060 (1900).

41. Sobel, *They Satisfy,* 136, 150. American suspended production of Herbert Tareyton for several months in 1945 in favor of Lucky Strike.

42. On commodity price controls during World War II, see Gold, *Wartime Economic Planning,* 386–96; *Columbia State,* 13 August 1944.

43. *Columbia State,* 9, 10 August 1944.

44. Total returns in constant dollars (1900) were $7,616,850 in 1940, $9,822,060 in 1941, and $26,993,375 in 1944.

45. On changes in tobacco allotments in the 1940s, see Brooks and Williamson, *Flue-Cured Tobacco Programs,* 58.

46. *Columbia State,* 10, 13 August 1944.

47. Based on USDA data, the study found tobacco prices up 383 percent and costs up 39 percent. See Gold, *Wartime Economic Planning,* 388–89, 393. Grapefruit

had the highest ratio. On parity payments in the early 1940s, see Brooks and Williamson, *Flue-Cured Tobacco Programs,* 39.

48. See also Johnson, *Economics of the Tobacco Industry,* 54. Johnson calculated flue-cured tobacco prices from 1934 to 1980 in constant 1967 dollars. The years 1944–48 averaged 73.9 cents (1967). No other five-year period comes close to equaling this.

49. See issues of *Life* magazine 1942, 1943, passim; also Sobel, *They Satisfy,* 131–32.

50. The USDA's six basic commodities were corn, wheat, cotton, rice, tobacco, and peanuts. See Willard W. Cochrane and Mary E. Ryan, *American Farm Policy, 1948–1973* (Minneapolis: University of Minnesota Press, 1976), 73.

51. Gold, *Wartime Economic Planning,* 126–28, 301–8. See also Charles Pugh, "Landmarks in the Tobacco Program," in *The Tobacco Industry in Transition: Policies for the 1980s,* ed. William R. Finger (Lexington, Mass.: Lexington Books, 1981), 32. On Lend-Lease policy with respect to Bright Leaf exports, see Brooks and Williamson, *Flue-Cured Tobacco Programs,* 40–41. One objection was tobacco's abnormally high fertilizer requirements. Tobacco occupied only one-half of 1 percent of the nation's cropland, but it consumed 5 percent of the fertilizer, a use factor of ten for one.

52. Cochrane and Ryan, *American Farm Policy,* 24.

53. Brooks and Williamson, *Flue-Cured Tobacco Programs,* 42–43. The quote is from a report of Carl T. Hicks, president, Flue-Cured Tobacco Growers Cooperative, *Raleigh News and Observer,* 4 June 1947.

54. *Flue-Cured Tobacco Cooperative Annual Report, 1996* (Raleigh: Flue-Cured Tobacco Cooperative, 1997), Blount served on the board from 1947 to 1959 and 1973 to 1976.

55. Brooks and Williamson, *Flue-Cured Tobacco Programs,* 42–45.

56. On tobacco prices in South Carolina, see Appendix table "Bright Leaf Tobacco Production in South Carolina." Real prices remained remarkably stable in the 1950s and 1960s. Increases in current prices resulted mainly from inflation. See Johnson, *Economics of the Tobacco Industry,* 54. Johnson indexes to the 1967 dollar. Small write-offs were made for spoiled leaf. See Laverne Creek, Tom Capehart, and Verner Grise, *U.S. Tobacco Statistics, 1935–92,* Statistical Bulletin 869 (Washington, D.C.: U.S. Department of Agriculture, Economic Research Service, 1994), 160.

57. Cochrane and Ryan, *American Farm Policy,* 72–76; Brooks and Williamson, *Flue-Cured Tobacco Programs,* 42.

CHAPTER EIGHT: Advance, Retreat, and Retrenchment, 1950–1990s

1. On the mechanization of American agriculture after World War II, see Gilbert C. Fite, *Cotton Fields No More: Southern Agriculture, 1865–1980* (Lexington: University Press of Kentucky, 1984).

2. See Charles K. Mann, "The Tobacco Franchise for Whom?" in *The Tobacco*

Industry in Transition: Policies for the 1980s, ed. William R. Finger (Lexington, Mass.: Lexington Books, 1981), 37–38; see also Anthony J. Badger, *Prosperity Road: The New Deal, Tobacco, and North Carolina* (Chapel Hill: University of North Carolina Press, 1980), 200.

3. Interview with C. P. Brewer by Eldred E. Prince Jr. and Robert Simpson, Loris, S.C., 18 May 1992.

4. Harold B. Rowe, *Tobacco Under the AAA* (Washington, D.C.: Brookings Institution, 1935), 149.

5. Drew Gilpin Faust, "The Rhetoric and Ritual of Agriculture in Antebellum South Carolina," *Journal of Southern History* 45 (November 1979): 541–68.

6. U.S. Department of Agriculture, *Census of Agriculture, 1949,* compiled from county tables, land use, and livestock census.

7. Paul R. Johnson, *The Economics of the Tobacco Industry* (New York: Praeger, 1984), 63–65. One outcome of the filter-tip trend was to reduce the amount of tobacco in cigarettes even as cigarette consumption increased. For example, in 1950, when filtered cigarettes constituted 1 percent of the market, 9.5 pounds of raw leaf were required to make 3,500 cigarettes. In 1983, when 95 percent of cigarettes had filters, only about 6 pounds of tobacco were needed for the same production. See Laverne Creek, Tom Capehart, and Verner Grise, *U.S. Tobacco Statistics, 1935–92,* Statistical Bulletin 869 (Washington, D.C.: U.S. Department of Agriculture, Economic Research Service, 1994), 14.

8. After 1965, *quota* referred to the number of pounds farmers could sell and *allotment* to the acreage they could plant. See Willard W. Cochrane and Mary E. Ryan, *American Farm Policy, 1948–1973* (Minneapolis: University of Minnesota Press, 1976), 241; Johnson, *Economics of the Tobacco Industry,* 48–49. On co-op operations, see Creek, Capehart, and Grise, *U.S. Tobacco Statistics,* 160.

9. For a detailed study of the lease and transfer system in the Pee Dee region, see Linda Marie Pett, "Changing Spatial Patterns of Tobacco Production in South Carolina" (M.A. thesis, University of South Carolina, 1976), 51–55.

10. Interview with Harvey Graham by Eldred E. Prince Jr. and Robert Simpson, Loris, S.C., 23 June 1992.

11. Pett, "Changing Spatial Patterns," 51–55; also Johnson, *Economics of the Tobacco Industry,* 49.

12. The Census of Agriculture reported 6,632 tobacco farms in South Carolina in 1974 and 1,965 farms in 1992, a decline of 70.3 percent. See *1992 Census of Agriculture,* Part 40 (South Carolina) County Tables, 275, and *1978 Census of Agriculture,* Part 40 (South Carolina) County Tables, 170.

13. Annette L. Clauson and Verner N. Grise, *Flue Cured Tobacco Farming: Two Decades of Change,* Agricultural Economic Report 692 (Washington, D.C.: U.S. Department of Agriculture, Economic Research Service, 1994), 3–4. On the disappearance of black-owned tobacco farms, see John Hatch, "Black Americans in the Tobacco Culture," in *Tobacco Farming: Current Challenges and Future Alternatives,* Southern Research Report No. 10 (Chapel Hill: Center for the Study of the

American South, Southern Historical Collection, 1998), 21–26. In the same volume, see also Robert Robinson, "African American Farmers and Workers in the Tobacco Industry," 27–33.

14. On the development of mechanical harvesters, see Verner N. Grise, *Structural Characteristics of Flue-Cured Tobacco Farms and Prospects for Mechanization,* Agricultural Economics Report No. 277 (Washington, D.C.: U.S. Department of Agriculture, Economic Research Service, 1975). See also Gigi Berardi, "Can Tobacco Farmers Adjust to Mechanization?" in Finger, ed., *Tobacco Industry in Transition,* 47–59. On labor savings, see Clauson and Grise, *Flue Cured Tobacco Farming,* 24–29.

15. Pett, "Changing Spatial Patterns," 55–60; Clauson and Grise, *Flue Cured Tobacco Farming,* 9; Pete Daniel, *Breaking the Land: The Transformation of Cotton, Rice, and Tobacco Culture Since 1880* (Urbana: University of Illinois Press, 1985), 264–65. Interview with Graham, 23 June 1992.

16. The 1955 crop had a total value of $33.5 million (1900). See Appendix table "Bright Leaf Tobacco Production in South Carolina."

17. Computed from Creek, Capehart, and Grise, *U.S. Tobacco Statistics,* 64.

18. Excise taxes and wholesale and retail profits round out the dollar. See Wayne Purcell, "Who Gets the Tobacco Dollar?" in *Tobacco Farming: Current Challenges and Future Alternatives,* Southern Research Report No. 10 (Chapel Hill: Center for the Study of the American South, Southern Historical Collection, 1998).

19. On the decline of tenantry after World War II, see Jack Temple Kirby, *Rural Worlds Lost: The American South, 1920–1960* (Baton Rouge: Louisiana State University Press, 1987).

20. On migrant labor, see Clauson and Grise, *Flue Cured Tobacco Farming,* 24–29.

21. On black out-migration and the rural work ethic as resource, see Hatch, "Black Americans in the Tobacco Culture."

22. Johnson, *Economics of the Tobacco Industry,* 64. Annual per capita cigarette consumption peaked at 4,345 in 1963; it was 2,640 in 1992. See Creek, Capehart, and Grise, *U.S. Tobacco Statistics,* 14.

23. Besides the health and moral questions raised about smoking in Jacobean England, the tobacco controversy assumed political overtones as well. By the early 1600s, smoking was firmly associated with the Cavaliers, and Puritans denounced tobacco smoke as "the vapors of Hell." See David Harley, "The Beginnings of the Tobacco Controversy: Puritanism, James I, and the Royal Physicians," *Bulletin of the History of Medicine* 67 (Spring 1993): 28–50. On the history of antismoking sentiment, see Joseph C. Robert, *Columbia Story of Tobacco in America* (Chapel Hill: University of North Carolina, 1967).

24. See U.S. Surgeon General Luther L. Terry, *Smoking and Health: Report of the Advisory Committee to the Surgeon General of the Public Health Service,* U.S. Department of Health, Education, and Welfare, Public Health Service Publication 1103 (Washington, D.C.: U.S. Government Printing Office, 1964).

25. Johnson, *Economics of the Tobacco Industry*, 61.

26. The No-Net-Cost Tobacco Program Act of 1982 (P.L. 97–218), "Federal Tobacco Price Supports," *Congressional Digest* 73 (May 1994); Johnson, *Economics of
the Tobacco Industry*, 50; Creek, Capehart, and Grise, *U.S. Tobacco Statistics*, 161–62.

27. In 1991–92, the inspection and grading fee for flue-cured tobacco was sev-
enty cents per hundred pounds; the no-net-cost assessment was twenty-two cents
per hundred pounds. See Creek, Capehart, and Grise, *U.S. Tobacco Statistics*, 70. In
1996, farmers paid 1 cent per pound and purchasers 1.8 cents per pound. See *Flue-
Cured Tobacco Cooperative Annual Report, 1996* (Raleigh: The Cooperative, 1997);
also David G. Altman and Adam O. Goldstein, "The Federal Tobacco Price Support Program and Public Health," in *Tobacco Farming: Current Challenges and
Future Alternatives*, Southern Research Report No. 10 (Chapel Hill: Center for the
Study of the American South, Southern Historical Collection, 1998), 71–72.

28. Grading and inspection costs fell from $7.8 million to about $100,000 in
1983. See Creek, Capehart, and Grise, *U.S. Tobacco Statistics*, 162.

29. *Flue-Cured Tobacco Cooperative Stabilization Corporation: The Growers' Cooperative* (Raleigh: The Cooperative, 1996).

30. The average support price for flue-cured tobacco fell from $1.70 to $1.44 a
pound. See U.S. Department of Agriculture, *Agricultural Statistics, 1994* (Washington, D.C.: National Agricultural Statistics Service, 1994), 86. On the no-net-cost
program, see *Congressional Digest*, May 1994, 160. In the 1990s, flue-cured tobacco
exports were about 75 percent of their 1970s levels. See Creek, Capehart, and Grise,
U.S. Tobacco Statistics, 249–53.

31. Government stocks of flue-cured tobacco declined from 1.302 billion pounds
in 1985 to 209 million in 1992. See Creek, Capehart, and Grise, *U.S. Tobacco Statistics*, 161–62.

32. Ibid., 3.

33. The percentage estimate is based on net tobacco expenses of $17 million di-
vided by total government commodity support of about $10 billion. See Altman
and Goldstein, "Federal Tobacco Price Support Program and Public Health,"
73–74.

34. Calculated by Minnesota Department of Revenues; see Arlene Levinson (for
Associated Press), "Tobacco Tax Goes Up in Smoke," *Myrtle Beach Sun News*,
19 March 1993. In 1993, cigarette taxes averaged fifty-one cents a pack in the United
States including twenty-four cents federal tax. See "Federal Tobacco Price Supports," *Congressional Digest* 73 (May 1994): 137.

35. On the prospects for leaf exports, see Charles Pugh, "The Federal Tobacco
Program," in *Tobacco Industry in Transition*, ed. Finger, 18–19. See also Daniel A.
Sumner and Julian A. Alston, *Consequences of Elimination of the Tobacco Program*,
North Carolina Agricultural Research Service Bulletin 469 (Raleigh: State of North
Carolina, 1984).

36. Leaf costs account for about 8 percent of the retail price of cigarettes. See

Pugh, "Federal Tobacco Program," 18. It is estimated that retail price reductions of about 3 percent would accompany deregulation.

37. Interview with Ted Boyd by the author, Loris, S.C., 21 March 1993.

38. See Pugh, "Federal Tobacco Program," 13–25.

39. An excellent analysis is Wendell Berry, "Our Tobacco Problem: Why Driving Tobacco Farmers Out of Business Isn't the Answer," *Utne Reader*, September–October 1992, 84–91. The article was excerpted from the *Progressive*, May 1992.

40. Altman and Goldstein, "The Federal Tobacco Price Support Program and Public Health," 78.

41. Creek, Capehart, and Grise, *U.S. Tobacco Statistics*, 270.

42. The domestic tobacco requirement was included in the Omnibus Budget Reconciliation Act of 1993 (P.L. 103–66) effective 1 January 1994. See *Congressional Digest* 73 (May 1994): 137.

43. Altman and Goldstein, "The Federal Tobacco Price Support Program and Public Health," 75.

44. Clauson and Grise, *Flu Cured Tobacco Farming*, figs. 4 and 14 compared, pp. 5, 14.

45. See *South Carolina Crop, Livestock, and Poultry Statistics, 1992–1994* (Columbia: South Carolina Agricultural Statistics Service, 1994), 12–24.

46. On values per acre, see Creek, Capehart, and Grise, *U.S. Tobacco Statistics*, 3.

47. Seasonal fruits, vegetables, berries, and flowers have shown promise in the market setting. In the Pee Dee, about 30 percent of tobacco-producing families earn income off the farm. Younger growers are more likely to have off-farm employment. See Clauson and Grise, *Flu Cured Tobacco Farming*, 14–15.

48. See Altman and Goldstein, "The Federal Tobacco Price Support Program and Public Health," 86–91.

49. On tobacco taxation, see Johnson, *Economics of the Tobacco Industry*, 125–33. From 1935 to 1992, tobacco taxes paid to government entities totaled 250 billion current dollars. Adjusting this sum for inflation would yield nearly one trillion 1995 dollars. Cigarette tax collections in 1993 exceeded $12 billion. See Creek, Capehart, and Grise, *U.S. Tobacco Statistics*, 63.

Bibliography

Manuscripts and Published Primary Sources

Allston Family Papers. South Caroliniana Library, University of South Carolina, Columbia.

Bacot, Peter B. Papers. Southern Historical Collection, University of North Carolina, Chapel Hill.

Berry, C. Burgin. "Diary of Col. Daniel Jordan." *Independent Republic Quarterly* 15 (April 1981): 25–35.

Browning, Andrew, ed. *English Historical Documents, 1660–1714*. Vol. 8. New York: Oxford University Press, 1953.

Carson, James M. Papers. South Caroliniana Library, University of South Carolina, Columbia.

Cheves, Langdon, ed. "The Shaftesbury Papers and Other Records Relating to Carolina and the First Settlement on the Ashley River Prior to the Year 1676." *Collections of the South Carolina Historical Society,* Vol. 5. Richmond: William E. Jones, 1897.

Coker Papers. South Caroliniana Library, University of South Carolina, Columbia.

Cole, Arthur H. *Wholesale Commodity Prices in the United States, 1700–1861.* 1938. Reprint. New York: Johnson Reprint Co., 1969.

Congdon Papers. Horry County Memorial Library, Conway, S.C.

Cooper, Thomas, and David McCord, eds. *The Statutes at Large of South Carolina.* Columbia: A. S. Johnston, 1839.

Coxe, Tench. *A Statement of the Arts and Manufactures of the United States of America for the Year 1810.* Philadelphia: A. Corman Jr., 1814.

Cyclopedia of Eminent and Representative Men of the Carolinas of the Nineteenth Century. Vol. 1. Madison: Brant and Fuller, 1892.

Darlington Agricultural Society. Minute Book. Vol. 1 (1846–80). Darlington County Historical Commission, Darlington, S.C.

Deas, Horry. Papers. South Caroliniana Library, University of South Carolina, Columbia.

De Bow, J. D. B. *A Statistical View of the United States . . . Being a Compendium of the Seventh Census.* Washington, D.C.: Beverly Tucker, 1854.

Dwight, Francis Marion. Papers. South Caroliniana Library, University of South Carolina, Columbia.

Glover, Joseph. Papers. South Caroliniana Library, University of South Carolina, Columbia.

Holliday Company Papers. South Caroliniana Library, University of South Carolina, Columbia.

Manning, Woodward. Papers. South Carolina Historical Society, Charleston.

Merrens, H. Roy, ed. *The Colonial South Carolina Scene: Contemporary Views, 1697–1774*. Columbia: University of South Carolina Press, 1977.

Poe, Clarence Hamilton. Papers. North Carolina Division of Archives and History, Raleigh.

Powell, William S., ed. *Dictionary of North Carolina Biography*. Chapel Hill: University of North Carolina Press, 1979.

Rawick, George, ed. *The American Slave: A Composite Autobiography*. 41 vols. Westport, Conn.: Greenwood Press, 1972–79.

Rogers, Frank M. Papers. Darlington Historical Commission, Darlington, S.C.

Sainsbury, Noel, transcriber. *Records in the British Public Records Office Relating to South Carolina, 1663–1684*. 5 vols. Columbia: Crowson-Stone, 1928–46.

Salley, Alexander S., comp. and ed. *Narratives of Early Carolina, 1650–1708*. New York: Charles Scribner's Sons, 1911.

Selected Series of Records Issued by the Commissioner of the Bureau of Refugees, Freedmen, and Abandoned Lands, 1865–1872. Washington, D.C.: National Archives Microfilm Publications, 1968.

Stevens, Michael E., ed. *Journal of the House of Representatives, 1789–1790*. Columbia: University of South Carolina Press, 1984.

Williamson, Benjamin F. Papers. Darlington Historical Commission, Darlington, S.C.

Williamson, Bright. Papers. Darlington Historical Commission, Darlington, S.C.

Woodard, Janet H., ed. *1850 Census of Horry County, South Carolina*. Greenville: A Press, 1980.

Government Records and Publications

North Carolina Agricultural Experiment Station. *Bulletin No. 86: Tobacco Curing by the Leaf Cure on Wire and the Stalk Process*. Raleigh: North Carolina College of Agriculture and Mechanical Arts, 1892.

South Carolina Department of Agriculture, Commerce and Industries.
Eleventh Annual Report, 1914. Columbia: Gonzales and Bryan, 1915.
Fourteenth Annual Report, 1917. Columbia: Gonzales and Bryan, 1918.
Sixteenth Annual Report, 1919. Columbia: Gonzales and Bryan, 1920.
Seventeenth Annual Report, 1920. Columbia: State Printing, 1921.
Twenty-first Annual Report, 1924. Columbia: State Printing, 1925.
Twenty-second Annual Report, 1925. Columbia: State Printing, 1926.
Tobacco Report, 1920. Columbia: Gonzales and Bryan, 1921.
Tobacco Report, 1938. Columbia: Gonzales and Bryan, 1939.
Tobacco Report, 1947. Columbia: State Printers, 1948.
Yearbook, 1926. Columbia: General Assembly, 1927.
Yearbook, 1927. Columbia: General Assembly, 1928.
Yearbook, 1928. Columbia: General Assembly, 1929.

Yearbook, 1929. Columbia: General Assembly, 1930.

Yearbook, 1930. Columbia: General Assembly, 1931.

Yearbook, 1931. Columbia: General Assembly, 1932.

South Carolina Division of Research and Statistical Services. *South Carolina Statistical Abstract*. Columbia: State Printers, 1977.

————. General Assembly. *Acts and Resolutions of the South Carolina Assembly, 1921*. Columbia: State Printers, 1922.

————. ————. *Acts of South Carolina, 1899*. Columbia: State Printers, 1900.

————. ————. *Journal of the House of Representatives, General Assembly, 1915*. Columbia: State Printers, 1916.

————. ————. *Papers of the General Assembly*. Petitions, 1789–96. South Carolina Department of Archives and History.

U.S. Department of Commerce, Bureau of the Census.

Tenth Census, 1880.

Eleventh Census, 1890.

Thirteenth Census, 1910.

Fourteenth Census, 1920.

Twenty-first Census, 1990.

Census of Agriculture, 1978, 1982, 1987, 1992.

————. *Historical Statistics of the United States: Colonial Times to 1970*. Washington, D.C.: U.S. Government Printing Office, 1976.

————. *Statistics of Agriculture, 1895*.

————. *Statistical Abstracts, 1900*.

————. *Statistical Abstracts, 1915*.

U.S. Department of Agriculture. *Agricultural Statistics 1994*. Washington, D.C.: Agricultural Statistics Service, 1994.

————. *Statistical Bulletin No. 58: First Annual Report on Tobacco Statistics*. Washington, D.C.: U.S. Government Printing Office, 1937.

————. *Yearbook, 1922*. Washington, D.C.: U.S. Government Printing Office, 1923.

Newspapers

Bennetsville, S.C.	*Marlboro Herald-Advocate*
Charleston, S.C.	*City Gazette and Daily Advertizer*
Charleston, S.C.	*Daily Courier*
Charleston, S.C.	*Mercury*
Charleston, S.C.	*News and Courier*
Charleston, S.C.	*South Carolina Leader*
Cheraw, S.C.	*Cheraw Chronicle*
Columbia, S.C.	*State*
Conway, S.C.	*Horry Herald*
Conway, S.C.	*Horry Weekly News*
Darlington, S.C.	*Darlington News*

Darlington, S.C.	*Darlington News and Press*
Darlington, S.C.	*Darlington Southerner*
Darlington, S.C.	*New Era*
Dillon, S.C.	*Dillon Herald*
Florence, S.C.	*Daily Times*
Florence, S.C.	*Florence Morning News*
Florence, S.C.	*Florence Weekly Times*
Georgetown, S.C.	*Georgetown Times*
Georgetown, S.C.	*Georgetown Times-Index*
Greenville, S.C.	*Baptist Courier*
Hartsville, S.C.	*Hartsville Messenger*
Kingstree, S.C.	*County Record*
Macon, Ga.	*Macon News*
Marion, S.C.	*Marion Crescent*
Marion, S.C.	*Marion Star*
Mullins, S.C.	*Mullins Enterprise*
Myrtle Beach, S.C.	*Sun News*
New York, N.Y.	*New York Times*
Raleigh, N.C.	*Progressive Farmer*
Sumter, S.C.	*South Carolina Tobacconist*

Selected Secondary Sources

Abbott, Martin. *The Freedmen's Bureau in South Carolina, 1865–1872.* Chapel Hill: University of North Carolina Press, 1967.

Altman, David G., and Adam O. Goldstein. "The Federal Tobacco Price Support Program and Public Health." In *Tobacco Farming: Current Challenges and Future Alternatives.* Southern Research Report No. 10. Chapel Hill: Center for the Study of the American South, Southern Historical Collection, 1998.

American Tobacco Company. "*Sold American!*": *The First Fifty Years.* New York: American Tobacco Company, 1954.

Bacot, D. Huger. "The South Carolina Upcountry at the End of the Eighteenth Century." *American Historical Review* 28 (July 1923): 682–98.

Badger, Anthony J. *Prosperity Road: The New Deal, Tobacco, and North Carolina.* Chapel Hill: University of North Carolina Press, 1980.

Ball, William Watts. *The State That Forgot: South Carolina's Surrender to Democracy.* Indianapolis: Bobbs-Merrill, 1932.

Bates, Edward C. "The Story of the Cotton Gin." *New England Magazine,* May 1890, 288–92.

Berry, C. Burgin. "Area Tobacco Goes Back More Than a Century." *Cheraw Chronicle,* 31 October 1991.

Berry, Wendell. "Our Tobacco Problem." *Utne Reader,* September–October 1992, 84–91.

Bleser, Carol R. *The Promised Land: The History of the South Carolina Land Commission, 1869–1890.* Columbia: University of South Carolina Press, 1969.

Boddie, William Willis. *History of Williamsburg County.* 1924. Reprint. Spartanburg: Reprint Company, 1980.

Boyd, W. K. *The Story of Durham, City of the New South.* Durham: Duke University Press, 1925.

Brooks, R. Charles, and J. C. Williamson Jr. *Flue-Cured Tobacco Programs, 1933–1958.* Agricultural Economics Information Series No. 66. Raleigh: North Carolina State College, 1958.

Browder, Nathaniel C. *The Tri-State Tobacco Growers' Association: The Co-op That Failed.* 1940. Reprint. Raleigh, 1983.

Carlton, David L. *Mill and Town in South Carolina.* Baton Rouge: Louisiana State University Press, 1982.

————. "The Piedmont and Waccamaw Regions: An Economic Comparison." *South Carolina Historical Magazine* 88 (April 1987): 83–100.

Cell, John W. *The Highest Stage of White Supremacy: The Origins of Segregation in South Africa and the American South.* Cambridge, Eng.: Cambridge University Press, 1982.

Chaplin, Joyce E. *An Anxious Pursuit: Agricultural Innovation and Modernity in the Lower South, 1730–1815.* Chapel Hill: University of North Carolina Press, 1993.

Clark, Thomas D. *Pills, Petticoats, and Plows: The Southern Country Store.* Norman: University of Oklahoma Press, 1944.

Clauson, Annette L., and Verner N. Grise. *Flue Cured Tobacco Farming: Two Decades of Change.* Agricultural Economic Report 692. Washington, D.C.: U.S. Department of Agriculture, Economic Research Service, 1994.

Clowse, Converse D. *Economic Beginnings in Colonial South Carolina, 1670–1730.* Columbia: University of South Carolina Press, 1971.

Cochrane, Willard W., and Mary E. Ryan. *American Farm Policy, 1948–1973.* Minneapolis: University of Minnesota Press, 1976.

Coclanis, Peter A. *The Shadow of a Dream: Economic Life and Death in the South Carolina Low Country, 1670–1920.* New York: Oxford University Press, 1989.

Coclanis, Peter A., and Lacy K. Ford. "The South Carolina Economy Reconstructed and Reconsidered: Structure, Output, and Performance, 1670–1985." In *Developing Dixie: Modernization in a Traditional Society,* edited by Winifred B. Moore. New York: Greenwood Press, 1990.

Cox, Reaves. *Competition in the American Tobacco Industry, 1911–1932: A Study of the Effects of the Partition of the American Tobacco Company by the Supreme Court.* New York: Columbia University Press, 1942.

Creek, Laverne, Tom Capehart, and Verner Grise. *U.S. Tobacco Statistics, 1935–92.* Statistical Bulletin 869. Washington, D.C.: U.S. Department of Agriculture, Economic Research Service, 1994.

Dabbs, James McBride, and Carl Julien. *Pee Dee Panorama.* Columbia: University of South Carolina Press, 1951.

Daniel, Pete. *Breaking the Land: The Transformation of Cotton, Rice, and Tobacco Culture Since 1880*. Urbana: University of Illinois Press, 1985.

———. "The Metamorphosis of Slavery, 1865–1900." *Journal of American History* 65 (June 1969): 88–99.

———. *The Shadow of Slavery: Peonage in the South, 1901–1969*. Urbana: University of Illinois Press, 1972.

DeCanio, Stephen. *Agriculture in the Postbellum South: The Economics of Production and Supply*. Cambridge, Mass.: MIT Press, 1974.

Drayton, John. *A View of South Carolina as Respects Her Natural and Civil Concerns*. Charleston: W. P. Young, 1802.

Dunn, Richard S. *Sugar and Slaves: The Rise of the Planter Class in the English West Indies, 1624–1713*. New York: Norton, 1972.

Durden, Robert F. *The Dukes of Durham, 1865–1929*. Durham: Duke University Press, 1975.

Easterlin, Richard. "Regional Income Trends, 1840–1950." In *American Economic History*, edited by Seymour Harris. New York: McGraw-Hill, 1961.

Engerman, Stanley. "The Effects of Slavery on the Southern Economy: The Recent Debate." *Explorations in Entrepreneurial History* 4 (Winter 1967).

Etheridge, Elizabeth. *The Butterfly Caste: A Social History of Pellagra in the South*. Westport, Conn.: Greenwood Press, 1972.

Faust, Drew Gilpin. "The Rhetoric and Ritual of Agriculture in Antebellum South Carolina." *Journal of Southern History* 45 (November 1979): 541–68.

Finger, William R., ed. *The Tobacco Industry in Transition: Policies for the 1980s*. Lexington, Mass.: Lexington Books, 1981.

Fite, Gilbert C. *Cotton Fields No More: Southern Agriculture, 1865–1980*. Lexington: University Press of Kentucky, 1984.

Foner, Eric. *Free Soil, Free Labor, Free Men: The Ideology of the Republican Party Before the Civil War*. New York: Oxford University Press, 1970.

———. *Politics and Ideology in the Age of the Civil War*. New York: Oxford University Press, 1980.

———. *Reconstruction: America's Unfinished Revolution, 1863–1877*. New York: Harper & Row, 1988.

Ford, Lacy K. *Origins of Southern Radicalism: The South Carolina Upcountry, 1800–1860*. New York: Oxford University Press, 1988.

Gayle, Charles J. "The Nature and Volume of Exports from Charleston, 1724–1774." *Proceedings of the South Carolina Historical Society* (1937): 33.

Glen, James. *A Description of South Carolina. . . . 1761*. Reprint, 1951.

Gold, Bella. *Wartime Economic Planning in Agriculture: A Study in the Allocation of Resources*. New York: Columbia University Press, 1949.

Gray, Lewis C. *The History of Agriculture in the Southern United States to 1860*. 2 vols. 1932. Reprint. Gloucester: Peter Smith, 1958.

Grise, Verner N. *Structural Characteristics of Flue-Cured Tobacco Farms and Pros-*

pects for Mechanization. Agricultural Economics Report No. 277. Washington, D.C.: U.S. Department of Agriculture, Economic Research Service, 1975.

Hahn, Steven. *The Roots of Southern Populism: Yeoman Farmers and the Transformation of the Georgia Upcountry, 1850–1890*. New York: Oxford University Press, 1983.

Hamilton, David E. *From New Day to New Deal: American Farm Policy from Hoover to Roosevelt, 1928–1933*. Chapel Hill: University of North Carolina Press, 1991.

Hammond, Matthew B. "Correspondence of Eli Whitney Relative to the Invention of the Cotton Gin." *American Historical Review* 3 (October 1897): 99–101.

Harlan, Louis R. *Separate and Unequal: Public School Campaigns and Racism in the Southern Seaboard States, 1900–1915*. New York: Atheneum, 1968.

Harley, David. "The Beginnings of the Tobacco Controversy: Puritanism, James I, and the Royal Physicians." *Bulletin of the History of Medicine* 67 (Spring 1993): 28–50.

Hatch, John. "Black Americans in the Tobacco Culture." In *Tobacco Farming: Current Challenges and Future Alternatives*. Southern Research Report No. 10. Chapel Hill: Center for the Study of the American South, Southern Historical Collection, 1998.

Headrick, Daniel R. *The Tools of Empire: Technology and European Imperialism in the Nineteenth Century*. New York: Oxford University Press, 1981.

Higgs, Robert. *Competition and Coercion: Blacks in the American Economy, 1865–1914*. Cambridge, Eng.: Cambridge University Press, 1977.

Holliday, Joseph W. "Horry and the Tobacco Industry." *Independent Republic Quarterly* 2 (April 1968): 7–8.

Imperial Tobacco Company. *A History of the Tobacco Trade: Information Brochure No. 2*. Nottingham: Forman and Sons, n.d.

Johnson, Paul R. *The Economics of the Tobacco Industry*. New York: Praeger, 1984.

Jones, Lewis P. "History of Public Education in South Carolina." In *Public Education in South Carolina: Historical, Political and Legal Perspectives*, edited by Thomas R. McDaniel. Spartanburg: Converse College, 1984.

———. *South Carolina: A Synoptic History for Laymen*. 4th ed. Orangeburg, S.C.: Sandlapper Press, 1971.

Jordon, Frank E. Jr. *The Primary State: A History of the Democratic Party of South Carolina*. N.p.: Author, n.d.

Joyner, Charles W. *Down by the Riverside: A South Carolina Slave Community*. Urbana: University of Illinois Press, 1984.

———. "The Far Side of the Forest." *Independent Republic Quarterly* 18 (Fall 1984): 13–17.

King, G. Wayne. *Rise Up So Early: A History of Florence County, South Carolina*. Spartanburg: Reprint Company, 1981.

Kirby, Jack Temple. *Rural Worlds Lost: The American South, 1920–1960*. Baton Rouge: Louisiana State University Press, 1987.

Klein, Rachel N. *Unification of a Slave State: The Rise of the Planter Class in the South Carolina Backcountry, 1760–1808*. Chapel Hill: University of North Carolina Press, 1990.

Kovacik, Charles F., and John J. Winberry. *South Carolina: A Geography*. Boulder: Westview Press, 1987.

Larsen, Grace, and Henry Erdman. "Aaron Sapiro: Genius of Farm Cooperative Marketing." *Mississippi Valley Historical Review* 49 (September 1962): 242–68.

Lerner, Eugene. "Southern Output and Agricultural Income, 1860–1880." *Agricultural History* 33 (1959): 117.

Litwack, Leon F. *Been in the Storm So Long: The Aftermath of Slavery*. New York: Knopf, 1979.

McCay, C. F. "An American Professor Sketches the Principal American Inventions Affecting Textiles." In *Cotton and the Growth of the American Economy, 1790–1860*, compiled and edited by Stuart Bruchey. New York: Brace and World, 1967.

McCusker, John J. *How Much Is That in Real Money?: A Historical Price Index for Use as a Deflator of Money Values in the Economy of the United States*. Worcester, Mass.: American Antiquarian Society, 1992.

McLear, Patrick E. "The Agrarian Revolt in the South: A Historiographical Essay." *Louisiana Studies* 12 (Summer 1973): 443–63.

McMath, Robert C. Jr. *Populist Vanguard: A History of the Southern Farmers' Alliance*. Chapel Hill: University of North Carolina Press, 1975.

Mantoux, Paul J. *The Industrial Revolution in the Eighteenth Century*. London: J. Cape, 1961.

Mendenhall, Marjorie S. "A History of Agriculture in South Carolina, 1790–1860: An Economic and Social Study." Ph.D. dissertation, University of North Carolina, 1940.

Meriwether, Robert L. *The Expansion of South Carolina, 1729–1765*. Kingsport, Tenn.: Southern Publishers, 1940.

Moltke-Hansen, David. "Protecting Interests, Maintaining Rights, Emulating Ancestors: U.S. Constitution Bicentennial Reflections on 'The Problem of South Carolina,' 1787–1860." *South Carolina Historical Magazine* 89 (July 1988): 160–82.

Nicholls, William H. *Price Policies in the Cigarette Industry*. Nashville: Vanderbilt University Press, 1951.

Norment, J. E. *The Pee Dee Tobacco Belt of South Carolina: A Condensed Review of the Tobacco Industry, with Special Reference to the Home Markets at Mullins, Timmonsville, Florence, and Darlington*. Columbia: State Publishing, 1903.

O'Brien, Michael, and David Moltke-Hansen, eds. *Intellectual Life in Antebellum Charleston*. Knoxville: University of Tennessee Press, 1986.

Ogg, David. *England in the Reign of Charles II*. 2d ed. Oxford: Clarendon Press, 1956.

Owsley, Frank. *Plain Folk of the Old South*. Baton Rouge: Louisiana State University Press, 1949.

Paarlberg, Don. *American Farm Policy*. New York: Wiley, 1964.

Parramore, Mary. "Preservation Plan for Historic Tobacco Related Resources." State Historic Preservation Office, South Carolina Department of Archives and History, Columbia, 1990.

Pee Dee Heritage Center. *Pee Dee Panorama Revisited*. Greenville: A Press, 1984.

Peterson, William H. *The Great Farm Problem*. Chicago: Henry Regnery, 1959.

Pett, Linda Marie. "Changing Spatial Patterns of Tobacco Production in South Carolina." M.A. thesis, University of South Carolina, 1976.

Petty, Julian J. *The Growth and Distribution of Population in South Carolina*. 1943. Reprint. Spartanburg: Reprint Company, 1975.

Poe, Clarence H. *How Farmers Co-operate and Double Profits: First Hand Reports on All the Leading Forms of Rural Co-operation in the United States and Europe—Stories That Show How Farmers Can Co-operate by Showing How They Have Done It and Are Doing It*. New York: Orange Judd Co., 1915.

————. *My First 80 Years*. Chapel Hill: University of North Carolina Press, 1963.

Price, Jacob. *Capital and Credit in British Overseas Trade: The View from the Chesapeake, 1700–1776*. Cambridge, Mass.: Harvard University Press, 1980.

Ramsay, David. *Ramsay's History of South Carolina from Its First Settlement in 1670 to the Year 1809*. 1809. Reprint. Newberry: W. J. Duffie, 1858.

Ransom, Roger, and Richard Sutch. *One Kind of Freedom: The Economic Consequences of Emancipation*. Cambridge, Eng.: Cambridge University Press, 1977.

Ravenel, Charles. "Southern Deficits." *Business and Economic Review*, July 1984, 22–28.

Reid, Joseph D. Jr. "Sharecropping as an Understandable Market Response: The Post-Bellum South." *Journal of Economic History* 33 (March 1973): 106–30.

Robinson, Robert. "African American Farmers and Workers in the Tobacco Industry." In *Tobacco Farming: Current Challenges and Future Alternatives*. Southern Research Report No. 10. Chapel Hill: Center for the Study of the American South, Southern Historical Collection, 1998.

Rodgers, Daniel T. *The Work Ethic in Industrial America, 1850–1920*. Chicago: University of Chicago Press, 1978.

Rogers, George C. Jr. *The History of Georgetown County, South Carolina*. Columbia: University of South Carolina Press, 1970.

Rogers, James A., with Larry E. Nelson. *Mr. D. R.: A Biography of David R. Coker*. Hartsville, S.C.: Coker College Press, 1994.

Rogers, James S. III. "The History of Horry County, South Carolina." M.A. thesis, University of South Carolina, 1972.

Rosengarten, Theodore. *All God's Dangers: The Life of Nate Shaw*. New York: Knopf, 1974.

Salley, Alexander S. Jr. *The Introduction of Rice Culture into South Carolina*. Columbia: Historical Commission of South Carolina, 1919.

Saloutos, Theodore. *Farmer Movements in the South, 1865–1933*. Berkeley and Los Angeles: University of California Press, 1960.

Saloutos, Theodore, and John D. Hicks. *Agricultural Discontent in the Middle West*. Madison: University of Wisconsin Press, 1951.

Sass, Herbert Ravenel. *The Story of the South Carolina Lowcountry*. 3 vols. West Columbia, S.C.: J. F. Hyer, 1956.

Schivelsbusch, Wolfgang. *Tastes of Paradise: A Social History of Spices, Stimulants, and Intoxicants*. New York: Pantheon Books, 1992.

Simpson, George. *The Cokers of Carolina*. Chapel Hill: University of North Carolina Press, 1956.

Snow, W. H. *Snow's Modern Barn System of Raising and Curing Tobacco*. 4th ed. Baltimore: Friedenwald, 1895.

Sobel, Robert. *They Satisfy: The Cigarette in American Life*. New York: Anchor Press, 1978.

Sproat, John G., and Larry Schweikart. *Making Change: South Carolina Banking in the Twentieth Century*. Columbia: South Carolina Bankers Association, 1990.

Stampp, Kenneth. *The Peculiar Institution: Slavery in the Ante-Bellum South*. New York: Knopf, 1956.

Stokes, Durwood T. *The History of Dillon County, South Carolina*. Columbia: University of South Carolina Press, 1978.

Summer, Daniel A., and Julian A. Alston. *Consequences of Elimination of the Tobacco Program*. North Carolina Agricultural Research Service Bulletin 469, 1984.

Tilley, Nannie May. *The Bright Tobacco Industry, 1860–1929*. Chapel Hill: University of North Carolina Press, 1948.

Tobacco Institute. *South Carolina and Tobacco: A Chapter in America's Industrial Growth*. Washington, D.C.: Tobacco Institute, 1977.

Turkel, Studs. *Hard Times*. New York: Pantheon Books, 1970.

Vernon, Amelia Wallace. *African Americans at Mars Bluff, South Carolina*. Baton Rouge: Louisiana State University Press, 1993.

Wallace, David Duncan. *The History of South Carolina*. Vol. 4. New York: American Historical Society, 1934.

Weir, Robert M. *Colonial South Carolina: A History*. Millwood, N.Y.: KTO Press, 1983.

Wilson, Charles Reagan, and William Ferris, eds. *Encyclopedia of Southern Culture*. S. v. "Dabbs, James McBride," by Robert M. Randolph. Chapel Hill: University of North Carolina University Press, 1989.

Williamson, Joel. *After Slavery: The Negro in South Carolina During Reconstruction*. Chapel Hill: University of North Carolina Press, 1965.

Wood, Peter. *Black Majority: Negroes in Colonial South Carolina from 1670 Through the Stono Rebellion*. New York: Norton, 1974.

Woodman, Harold D. "The Decline of Cotton Factorage After the Civil War." *American Historical Review* 71 (July 1976): 1219–36.

———. *King Cotton and His Retainers: Financing and Marketing the Cotton Crop of the South, 1800–1925*. 1968. Reprint. Columbia: University of South Carolina Press, 1990.

————. "Post–Civil War Agriculture and Agricultural Law." *Agricultural History* 53 (1979): 311.

Wright, Gavin. "Cotton Competition and the Post-Bellum Recovery of the American South." *Journal of Economic History* 34 (September 1974): 610–35.

————. *Old South, New South: Revolutions in the Southern Economy Since the Civil War.* New York: Basic Books, 1986.

————. *Political Economy of the Cotton South: Households, Markets, and Wealth in the Nineteenth Century.* New York: Norton, 1978.

Young, Thomas Benton for Clemson College. *Tobacco Culture in South Carolina: Popular Bulletin No. 86.* Columbia: R. L. Bryan, 1904.

Index